DARBY'S RANGERS

WE LED
THE WAY

Darby's Rangers

We Led the Way

The Way

WILLIAM O. DARBY / WILLIAM H. BAUMER

Copyright © 1980 by Presidio Press

Published by Presidio Press
P.O. Box 3515, San Rafael, California 94902

Library of Congress Cataloging in Publication Data
Darby, William Orlando.
We led the way.
1. World War, 1939–1945—Regimental histories—United States
1st Ranger Battalion. 2. World War, 1939–1945—Regimental histories—United
States—3d Ranger Battalion. 3. World War, 1939–1945—Regimental
histories—United States—4th Ranger Battalion. 4. United States. Army.
1st Ranger Battalion—History. 5. United States. Army. 3d Ranger Battalion—
History. 6. United States. Army. 4th Ranger Battalion—History.
7. World War, 1939–1945—Personal narratives, American. 8. Darby, William
Orlando. 9. World War, 1939–1945—Mediterranean region. I. Baumer,
William Henry, 1909– joint author. II. Title.
D769.311st.D37   940.54'12'73   80-10431
ISBN 0-89141-082-1

Text design by Howard Jacobsen
Composed by Community Type & Design, Fairfax, California
Printed in the United States of America

TO
THE RANGERS WHO GAVE THEIR LIVES
FOR THEIR COUNTRY

CONTENTS

LIST OF ILLUSTRATIONS

ix

PREFACE

xi

INTRODUCTION

Darby's Early Days

1

CHAPTER I

North African Spearhead—Arzew · November 1942

5

CHAPTER II

Training in Northern Scotland · June–September 1942

24

CHAPTER III

Dieppe and Training at Dundee · August–October 1942

41

CHAPTER IV

Tunisian Combat · February–March 1943

51

CHAPTER V

The Battle of El Guettar · March 1943

66

CHAPTER VI

Landings in Sicily · July 1943

79

CHAPTER VII

To Messina · July–August 1943

101

CHAPTER VIII

Sorrento—Salerno's Left Flank · September 1943

111

CHAPTER IX

Up the "Boot" to Venafro · October–December 1943

124

CHAPTER X

Landing at Anzio · 22 January 1944

141

CHAPTER XI

Cisterna—Death at Dawn · 29 January 1944

154

CHAPTER XII

The Rangers Live On

169

EPILOGUE

Darby's Later Assignments

173

APPENDIX A

Darby's Message to the Officers and Men of the Ranger Battalions

181

APPENDIX B

The Other Ranger Battalions

183

LIST OF ABBREVIATIONS

198

LIST OF ILLUSTRATIONS

MAPS

Ranger Attack at Arzew · 8 November 1942
4

Ranger Actions in Tunisia · February to April 1943
54

Ranger Actions in Sicily · July to August 1943
82

Ranger Attack on the Sorrento Peninsula (near Salerno)
9 September 1943
110

Ranger Operations, Anzio and Cisterna · January 1944
140

PHOTOGRAPHS

Ranger Training, Achnacarry, Scotland
Following page 40

The Rangers in North Africa
Following page 78

The Rangers in Sicily and Italy
Following page 153

PREFACE

THIS BOOK HAS HAD AN UNUSUAL HISTORY. BILL
Darby, my West Point classmate, reported for duty in the Operations
Division (OPD), War Department General Staff, in May 1944. I had
just returned from military duty in Moscow and London and was
assigned to OPD.

Knowing Darby had a story to tell, I contacted him with the news
that a publishing house was interested in Darby's Rangers. Darby
and sometimes Herman Dammer, his executive, came to my home
in Washington to tell about the Rangers, probably on six to eight eve-
nings altogether. I had a stenographer in the next room taking down
Darby's words.

In approximately six weeks of night work, the manuscript was completed. D-day for the Normandy Invasion had passed and, according to my publishers, the market for war books had taken a nose dive.

Shortly thereafter I went to France and didn't return to the United
States for two years. The manuscript for Darby's Rangers survived a
half dozen moves in my file cabinet. Bill Darby's younger sister,
Doris (Mrs. Lyndell Watkins), never gave up her desire to see the
story published. We agreed to leave the manuscript as Darby had

told the story but adding perspective to put the Ranger operations in context during World War II. I have also supplied some biographical information about Darby as well as comments about the Rangers.

I wish to thank a number of people for their assistance on this book. My late wife, Alice Baumer, helped immeasurably on the original manuscript, as did Colonel Herman Dammer, Darby's right-hand man through all the Ranger battles, and Colonel Dammer's wife Elizabeth. Charles MacDonald of the Office of the Chief of Military History gave me good advice, supplied many of the history books, and directed me to the National Archives where I got copies of the Ranger "After-Action Reports." Bill Darby's wife, Natalie (now Mrs. Conger Beasley), has furnished information and photographs. I deeply appreciate her help. I also wish to thank Dr. Michael King, whose Ph.D. dissertation, "William Orlando Darby: A Military Biography," offered interesting biographical data.

Most particularly, I want to thank the Rangers who gave their impressions of Bill Darby. Lt. James J. Altieri, who served with the Rangers through all their campaigns, was the editor of *Darby's Rangers,* another book on the Rangers, and organizer of Ranger conventions, has helped immeasurably with suggestions and advice. Phil Stern, photographer of the Rangers until wounded in Tunisia, has opened his files and printed numerous photographs, some of them now published for the first time. For other recollections of Darby, I quite naturally turned to our classmates.

A good friend, Ralph Ingersoll, accompanied Darby's Rangers as a captain on the night attack at Djebel el Ank, east of El Guettar in Tunisia. He wrote of this experience in *The Battle Is the Pay-Off.* Graciously he gave permission to utilize any part of his book.

My thanks also go to Gail Testa and Virginia Niedringhaus who somehow got all the military terms through their typewriters.

William H. Baumer
January 1980

Darby's Early Days

WILLIAM DARBY WAS BORN 9 FEBRUARY 1911 AND grew up in Fort Smith, Arkansas; his family had been part of the nineteenth-century westward migration. Bill—as he was called— grew up in the usual way of small-town America in the 1920s. He was a Boy Scout, part-time delivery boy, churchgoer, and an avid reader.

In high school he demonstrated a capacity for leadership and showed the traits of a born salesman. He was handsome—with a high forehead, blue eyes, firm mouth and jaw, and a ready smile. He had a friendly willingness to help out at any time.

Bill was interested in a military career and had his sights set on the United States Military Academy at West Point. It was quite difficult in 1929 to get an appointment to West Point—and to be accepted. The Darby's local congressman, Otis Wingo, was persuaded to include Bill in his nominations for the Academy as a second alternative candidate. As such, his selection for appointment was contingent on whether the principal and first alternative candidates were qualified. When both withdrew or were disqualified, Darby was named.

A member of the Class of 1933 at West Point, Darby was an exemplary cadet—a good student and a cadet company commander. He

1

was known as a charming, persuasive, extremely likeable person. He had lots of energy and was always willing to jump in and do a job.

On 13 June 1933 Darby graduated from West Point with a bachelor of science degree and a commission as second lieutenant in the field artillery. His class rank—based on classroom grades and military performance—was 177 out of 346. After graduation he reported to Fort Bliss, Texas, where he was assigned to the 1st Battalion, 82nd Field Artillery of the 1st Cavalry Division. The 82nd was the only unit of horse artillery in the army, with all its officers and men mounted.

For the next eight and one-half years, Darby served in various field-artillery assignments, attended school courses, and gained experience as a troop leader. His efficiency reports showed him to be progressing well in his chosen profession: he was a superior young officer. On 1 October 1940 he was promoted to captain, along with other members of his West Point class.

In early 1941 Darby participated in a joint army-navy training operation in Puerto Rico: it was his first experience with landing exercises, a skill he was to develop extensively during operations in Morocco and Sicily. He took part in additional ship-to-shore landing operations with the Carib force in the New River area of North Carolina. Amphibious training was an experience given to a very limited number of officers.

In November, Darby was ordered to Hawaii. Before he left, however, Pearl Harbor was attacked. He received new orders to report to Maj. Gen. Russell P. Hartle, commanding general of the 34th Infantry Division, in New York City. He appointed Darby as his aide.

On 15 January 1942 Hartle, Darby, and leading elements of the 34th sailed from Brooklyn for Belfast, Northern Ireland. They arrived on the twenty-sixth, and the next day Hartle assumed command of U.S. Army Northern Ireland.

It was early May before all of the 34th Division's units were landed in Northern Ireland. During this period, Darby was unhappy at the lack of activity. He requested a transfer, but it couldn't be arranged immediately. Plans were afoot, however, which would be to Darby's advantage.

Gen. George C. Marshall, chief of staff of the army, was anxious for American forces to get combat experience before the invasion of

Europe. The best opportunity seemed to be with Lord Louis Mount-batten, chief of combined operations, the headquarters of the British Commandos. Col. Lucian K. Truscott, Jr., was called upon to implement this project, and on 1 June he wrote instructions to General Hartle to organize a commando-type American unit.

On 8 June Bill Darby's hopes were realized: he was assigned to this new unit, to be called the Rangers. Thus does lightning strike in war time. Darby had the requisite training; he was on the spot; and he knew how to react to his good fortune.

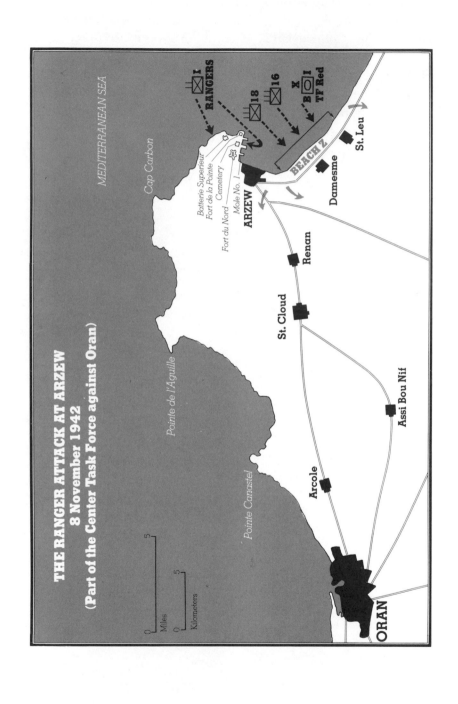

THE RANGER ATTACK AT ARZEW
8 November 1942
(Part of the Center Task Force against Oran)

MEDITERRANEAN SEA

Cap Carbon

Pointe de l'Aiguille

Pointe Canastel

ORAN

Arcole

Assi Bou Nif

St. Cloud

Renan

ARZEW

Batterie Supérieur
Fort de la Pointe
Cemetery
Fort du Nord
Mole No. 1

RANGERS
I

18

16

X
B I
TF Red

BEACH Z

Damesme

St. Leu

Miles
0   5

Kilometers
0   5

1

North African
Spearhead—Arzew

NOVEMBER 1942

PERSPECTIVE   The summer of 1942 was an unforgettable time for the World War II Allies. Until that year, defeat had followed defeat. Pearl Harbor came first for the United States, and then the loss of the Philippines; Britain had its Dunkirk and had lost Singapore; and the Soviet Union was fighting a desperate battle against the Nazi Army on its entire Western front.

Darby's Rangers' first operations—Operation Torch of 8 November 1942 —began with the war in North Africa in support of the Allied landing. This invasion had the backing of both British Prime Minister Winston Churchill and American President Franklin Roosevelt, and the opposition of practically all the military staffs. It was first mentioned by the British at the Arcadia Conference in December 1941. They stressed the desirability of bringing French forces back into the war against Germany and thought of the North African opera-tion as a relatively cheap means of seizing the initiative from Hitler. At the same time, the United States was busily engaged in the Pacific, particularly with the Guadalcanal operation which began on 7 August 1942. In late August 1942 the Soviet Union was to see the beginning of the Stalingrad attack by the Germans.

Churchill journeyed to Moscow to take news to Joseph Stalin, premier of the Soviet Union: the Western Allies were not going to invade the continent in 1942 but instead were to attack northwest Africa before the end of October. He gave Stalin the reasons for the inability of the Allies to help his beleaguered

5

forces by drawing German divisions away through a continental attack. Churchill explained Operation Torch and what was hoped it would do; he was greatly surprised when Stalin agreed with its concept.

After Churchill's visit to Moscow, and with Roosevelt's complete approval, plans went ahead swiftly for the Allied invasion of North Africa. On 14 August the Combined Chiefs of Staff appointed Gen. Dwight D. Eisenhower, then in command of the American forces in England, to be commander of the Allied expeditionary force and directed him to prepare plans for the landing. Three task forces were developed for the operation. The Western Task Force was to capture Casablanca, the Center Task Force the city of Oran, and the Eastern Task Force the seaport of Algiers. In each case these amphibious landings were to be made in the classical historic mode of pinching off a seaport by attacking from the flanks, rather than head on.

The Western Task Force, under the command of Maj. Gen. George S. Patton, included infantry troops and Maj. Gen. Ernest Harmon's armored forces. Harmon had elements of the 2nd Armored Division while the infantry was part of the 9th Infantry Division. The Central Task Force at Oran was commanded by Maj. Gen. Lloyd Fredendall and included the 1st Infantry Division and Maj. William Darby's Ranger Battalion. At Algiers the landing force consisted of a British division, a regimental combat team from the American forces, and three British Commando units.

¶   IT WAS JUST THREE HOURS BEFORE THE START OF the greatest amphibious operation in history with the hands of the ship's clock into 8 November 1942. I was standing on the bridge of H.M.S. *Ulster Monarch* with the master of the ship, trying to pierce the fog. Pricks of doubt ran through both our minds as we considered the assault landing to be made at Arzew, east of Oran, by my command, the 1st Ranger Battalion. Arzew was now some thirty miles off our starboard bow. Strange lights flickered in the distance along the shore, raising questions as to whether the landing force had been discovered. Knowing the importance of the assault landing, we were rubbing our hands nervously. What would the French do? Would they fight bitterly, or would they give up after their honor had been satisfied by strong resistance against an aggressive assault? A beacon, flashing its signal in a circle, spoke reassuringly. Perhaps the Rangers were going to make a landing in the dark without blue jets of flame crossing their path or large shells sending up waterspouts close by the landing boats.

The fog was growing thicker. I drifted over to the port side of the bridge and stared into the water, but close astern I could barely make out the misty outlines of H.M.S. *Royal Scotsman* and H.M.S *Royal Ulsterman,* bearing the remainder of the 1st Ranger Battalion.

Suddenly I stiffened with fright. Cold chills ran down my spine and my hair literally stood on end. Two silver objects, racing with terrific speed, were heading for the ships. "My God, torpedoes! We've been discovered."

Clutching the master of the ship by the arm, I pointed shakily towards those streaks of foam in the sea. For a few seconds we stared at them in numbed silence. Nothing could be done since it was too late to take any evasive action. The streaks were within twenty-five yards of the ship and closing fast. As they approached nearer and nearer, I instinctively threw my hands to my head as if to protect myself from the expected explosion. Then as the objects were within a few yards of the ship, they leaped out of the water throwing a fountain of spray. Diving gracefully, the two porpoises—for that was what they were—changed course to follow the ship. We mopped the perspiration from our foreheads and laughed weakly at one another's fears.

The North African invasion by United Nations forces was an awesome venture. The operation, carrying the hopes of many Allied peoples, was on a shoestring. Some of the landing craft, ships, and men had been made available just as the convoys were casting off from Great Britain and the United States. For months the public of the various countries of the United Nations had called for a second front; and when American troops first went to Northern Ireland and England, there was some feeling that the invasion of the continent was imminent. The soldiers on this expedition were not aware of any strategic decisions but knew only that they were going to the north coast of Africa, an area new to them and practically unknown to the average person on the streets at home.

As commanding officer of the 1st Ranger Battalion, I was well aware of the importance of the mission. Nervously I continued to scan the dim shapes all around. Beyond and to the rear of the three British ships bearing my battalion was a vast armada of assault ships protected by units of the British and American battle fleets. The

Mediterranean was calm, but the fog and darkness gave little information as to the size of the swells through which the ships were pounding their deliberate passage.

I pondered the job ahead, certain that my unit—British-trained under Commando instructors and experienced in landing exercises in all kinds of weather on the islands west of Scotland—would fight smartly and courageously. There were nearly five hundred of us, each man versed in the use of weapons and aware of the importance of scrambling ashore and vaulting over the parapets of the forts. The coastal guns within had to be knocked out to make the landings of the main forces safe.

The three ships on which the Rangers were being carried to battle were British, British-manned, and bore the resounding title of His Majesty's Ships. Taken from the Glasgow-Belfast ferry run, they were small ships—never intended for battle.

When my men had first boarded the former ferryboats, they had a twinge of self-pity since they were obviously not built for combat, they were just the best available. Though Great Britain had a large merchant marine at the beginning of the war, they had had to scrape the barrel by 1942. Ships of all types and classes were handed their orders to join the military service and be converted, like these ferryboats, for assault use. The primary method of conversion was to rip out the luxury items and place davits inboard on the promenade deck to hold the landing craft.

The North African landing was to be a ship-to-shore operation rather than shore-to-shore. In the latter, men enter a large landing craft at a port, proceed across water, and land directly on a beach. This is the easier of the two, but for longer distances, ship-to-shore is a necessity. Men could not stay in even large landing craft over many hundreds of miles of open water without suffering from exposure which would make them unfit for an assault landing. By utilizing large ships carrying a number of small landing craft, fighting men can travel distances of more than a thousand miles and be disembarked several miles out to sea from their landing beach. This was the procedure for the North African operation.

The mother vessel is called an assault ship for another reason. Carrying necessary weapons, equipment, and supplies for the men

NORTH AFRICAN SPEARHEAD—ARZEW

aboard, it is "combat-loaded" so that everything is available in the priority needed. Guns and ammunition come first; food, shelter, and clothing next.

After the initial beach has been crossed and the defenses set up inland, succeeding waves of troops go ashore from ships which are "convoy-loaded" instead of "combat-loaded." In the former case, a number of ships bearing a battalion, a regiment, or a division, have all the initial supplies stowed economically throughout the convoy.

On 26 October 1942 the three ferryboats left their home port of Glasgow bound for Oran. They must have seemed like trusty old streetcars being sent out on a new and untried rail line. They steamed southward at good speed and eventually joined other groups of larger transports. The armada, gathered together like chickens in a barnyard, was protected by the mother hens of the fleets hovering in the distance. Only the superstructures of some of the men-of-war could be seen. Planes floated above the convoy all day in great easy circles, assuring the troops that aircraft carriers were accompanying them. Zigzagging, the convoy steamed south, headed like others presumably on the long voyage around the Cape of Good Hope to Egypt and the battle there against Rommel.

En route to North Africa, the convoys were subjected to a rough storm. Ships rolled from side to side. The *Royal Scotsman* lost one of the vital LCAs (landing craft, assault), which broke loose from its davits. A destroyer dropped back to sink it with gunfire so that no trace would be left for U-boats to pick up the armada's trail.

Initially many Rangers were seasick. Although hard men physically, keyed for battle and better trained than other American comrades in the expedition, they shuddered under the same fears, experienced the same chills, and succumbed to the same relentless roll of the ships. Aboard ship, we kept up a rigorous schedule of physical training. Setting-up exercises and runs around the deck took up much of the day, but at sundown the convoy area took on the look of a gigantic Fourth of July celebration. It began with a sputter as the Rangers tossed bottles and cans overboard for target practice. Rifles, automatic rifles, and machine guns spattered gunfire from the ships' sterns at the bobbing objects. Lieutenant Shunstrom, a former weight lifter, exhibited his muscles when he fired a string of bullets from a light machine gun held high over his head. The ships' crews tuned up their larger weapons. One ship would fire its anti-aircraft guns; others trained on the shellbursts high in the air. The blazing sun dropped down on the ocean, halting the firing, and once more the convoy was wrapped in its protective coat of darkness.

Each day the Rangers had "skull practice." Like a good football team, we were planning and preparing for the payoff game. Officers discussed their plans on a large-scale plaster-of-paris model. Every section and platoon had maps and air photographs that showed the coast in the vicinity of Arzew in great detail. British and American intelligence agencies had supplied us with the most minute information about beaches, coastal guns, fortifications, and the arms of the French defenders.

Our objective area, the coast between Oran and Arzew, resembled a camel's back. Oran was on the eastern side of one hump, fronting on a large bay, and Arzew was thirty miles east on the eastern side of the next hump. The latter town looked across the broad Arzew Bay to the town of Mostaganem.

The plan was to land the 1st Division with the 16th and 18th Infantry Regiments to the east of Oran across the beaches of Arzew Bay and the 26th Infantry Regiment far to the west of Oran, to converge on Oran with two pincer movements and squeeze it off, thereby giving us the excellent naval base of Mers-el-Kebir and the port of Arzew itself.

I knew a month before we sailed that our mission was to capture, ahead of the 1st Division, the two gun batteries that dominated the long beach at Arzew.

Two separate coastal batteries were at Arzew: a small one at the harbor's edge named Fort de la Pointe and a larger position, Batterie du Nord, on a hill overlooking the harbor and the bay to the east. The latter was a more pretentious fort with a four-gun battery equipped with long-range rifles that could keep our fleet five miles at bay. They had the facilities for shooting in almost any direction. The guns were well sited and well controlled.

Our search for landing beaches disclosed only two between Arzew and Oran. Four miles northwest of Arzew at the top of the hump near Cap Carbon, was a beach suitable for the landing of a small force. Up the hump a short distance from Arzew was another small beach, appropriately named Cemetery Beach; the many offshore rocks noticeable in the air photographs made us shy away from a landing there. Assault boats would be broken up before they reached shore. The harbor of Arzew was the sole remaining possibility for a landing within our allotted sector.

The selection of landing locations was part of the problem confronting the Rangers. Knocking out two separate coastal batteries was another. We faced a dilemma: If the entire battalion attacked the smaller fort at the water's edge, we would very probably alert Batterie du Nord on the hill. If the Rangers attacked the larger fort first, French defenders would be alert and at "action stations" at Fort de la Pointe and other coastal defenses, and the boom in the harbor would be closed.

Contrary to standard practice, it was decided to split the 1st Ranger Battalion so as to attack both positions in a one-two punch. Four companies under my command were to attack the larger fort, while my executive officer, Maj. Herman Dammer, was to lead the remaining two companies against the harbor fort. (In the Rangers, every unit or task force was designated by the commanding officer's name, thus adding personality to their fighting.)

The Dammer Force aboard the *Royal Scotsman* had to replan their boat loading after the loss of the assault craft in the heavy Atlantic storm. Air photographs showed that Arzew on the eastern slope of the coastal hump had an artificial harbor enclosed by two jetties—the outer, or seaside jetty, pointing due south. Fort de la Pointe was situated at the land end of this sea jetty where it made a right angle with another sea jetty. The fort was composed of two separate positions. A barbed-wire enclosure guarded three coastal guns, and directly behind, there was a small French fort whose vertical walls were about twenty feet high. There were no guns in the walled fort.

For the attack in the harbor, the assault forces would have to enter through a boom connecting the harbor jetties. The boom was a string of buoys connected by cable and from which antitorpedo nets were suspended. Photographs taken at irregular intervals showed the boom was open or shut at varying times. The Rangers couldn't plan on the boom being open, so placed improvised steel skids or bumpers on the underside of the LCAs' hulls to protect the propellers and rudders. They could thus slide on top of the cable boom without fouling their propellers. A toboggan effect was added by extending the keel and making it deeper.

The Dammer group was prepared for assault, save one detail. How high was the dock where they would unload? The few Rangers who had accompanied British Commandos on the Dieppe raid the previous August stressed the importance of knowing whether scaling ladders would be needed. Survey files and photographs failed to give the height of the Arzew dock above the water. Ten days before sailing from Scotland, an intelligence officer sent us a faded photograph showing a fisherman reaching up to lay his catch on the dock. Standing in his boat he was just able to lay his hands on the dock's edge. This gave the needed information.

After ten days the ships reached a point west of Gibraltar. Then turning eastward in the darkness, they hurried through the Straits. Aboard ship, rumors of U-boats, of sinkings within the convoy, of enemy knowledge of Allied plans moved among the troops. For one awful day after passing through the Straits, the three converted ferryboats circled inside the Mediterranean under guard of two corvettes disguised as landing craft assault (LCA). Swinging clockwise, the small ships brushed close to the Spanish coast near Granada and then steamed near the African shore. At dawn, when halfway around the first circle, a U-boat alarm was sounded. Simultaneously a deep bang, bang, bang was heard. The explosions sent huge billows of water high in the air near the corvettes, which were dropping depth charges.

A haze hid the African coast, and the British ships continued on the great circle course. Suddenly the cry of "Action Stations" went up. The ships' crews ran to their guns; the Rangers hustled into their life belts. Dead ahead about a mile and in the fringe of the haze stood three shapes that looked like destroyers to the untrained eye. They were huge French submarines on the surface. Following them was another craft that looked like a tender.

The British captains saw the enemy craft. In turn, they were positive French eyes were peering at them. The master of the *Ulster Monarch* wished to hide the giveaway landing craft on board, but it was too late. "The gaff is blown," he stated positively, as he mentally brushed aside the possibility of surprise in the landings. Rapidly deciding against breaking radio silence, he boldly continued his course toward the enemy. Sailors and soldiers held their breath. The small ships swiftly closed half the distance to the subs. Then the subs turned tail and disappeared in the fog.

At dusk the Rangers were happy to see the large convoy approach. We joined it on a course for Malta, a course set in the hope that the enemy would believe it was the usual supply convoy for the mighty little fortress. When darkness on the night of 7 November hid their actions, the ships wheeled to the right in the direction of Oran.

I turned away from the bridge of the *Ulster Monarch* to go below, still feeling a bit ridiculous after the porpoise scare. I had just entered my cabin to make a last-minute check of equipment when a loud and insistent knocking rattled the door. Through it burst a wild-eyed lieutenant—the one selected to lead the advance guard platoon against the main coastal battery positions. His face was chalky and drawn. He blurted out, "My God, Colonel, I've drawn a blank. I can't seem to remember a thing. Please go over my job with me once more."

With a sinking heart I tried to hide my own fears and attempted to calm those of the numbed lieutenant. Carefully, for what seemed the hundredth time, I outlined the plan of attack of the Darby Force.

Two ships, the *Ulster Monarch* and the *Royal Ulsterman*, bearing four companies of the 1st Ranger Battalion were to drop off from the convoy as it proceeded eastward for Arzew Bay. Then after locating the Cap Carbon headland at the top of the hump, they would proceed down the coast a short distance to our small landing beach. Ashore, we would follow the coastal road running southeast toward Arzew for four miles. Close to the town, we would turn inland up a wadi, or valley, to attack Batterie du Nord on the ridgeline, where four 105-mm guns in concrete emplacements were heavily wired in. Five hundred yards south was a pentagonal French fortification named Fort du Nord, which was also to be captured.

The lieutenant's tenseness dissipated at the recital of the mission. He joined me in a smoke as together we laughed off his predicament. Then we went below to visit our Rangers in the troop decks.

The men were putting the final touches on their rifles and automatic weapons. One Ranger dropped a bit of oil onto the receiver of his automatic rifle and then carefully wiped it off. Minute adjustments were being made in their packs. One soldier, taking no chances, was pushing the cartridges out of his automatic rifle magazine with his thumb. Each one was inspected and carefully rolled in an oily rag. Mae Wests were being checked for airtightness. The Rangers, seated on the floor or on their equipment, were shifting uncomfortably. The look in their eyes said they could do the job ahead of them; they knew they could and were rarin' to go.

From the troop deck, I wandered to the rear mess deck where a religious service was in progress. A Catholic chaplain standing before an improvised altar was ministering to the Rangers without regard to their individual creeds. After the service, I returned to my cabin again to finish checking my equipment. Like the men, I poked at my pack, glanced feelingly at my Springfield rifle, and then grasped it with two hands for reassurance. All Ranger officers carried rifles so as to be indistinguishable from their men and not special targets for enemy snipers. I fretted about insignificant things. What to do about the two packages of cigarettes that I couldn't squeeze into my pack? Should I leave the bar of soap resting in the water basin? Then lying down fully clothed, I tried to gather my thoughts about the coming landing. Again there was a knock at my door. The priest, wearing a green beret, entered. Plainly distressed, he said questioningly, "My name is not on the list to make the initial landing."

I attempted to reassure him. "But don't you see, Chaplain, there is no need to risk your life uselessly. You'll be of far more benefit tomorrow after the battle is over."

The padre shook his head gravely. "I'm afraid you don't understand. It is most important that I be with the men in battle. Don't you see that if I could get to one dying soldier and bring him thoughts of his God, I'll be accomplishing my personal mission."

"I guess you win, Chaplain," I said. "Frankly, I never thought of it that way before. You'll go in boat Number Five in my wave."

Finally the hour for "embarkation stations" arrived. The signal was given over the ship's public-address system. The Rangers, letter perfect in the drill, filed noiselessly into their boats. They had practiced this many times during the voyage, and each man knew his way through the darkened ship by heart. The Rangers were soon in their places, and the command was given, "Off gripes, lower away!"

At that instant, five LCAs and one LCS (landing craft, support) from each of the two mother ships dropped towards the water. Their engines started quietly, and the misty shapes moved forward to rendezvous off the bow of the leading ship. But there was one hitch. One of the assault landing craft of the *Ulster Monarch* was hanging by its stern for some inexplicable reason. Its occupants had been dropped bodily into the sea and were swimming around, that is, except for one very short Ranger officer—the head of a demolitions party. When getting into the landing craft on deck, he had fuses, caps, primers, and even some TNT draped around his slight figure. In his hands he carried a rifle and a contraption known as a "beehive," a steel device for constricting a TNT explosion. The officer went down and down into the water. His fight for buoyancy was futile until he released the beehive and threw off some of the explosives. When he surfaced, he still gripped his rifle. Nearby Rangers tugged for several minutes before they pulled the officer and his remaining load of explosives aboard. The other men in the water had been picked up by already crowded LCAs. There was no shouting or excitement, and the Rangers still had a firm grip on their weapons. Their past training had paid off. They were not surprised or terrified—just angry about getting wet so prematurely.

The LCAs carried thirty-two to thirty-five soldiers in addition to the British crew of five. A Ranger platoon filled one LCA, a company, two; and the entire battalion with its headquarters filled fourteen LCAs. The LCSs carried no assault troops but hovered about the forces while landing, their machine guns and other weapons prepared to fight off torpedo boats or to match fire with machine guns or small weapons opposing the landing from the shore.

After the thoroughly wet Rangers had been dragged out of the water into the remaining landing boats, the flotilla started for shore. Apparently they had circled so long that they went off in the wrong direction. The captain of the *Ulster Monarch* steamed his ship alongside, in an unplanned maneuver, saying, "You're off course; follow me." And he coursed the small boats for a mile. Then he shouted over the bridge, "Keep whatever you have on your compasses and go right in."

The landing boats hit their objective right on the nose. It was very hazy—visibility being limited to about two hundred feet, so Cap

Carbon could not be seen from out at sea. The landing units had to depend on their compasses and on the faintly visible stars above. The flotilla charged towards shore, making no noise and leaving a very slight wake.

Suddenly a shape developed menacingly out of the gloom, and the leading LCA narrowly avoided collision. It was a fishing boat harmlessly bent on its trade. A hundred rifles were leveled at the boat; machine guns from twelve craft were trained on it. If the poor terrified fisherman had so much as coughed, he would undoubtedly have been blown out of the water. No shot was fired, and the fisherman for once had a story that none of his fellows could equal.

There was still another scare in store. The assault boats were suddenly illuminated from below. Was it possible that there were lights under the water? The Rangers jumped to the conclusion that a submarine was about to surface and stared at the water with many misgivings. Before their wild imaginings could produce the picture of a Nazi submarine pen or something similar, they had passed into darkness again. No one was able to understand the reason for the lights at the time. Later we learned that they were actually underwater lights used to lure unwary sardines into fishnets.

The fog began to lift slightly and dead ahead stood the huge mass of Cap Carbon, recognized immediately by the Rangers from their long study of the maps and photographs. Along the shore southeastward toward Arzew, the small sandy scramble beach awaited us, if the photographs were correct. The reassuring gentle slap of waves on the sloping beach was sweet music compared to the crashing cymbals of the waves hitting the rocks and reefs which closely flanked the landing beach.

The Rangers were tense. They gripped their weapons tightly, shifted their feet, and tried not to look at one another as the keels slipped over a sandbar with a grating noise. A jar followed and then a complete stop. The men smiled inwardly for they had made a perfect landfall after all. The ramps were dropped noiselessly. Heavy shoes planked on them, but there was little sound as the Rangers rushed out to touch African soil for the first time. As if rehearsing a play, the men ran swiftly across the beach and tore into the cliffs. They knew they had a difficult climb ahead, and they wanted to get all the momentum possible.

So far the landing had been a complete surprise. The enemy was nowhere in sight. Then unexpectedly a sentry wandered toward them from his lookout post on Cap Carbon, perhaps attracted by some unfamiliar noise. Dazedly, he walked in among the Rangers and was taken prisoner before he could give warning. The lines around the Rangers' mouths relaxed: Like football players who had made the first tackle, they were now unconcerned about the crowd at the big game. The advance guard, led by a calm, confident lieutenant—the one who had been so badly shaken three hours previously—moved out as if on maneuvers. Noiselessly the snake-like procession formed behind them and started southeast across the rolling African foothills toward the four-gun position of Batterie du Nord.

While the Darby Force was striding over the four miles from our landing beach to Batterie du Nord, the Dammer Force had disembarked from the *Royal Scotsman* at 0100, 8 November. Proceeding in column, the five assault boats soon reached the area of Arzew harbor. Green and red lights glowed at the ends of the harbor's two jetties. Eyes searched for the boom. Then looking up from the harbor, they checked the location of Fort de la Pointe directly ahead, Cemetery Beach up the coast to the right, and the lighthouse on Ile d'Arzew off to their right rear towards the transport disembarkation area. The lighthouse beacon shone in the darkness.

Yes, the boom should be dead ahead. The British coxswains nervously pushed their fingers towards full throttle. Major Dammer in the lead boat peered ahead, nodded. Then with an expelling of air, he whispered loudly, "The boom is open!" Hands relaxed on the throttles, and the flotilla continued its rapid advance to the shore.

As the Dammer Force headed into the harbor along the harbor's outer, or sea, jetty, they intended to get between it and the main pier. In the darkness, they quickly found themselves on the west, or bay, side of the pier. With grand disdain for the danger of the situation, the flotilla swept around in a complete circle and moved as planned toward the dock.

The boats touched and men jumped out. The landing craft ramps dropped down but not flat as expected. One piece of information had been lacking. Though the height of the sea wall was known, there had been no indication that it sloped into the water. The men clambered out and slipped on the slime. Forgetting the need for quiet, they cursed violently as they fought their way up the slanting sea wall. As they slid back again and again, their equipment caught on the small buoys attached to the dock as fenders for the protection of ships. The Rangers got tangled up in these, and the swearing became more heated.

Strangely, all remained quiet ashore. Capt. Manning Jacob's platoon moved down the dock, encountering one bewildered Arab and two French soldiers returning with laundry bundles to the fort. The rest of Companies A and B made a sweep part way up the hill so as to come against the fort from the north. The two Ranger groups converged from opposite directions on the three emplaced guns. Cutters were jabbed into the rusty barbed wire and zipped through it. A sentinel silhouetted against the skyline asked unexcitedly who was there. Captain Jacob's answer in French sparred for time. The sentinel, unaware of danger, came down to where the Rangers were cutting wire to satisfy his curiosity. A Ranger struck him from behind. No shot was fired, no alarm given as the guard was taken prisoner.

The Americans poured through the wire, vaulted a low parapet, and after a few quick shots captured the guns and some sixty prisoners. The fight was over in fifteen minutes. French collaborationists had done their job well, for the surprise was complete. Even the wife of the adjutant of the post was captured in the fort. The Dammer Force then posted outguards around the area while the major was attempting to reach the main body over his walkie-talkie radio.

Meanwhile, the Darby Force, after our successful landing near Cap Carbon, proceeded still undiscovered along the coastal road towards Batterie du Nord. An LCS followed the column offshore, prepared to give flanking fire in case we were met by enemy fire. When still about two miles from Arzew, my curiosity overcame me, so I called the walkie-talkie operator and signaled for Major Dammer. By coincidence, this was the same time the latter was trying to reach me. Dammer spoke jubilantly, "I've captured *my* objective." I got the implication all right, that my subordinate had succeeded quickly. Now it was to be seen if I would do as well. I asked about indications of alertness in the battery on the hill, and received a disappointing, "Yes, sir," which meant a hard fight. But my Rangers were ready.

My main force had reached the wadi leading up into the hills from the coastal road. Companies C, F, and E advanced abreast. Company D, manhandling four 81-mm mortars, moved into a defiladed position five hundred yards to their rear, in a ditch previously selected from the map as the ideal location for the mortars. From that prearranged position and using a predetermined range, they were to hold their fire until called on.

The rifle companies proceeded stealthily towards the north side of the battery with concentric circles of barbed wire eight feet high and fourteen feet deep obstructing their approach. No sound was made until the Rangers began cutting through the wire. Cautiously they snipped the strands, expecting momentarily that machine-gun fire would streak acrosss their hands and in front of their faces, but none came.

Just as they reached the last strand, the stillness was blasted by the chatter of French machine guns. Tracers sputtered over the heads of the Rangers inside the bank of wire. No orders had been given yet, so I now called for Lieutenant Klefman and his men to pull back to the edge of the wire. The lieutenant hugged the edge of the wire trying to pull one of the Rangers who had been hit and was lying across the severed strands to safety.

In a matter of seconds I ordered Lieutenant Shunstrom to take his platoon and get ready to rush the control tower facing out to sea. After this movement, Lieutenant Klefman acted as a forward observer for the mortars. They fired one salvo, figuring as planned that by ranging slightly beyond the target, the Rangers in the shadow of the fort would be safe from shell fragments. Klefman called back, "Christ, the mortars are right on. Come back fifty yards and pour it on." Eighty 81-mm shells came in a flurry, turning the French machine guns off as if someone had pulled a switch. Ranger riflemen sprang from prone positions close to the wire and went over the parapet, shouting as they bored in. Needing no orders, several Rangers rushed the big guns, thrusting Bangalore torpedoes—four-foot sections of steel pipe crammed with explosives—into the muzzles.

At the same moment, a larger party of Rangers slammed through the main entrance of Batterie du Nord, shooting the sentry barring their path. The battle was practically over. The French soldiers had barricaded themselves in a powder magazine underground thinking the mortar shells were aerial bombs. They did not answer to the call in French that they give themselves up. Grenades were pushed down the ventilators along with a Bangalore torpedo. The French came out with their hands in the air, sixty prisoners in all. After the guns were completely demolished, outposts were established.

The Rangers had lost two men killed and eight wounded. We had taken out the coastal batteries by 0400 on 8 November and were ready to signal the support elements of the 1st Division five miles out to sea that the coastal batteries of Arzew would not hamper their landing.

Although I was jubilant about the victory, I found we had lost our most priceless piece of equipment—the long-range radio. It had been agreed upon beforehand that the success signal would be flashed by radio and authenticated by four green Very Lights fired in rapid succession followed by four white star shells. The latter were at the bottom of the sea along with their special projectors. One boat had been lost in the landing, and the large radio and all the white star shells had been loaded in it.

The Rangers atop the hill at Batterie du Nord shot green lights all over the place. Gen. Terry Allen, commanding the 1st Infantry Division, and Gen. Lloyd Fredendall, the corps commander, saw them and said to each other, "What does that mean? If it's Darby and he's been successful in knocking out the batteries, he will authenticate with white flares."

But I couldn't authenticate our success and began to get panicky. Finally we thought of the British naval forward observer party that had come ashore with the Rangers. They dried out their radio and an hour later got a message off to a British destroyer, which in turn transmitted it to the American forces. Though General Allen got the message two and a half hours later, he had moved his troops on seeing the green flares. By dawn the 16th and 18th Regimental Combat Teams of the 1st Division were well ashore.

Surprisingly, the action at the harbor fort by the Dammer Force had not alerted the larger fort. The battery commander, a French naval officer, had been so surprised that he had had time to grab only his naval coat and cap. Below his correct upper dress, pajama trousers and slippers stuck out ludicrously.

I directed him to call the commanding officer of Fort du Nord. Knowing that it contained no heavy guns and having been told it was a convalescent home for the French Foreign Legion, I felt there was no urgency about its surrender. I therefore asked the commander to meet me at dawn at Batterie du Nord for the surrender. The French commander assented.

A few minutes later a burst of machine-gun fire from the fort plunged into the Ranger positions but without injuring any of us. This firing continued, so again the telephone operator called, relaying a threat that mortar fire and naval gunfire would be turned on the fort if they did not stop shooting. While this conversation was in progress, the nettled Rangers laid a few 60- and 81-mm shells into the fort. The French commander, acceding to the American demands, called back with a "Oui, oui, mon Colonel." I then ordered the commander to come out of the fort with a white flag in hand.

The comic opera continued. Five men and I started across the intervening five or six hundred yards to the fort with a company of Rangers to cover us. No white flag appeared however. Instead there was a burst of machine-gun fire from the French. We were now thoroughly aroused and fighting mad. A company advanced to attack and and was stopped by the moat surrounding the fort. Then, thinking only of getting at the French, they rushed across the drawbridge heedlessly. Inside, drunken members of the garrison were throwing their rifles down a well. They were taken prisoner and sent to the magazine caves at Batterie du Nord.

While the Fort du Nord incident was going on, Major Dammer sent one group of his men to occupy the refinery area north of the harbor to prevent sabotage. Another group moving in the darkness was sent to dislodge snipers in the cemetery on the hillside between Fort de la Pointe and Fort du Nord.

Lieutenant Shunstrom's platoon was dispatched to assist in clearing the cemetery. Before dawn all the snipers except one had been captured or killed. A Foreign Legion captain of undetermined origin, but who spoke a good Brooklynese English, was holed up and continued sniping until overpowered. When captured he stated, "By God, if I hadn't run out of ammunition, you'd never have gotten me!"

Major Dammer's Force next went through the harbor area, knocking out enemy snipers on the main mole. Some resistance remained however in the warehouses at the foot of the pier. At this moment, several British and American naval officers on an LCS were entering the harbor to board the ships to prevent scuttling. They swung around to the bay side of the mole and moved the assault craft up close where their .50-caliber machine guns soon blasted out the snipers in the warehouse.

Continuing past the harbor, the Rangers met a battalion of the 1st Infantry Division that had landed on the other side of the town and marched through it. The infantry battalion commander reported the town cleared and turned over responsibility for its administration to the Rangers. When it was daylight, the Rangers discovered that the town had not been completely cleared. There were snipers everywhere. It took three days to clean them out.

Action began at dawn when a battery of French 75-mm guns started shooting at an Allied ship which had entered the harbor. They managed to put several shells on the decks before the Rangers captured the battery. Since Arabs were scavenging rifles from the dead Frenchmen, a thorough search of their village had to be made and weapons recovered.

With Arzew completely in our hands and the two regimental combat teams of the 1st Division ashore, the attack moved inland. On the afternoon of 8 November, our Company E, commanded by Lieutenant Max Schneider, was sent to join a battalion of the 16th Infantry at Port-aux-Poules southeast along the coast. The rest of the Ranger battalion remained for a time in Arzew, where I presided as the town mayor.

The Ranger company sent east made contact at about 0700 on 9 November with the 1st Battalion, 16th Infantry, and was instructed to proceed by road to La Macta, approximately four and a half miles farther east. About one half mile east of Port-aux-Poules light enemy fire came from a ridge south of the road. The Rangers pushed on and a mile west of La Macta were compelled to deploy because of heavy fire from rifles and machine guns. The second platoon of this company, assisted by two self-propelled 75-mm guns, swung around to the left or east flank while the other Rangers held the enemy at their front.

The French gave up, and our troops went unmolested into La Macta where they placed outposts for the protection of the town. The next day they were relieved by other infantry elements and returned by train to Arzew.

Meanwhile, I ordered Lt. Gordon Klefman to take C Company from Arzew on 8 November to defend the command post of the 1st Division at the village of Tourville, on the outskirts of Arzew. This company then moved overland the next morning to assist the 18th Infantry combat team near St. Cloud. Attached to the 1st Battalion of the 18th Infantry, Klefman and his Rangers moved after dark in an encircling movement to block the exits on the south of St. Cloud. During the night they got astride of the main road without incident. At dawn, they discovered an enemy mortar column at a standstill just outside town, so the company moved to attack. When they were within a quarter mile of the enemy column, artillery, mortar, and machine-gun fire was poured onto them from a blanketed artillery position alongside the road.

While one platoon kept the enemy engaged, Klefman sent the other westward to flank the enemy. The Rangers on the encircling move were brought to a standstill by machine-gun fire when about seventy-five yards from the enemy position. They dug in, sniping at the French and mortaring their position. Lieutenant Klefman was mortally wounded while leading the encircling platoon across an open field. In his last seconds he commanded, "Keep going! Keep going to the right and don't worry about me." About midafternoon, the French surrendered. C Company rejoined the battalion about dark on 10 November. The battle for Oran was won.

Our plan of attack on the Arzew batteries had been carried out as planned. The only hitch was the loading of the heavy radio and the white star shells in the same boat. We suffered rather light casualties, four killed and eleven wounded, while capturing several hundred prisoners and inflicting heavy casualties on the enemy. The training at the commando depot in Scotland, where individuals had been trained to size up a new tactical situation instantaneously, had paid off. They hit the ground, fired their weapons, crawled or ran forward without deliberate or conscious thought. Improvisation on the battlefield was not needed. Each Ranger knew his job and anticipated events.

II

Training in Northern Scotland

JUNE–SEPTEMBER 1942

PERSPECTIVE   When the 1st Ranger Battalion was organized, there was some debate in the United States Army as to what its purpose was and what was expected of it. In the original orders of 1 June 1942, the commanding general, United States Army Northern Ireland Forces, was told to form a "commando organization" as the first step in a program specifically directed by Chief of Staff Gen. George Marshall to give battle experience to the maximum number of American Army personnel.

The 1st Ranger Battalion was activated on 19 June 1942 at Carrickfergus, Northern Ireland. The Rangers had the usual infantry equipment with some notable additions: special equipment for amphibious landings and night attacks, e.g., collapsible rubber dinghies and life-preserver vests. They also had engineering gear including demolition equipment and camouflage nets.

The initial orders were explicit that the unit was to be formed by obtaining volunteers from units of the United States Army in Northern Ireland. It said that officers and noncommissioned officers should possess leadership qualities of a high order with particular emphasis on initiative and common sense. All officers and men were to possess natural athletic ability and physical stamina and, insofar as possible, be without physical defect.

Commando training likewise involved a number of specialties in addition to the usual physical training and qualifications in arms. Among the specialties included but not listed in the "Table of Organization" were demolition personnel, mechanics, truck and tractor drivers, and maintenance personnel. Other experience listed as particularly desirable related to judo, scouting, small boats, mountain climbing, weapons, power plants, and radio stations.

The Rangers were attached to the Special Services Brigade (British) for training and tactical control. It was expected that all applicable American doctrine, methods, and equipment would be retained, but some special procedures followed by the British Commandos would be adopted when necessary.

¶ THE WORLD WAR II AMERICAN RANGERS WERE born in June 1942. General George C. Marshall, chief of staff of the United States Army, had visited the British Commando Training Depot and upon returning home directed the creation of the new American Rangers. It was he who adopted the name "Rangers," after the famous band led by Maj. Robert Rogers against the French and Indians during that period of our prerevolutionary history.

Rogers' Rangers had been famous for hit-and-run raids into enemy country. This, in General Marshall's eyes, was to be one of the main tasks of the new Rangers, thus giving the men experience for the greater battles to come. In addition, they were to be trained in amphibious warfare and were to operate with the British Commandos.

American troops in Northern Ireland in the summer of 1942 were assigned to the V Corps, which consisted of the 34th Infantry and 1st Armored Divisions. For more than five months they had trained and maneuvered across Ireland's hedges and green fields. At first, an invasion of the continent seemed imminent, but when only a trickle of soldiers joined them, their hopes for action began to fade.

One day in June 1942 a circular letter appeared on every bulletin board in North Ireland, offering hardy soldiers a rugged future in a job where a man could call his soul his own.

"I joined this outfit," said Technician 5th Grade Clyde Thomson, of Ashland, Kentucky, "because they said in that letter they wanted men to work in small combat groups which would hit the enemy and run. Well we hit more'n we run, but I'm satisfied they kept most of their promises, and we were on our own most of the time. That's the way we wanted it, and that's the way it was."

At that time I was serving as aide to Maj. Gen. Russell P. Hartle, commanding general of the American Forces in Northern Ireland. I received orders 8 June 1942 that I was to organize the 1st Ranger

Battalion. Setting up headquarters in Carrickfergus, twenty miles north of Belfast, I spent the next dozen days interviewing the officer volunteers and with their help some two thousand volunteers from the V Corps. There was no intention of selecting a six-foot "Guards" unit. Physical condition, natural athletic ability, and stamina were sought without regard to a man's height. We naturally required thorough medical examinations for all soldiers. Looking beyond the physical, we attempted to determine whether a volunteer had good judgement and if his desire to be a Ranger was genuine. Our interviews had the object of weeding out the braggart and the volunteer looking for excitement but who, in return, expected to be a swashbuckling hero who could live as he pleased if only he exhibited courage and daring in battle.

When the 1st Ranger Battalion was officially activated on orders from the commanding general European theater of operations on 19 June 1942, to its 26 officers and 447 enlisted men a 10 percent overstrength was added to compensate for losses in training. The original 1st Ranger Battalion consisted of a headquarters company of 8 officers and 69 enlisted men and 6 companies of 3 officers and 63 enlisted men each. Six days after its establishment, we were inspected by Gen. Robert Laycock, chief of the British Commandos and then general officer commanding the British Special Services Brigade.

General Hartle took a personal interest in Ranger recruitment, ensuring that topnotch soldiers who volunteered were released from their units. His enthusiasm for the special battalion never waned, as he made many personal inspections, offering constructive suggestions in our training schedule and directing the supply of special clothing for hiking and climbing.

Among the original group of 575 Rangers were all types of Americans. There were few regular soldiers and no regular army officers other than myself. They ranged in age from seventeen to thirty-five, from boyish-looking soldiers just out of high school to an occasional grizzled "old soldier." They had come from practically every section of the Union, each claiming that the best fighting men come from Texas, or Iowa, or Georgia. A half dozen engagements later they were certain that no section of the broad United States produced better soldiers than another. Coming from Arkansas, I had to admit with a twinkle that there were no duds from Brooklyn, though as individual fighters, they were also equaled by men from elsewhere.

Sixty percent of the first group of Rangers came from the 34th Division, mainly from Iowa, Nebraska, and Minnesota. Thirty percent had joined from the 1st Armored Division. The remaining ten percent were from medical, quartermaster, and signal troops of the V Corps.

Although many were Middle Westerners, the Rangers also included Pvt. "Chico" Feranandez of Havana, an expert machine gunner, and lion-tamer Cpl. James Haines of Kentucky, who had worked with Frank Buck and believed that being with the Rangers "ain't no different." Another favorite character was Pvt. Samson P. Oneskunk, a Sioux Indian from South Dakota.

In high spirits, with their future before them, the men of the 1st Ranger Battalion stepped down from the train at Fort William in Northern Scotland. A Cameron Highlander band was piping its shrill music from bagpipes, sounding the call of battle. The great adventure was about to begin.

We were met by Lt. Col. Charles Vaughan, M.B.E., a ruddy-cheeked, husky British officer who radiated enthusiasm and goodwill. After a short preliminary welcome, we formed, carrying our packs and rifles. Colonel Vaughan took the head of the column and cheerfully stated that he would lead the way to Achnacarry Castle, the headquarters of the Commando Depot. The brawny Scots picked up their bagpipes and strode off up a hill tootling as if glad to show us their country. With the lift given by the band, we stretched our stride, lifted our heads, and set out behind them for the hills in the distance. The first mile or two was fun. The band played on and the Rangers' enthusiasm sparkled. The hill got steeper, the band played louder, and feet began to drag. Mile after mile, we plodded ahead, packs getting heavier, and perspiration trickling down our backs. Questions tore through the column. Where was this castle? How much farther? Feet were blistering, and the men's faces grew grimmer. The band, however, seemed to gain strength. Not a single Ranger dared to fall out. They were volunteers and had been told they had chosen a rugged life. At last Achnacarry Castle appeared on the horizon. Its vine-covered walls and well-kept lawn seemed to beckon in their greenness. We all managed to make it. The colonel complimented us on our splendid march and promised more difficult ones in the future. Had we not been so exhausted by our march, we might have detected an impish grin beneath his ruddy features.

Achnacarry Castle has its own place in Scottish history. It had served many centuries as the seat of Locheil, the chieftain of the Cameron clan. It had also been a refuge for Bonny Prince Charlie several centuries before. It is situated in a mountainous section, heavy in trees and undergrowth. The terrain is broken and dotted by many lakes. In general this part of Scotland is wild, with inhabitants few and towns far apart. Wildlife such as grouse and red deer are in abundance, and the ice-cold streams plunging down the mountains are filled with salmon and trout. Achnacarry had been requisitioned by the government and was now used as the headquarters of the British Commandos. There were no barracks around the main building, though there were several permanent structures, one of which was occupied by Locheil.

We were shown to a camp with eight of us assigned to each of the British-type Bell tents. Unlimited use of the icy Scottish stream that roared past Achnacarry was offered for bathing. The food was rough British fare consisting mainly of tea, fish, and beans for breakfast; tea, beans, and bully beef for lunch; and tea, beans, and beef for dinner. This fare was varied occasionally by porridge without sugar or milk and by some ungodly concoction peculiar to only the British and known as "Duff." Naturally there were howls of anguish among the American Rangers at this manner of living.

To all these complaints of the many discomforts of his depot, Colonel Vaughan's invariable answer to me was "It's all part of the training, William, it's all part of the training." And with a twinkle in his eye, he would walk away leaving me wondering what approach one could possibly use to get under his hide.

The British Commandos did all in their power to test us to find out what sort of men we were. Then, apparently liking us, they did all in their power to prepare us for battle. At the depot were soldiers of many United Nations; the fighting French and Dutch, as well as the British. There were British veterans who had raided Norway at

Vaagso and at the Lofoten Islands, men who had escaped from Singapore, and others who had slipped away from the Italians in Somaliland. As instructors at the depot, these men were a constant source of inspiration to my Rangers and, at the same time, a vivid reminder of the difficulties of the job ahead.

A new life opened for us. The training was characterized by its realism and its simplicity. Inexpensive equipment was utilized but did not detract from the never-failing enthusiasm displayed by the instructors.

At the beginning of the training, in the presence of the commanding officer of the Commando Depot, I told the Ranger officers they would receive the same training as their men. Colonel Vaughan agreed. Thereafter, during instruction periods by the British, my officers fell in ranks when the battalion formed. Furthermore, the ranking officer present was to be the first to tackle every new obstacle, no matter what its difficulty. I included myself in this rule, believing deeply that no American soldier will refuse to go as far forward in combat as his officer.

The tremendous personality of Colonel Vaughan pervaded the atmosphere at the Commando Depot. A former Guards drill sergeant and an officer in World War I with later experience in commando raids in World War II, he was highly qualified for his job. He had served with distinction during the commando raids against Vaagso and the Lofoten Islands in Norway. A burly man, about six-feet-two, strongly built and of ruddy complexion, he had a face which at times showed storm clouds and at other times, a warm sunniness. A man of about fifty years of age, he was in excellent physical condition and was remarkably agile.

Though not to his liking, being a man who naturally loved to be with troops, he organized the staff of the Commando Depot and built up its many courses of instruction. His drill schedule would have delighted the heart of a Napoleon. From early morning till late at night, seven days a week, he accounted for every minute.

Colonel Vaughan was constantly in the field, participating in, observing, and criticizing the training of the men. During it all he was highly enthusiastic. Observing a mistake he would jump in and personally demonstrate how to correct it. He insisted upon rigid discipline, and officers and men alike respected him. He was quick to think up means of harassing the poor weary Rangers, and as he put it, "To give all members the full benefit of the course."

The Commandos' first item in its trilogy of training was physical conditioning, developed by speed marching and execution of runs over increasingly difficult obstacle courses. Next we learned to use the portable weapons, including rifle, machine gun, bayonet, and mortar, which were needed by hit-and-run raiders. There were no specialists in the camp. All men had to meet intentionally high standards in employing these weapons. The third requirement was battle preparedness—the expert ability to execute small tactical problems. This know-how included such items as the practice and accomplishment of stalking a sentry, scouting in the advanced guard, patrolling for information in enemy territory, street fighting, and knocking out pillboxes on the forward and rear slopes of hills.

Northern Scotland was ideal for physical conditioning. Its rugged, scenic terrain included mountains, valleys, bogs, and heavily forested country with a stout heather undergrowth. We were astonished that in our climbs in the hills we encountered more ponds and swamps than in the lowlands.

Around the Commando Depot were man-made obstacles, including high walls, ladders, ditches, and hedges. The physical training course over them was strenuous but well within our capabilities. We marched swiftly, swam rivers or crossed them on bridges made of toggle ropes—a length of cord with a wood handle at one end and a loop at the other. Each man carried one. There were cliffs to climb, slides to tumble down, and when all that was not quite enough, we played hard games.

Borrowing from some of the ancient Scottish games, log exercises became ritual in our training. A group of men carrying a six-inch log on their shoulders tossed it about in an attempt to keep it off the ground.

There was boxing and close-in fighting. There was no particular emphasis on jujitsu, though the men were given a few good usable holds that each could be expected to remember and utilize when needed.

Famous, and cursed by the Rangers, were the speed marches at the Commando Depot. Starting out with three-mile hikes, the training worked up to courses of five-, seven-, ten-, twelve-, and sixteen-mile speed marches. On these we had to average better than four miles an hour over varied terrain, carrying full equipment. As we progressed in our physical training, we were sent on longer speed marches.

One night preceding the twenty-five-mile march Capt. Steve Meade, a horoscope fan, received a new forecast in the mail. The Rangers gathered around, reading, "You must avoid high places." The march was scheduled over the mountains. Meade read on, "Don't strain yourself on this particular date." Knowing the obstacles ahead the Rangers roared. Finally the horoscope warned, "Stay away from wet places." The writer had evidently not heard of northern Scotland.

Speed marches gave maximum development to lungs and legs, and most importantly, to feet. In the early stages we had blisters by the bushel. Finally, though, we became hardened, and our feet were able to stand up under any kind of pounding. On one occasion during the training in speed marching, the Rangers flew across ten miles in eighty-seven minutes, flashing that long stride that was to become our trademark in the Mediterranean war.

Another vital part of the training were three-day combat problems, each climaxed by a sham battle. It was the belief at the Commando Depot that any trained soldier can march the first day, even over obstacles, up and down hill, and through swamps. The good soldier will finish out the second day's march, but only the topnotch soldier will complete the march on the third day and still be able to fight effectively.

After the first three-day exercise with its climactic combat problem, the 10 percent overstrength we had had in the beginning melted away to a 10 percent deficit of our full strength of six companies. These "separations" from the Rangers, as the Army termed them, were greater in number than the casualties including killed, wounded, and sick throughout the Tunisian campaign.

The training in weapons was more comprehensive than that received by the average infantry soldier at the time. Great stress was given to field firing and the use of the bayonet at close quarters. To bring out this point, the Commandos had a unique bullet-and-bayonet course. Here men working in pairs, one covering the other, were required to climb difficult obstacles, such as a fourteen-foot wall, and to leap with fixed bayonet off its top to the muddy ground below. Many times men went in so deep that they had to be pulled out by the instructor. The course included pop-up targets to be fired at rapidly by a single member of the team. The course was ended by a climb up a steep slope at a high rate of speed under fire. At the top the trainee was expected aggressively to bayonet the targets there. This course demanded the utmost physical conditioning and skill in the use of rifle and bayonet. On reaching the top of the hill some of the men would be so exhausted that as they lunged with their bayonet into one of the dummies, they would fall to the ground. Any man who was unable to complete the course, after reasonable opportunities, was washed out.

Several of the courses were designed to test a man's courage, the outstanding one being the famous death slide. The trainee had to climb a tree some forty feet high. Here he found a single rope tied to the top of the tree and sloping down at a dizzy angle of about forty-five degrees to another tree on the far bank of a roaring river, with only a toggle rope thrown over a trolley as support. Though it sounds simple in words, it was quite terrifying the first time to leap out into space and go soaring across a narrow, swiftly flowing river while under fire. The landing was made in a huge mud puddle on the other side. A Ranger sergeant, talking out of the side of his mouth, commented, "Better to find out now instead of in battle the guys who've got no guts."

Another breathtaking exercise was the drop from one of the steep towers of Achnacarry Castle. Here, by means of rope and a method known as "absailing," the trainee would leap off the top of the castle and by playing out the rope under his left leg and through bare hands, would lower himself to the ground, using his two feet spread well apart as a brake.

Added to this the Commando training emphasized realism. One Ranger explained, "Those bastards tried to kill us or we thought they did. We always maneuvered under live fire." They went so far as to put opposing snipers and machine guns against the Rangers in most of their problems. "Enemy" soldiers were clothed in German uniforms and fired German weapons. The "enemy" looked real and sounded real. The only difference was that the snipers did not shoot to hit the Rangers but for near misses. The Americans learned caution and the reality of battle. It took only one such sniper shot and the Ranger who insisted on crawling with his tail in the air hugged the earth, from forehead to instep, forever afterward. Also, while scouting and patrolling or working on tactical problems, targets sprang up and small charges of TNT were exploded on contact. A Ranger's reaction was tested by the amount of time taken to swing his fire upon a cardboard target in front, to the flank, or behind him.

In addition to the special training for pairs and groups, the individual soldier's initiative was developed. Self-reliance and self-confidence became a part of the Rangers' makeup. We were required to do everything for ourselves without waiting for orders. We did sensible, sane things just because they were the sensible, sane things to do.

Colonel Vaughan and his staff had developed a large number of special battle preparedness courses utilizing the firing of enemy weapons by his own "enemy" troops. One was the "me-and-my-pal" course. The necessity of two men always working together was stressed. One of a pair covered his buddy as the latter approached a low building. The man being covered by his pal would knock out a window and while hugging the building toss in a grenade. Then under his buddy's cover, he would enter and make sure the room was clear. Quickly, thereafter, he would motion for his companion to join him. Throughout the course over stone fences, under barbed-wire entanglements, across streams, up hills, the constant requirement was for one man to cover the other. Targets would spring up unexpectedly, causing one to have to shoot over his pal's head. Dangerous as this was, it stressed the confidence that a soldier must have in his friends and the type of cooperation necessary in the Rangers.

When the ruddy-faced British colonel had carried us this far in his training program, he gave us a pat on the back and promised an equally rugged life in which we would live by our wits as well as by our physical strength, knowledge of weapons, and tactical know-how. His problems were written with imagination. A sense of both the dramatic and of the ridiculous would run through the knowledge of the "enemy," the situation of the Allied troops, and the problems confronting them.

One day's problem would place a group of Rangers as the

"enemy" at Spean Bridge. The information sheet would tell of Mac-Darby's roistering Rangers cutting up at the hotel nearby. This was obvious since there were screams coming from the women folk at the hotel. The friendly party of Rangers had found MacDarby's raga-muffins committing their usual loot and pillage, according to the story in the problem. The elements of battle having been presented, the commanders on each side were left to work out their own plans.

Colonel Vaughan couched another of his tactical situations in a running story which began with the information that the Ranger officers had been leaving camp quietly in jeeps to visit a nearby fort where they had outclassed the Commando officers with the local blondes and brunettes. The Commando chief, MacVaughan, aided by his henchman, Private Samson Oneskunk, had created jealousy among the company commanders and to teach the Rangers a lesson had ordered them to leave camp.

The latter formed themselves into two parties: the Meade Rangers and the Martin Sharpshooters. Martin, a lady killer, makes love to the hotel proprietress at Spean Bridge and is determined to keep Meade out.

By this device the Ranger problems were heightened in interest. The reason for battle was thus established. Obviously Martin had to make a defense of the town. Meade was to attack. Though each commander worked out his own plan, the problem contained enough requirements to sufficiently control the impending battle.

The attacking forces, limited to half rations and a canteen of water, were usually given a route of advance that would compel them to approach the town from a certain compass point. Similarly the defenders were placed in one part of the town if they interpreted the written situation correctly. The instructors also controlled the time of the battle so that it would occur in daylight or dark, as they chose. However, the greatest discretion was left to the commanders of the opposing forces.

Many of the problems centered around the village of Spean Bridge and its hotel. The latter was operated by two lovely middle-aged Scottish ladies, who joined in the fun, pretending not to mind if the soldiers threw grenades close by and broke their windows. When a battle was completed, they served tea to these rugged, hard men, treating them as neighbors and friends. The countryside, as well as the townspeople, entered into the problems, getting not only a vicarious thrill out of the training but also at times some rough action accidentally. The people had reason to feel they were actually in the war.

In one problem Spean Bridge was well guarded by the "enemy." The Rangers, when they had developed their plan, had to enter the town in order to destroy the enemy forces and to liberate the village. The Ranger group became shepherds for the day. Locating a large herd of sheep was no problem; there were many available. Attired in the ragged dress of the local shepherds, they moved into town among the sheep while the cold steel of their weapons rubbed their skin under the rags. On this problem the country scene was so casual that even the umpires were surprised when they found the Rangers in possession of the town after they had shown their arms from under their shepherds' clothing.

Captain Steve Meade had to get his Rangers into town to take the hotel on another problem. In his best midwestern accent he persuaded the good-natured stationmaster to join in the fun. When the daily train entered the station, the guards checked the incoming passengers, searching the train thoroughly. Meanwhile a switch engine was moving up and down the track away from the station. Finally a freight car, or goods wagon as the British termed them, was shunted behind the hotel. The stationmaster, deliberately and without show, walked up to the car and broke the seal. Out popped thirty or more Rangers who surrounded the hotel and cleaned out the enemy.

The Rangers were not above pulling any legitimate trick to gain their end, despite the fact that war is not a game but a dirty business. One day some Rangers borrowed a nurse's uniform and, in the best men's college dramatic-show manner, painted and powdered one of the officers who was able to walk into the rival headquarters, whip out his tommygun, and take over. Colonel Vaughan further, however, ruled this one out as not being "quite cricket." And the "female's" favorite story was that he was whistled at by British sailors while passing through Fort William en route to Achnacarry in his nurse's garb.

The training was not all comedy, of course. Even these situations were the final development in a problem that required the utmost use of the Rangers' newly acquired physical conditioning, expertness with weapons, and tactical training.

It soon came time for us to leave Achnacarry Castle. On 1 August 1942 the Ranger Battalion rode out in trucks to the railroad station—down the same long hill that we had hiked to Achnacarry. The British Army had given us the basic infantry training of Commandos. The Royal Navy would train us for amphibious assaults at H.M.S. *Dorlin*, Argyle, Scotland. His Majesty's Ship *Dorlin*, like one or two others in the fleet, such as the *Island of Ascension*, did not float. It was an amphibious training center on the western coast of Scotland.

The Ranger companies were assigned in pairs to Roshven, Glenborrodale, and Glencripesdale. The headquarters was at Shielbridge. Shortly, we dropped the "Glen" prefix and were calling two of the locations "Borrodale" and "Cripesdale." Only Borrodale and Shielbridge were connected by land; the others could be reached only by boat.

At Dorlin we were in for a new type of training. At Achnacarry the emphasis had been on developing the individual's strength as a soldier. Rarely did we move out on tactical problems and training exercises involving more than a single section or platoon. We had been given only the first elements of training in amphibious assaults; for example, we had an exercise in which one company had moved across the loch in canvas boats and then scrambled ashore under sniper fire.

Physically, the western islands of Scotland were perfect for amphibious assaults under the direction of the Royal Navy. There were islands and peninsulas offering sandy beaches and rocky beaches—some opening inland, others leading directly into cliffs. No finer place could have been selected, since nearby was practically every type of terrain and every type of beach that could reasonably be met in landing operations. It was a compact, consolidated place. In some cases we were able to wade ashore several hundred yards dropping from neck-high to knee-high water. In the western islands of Mull, Rhum, Eigg, Canna, and Soay, we found excellent training grounds—small landing areas of sand in an otherwise impossible rocky coast. We saw these as the finest assault sites for the hazardous missions of knocking out coastal batteries. Invariably they were less fortified and were weakly held, compared to the pillboxed, extensive sandy beaches where an enemy would reasonably maintain his main strength.

Kentra Beach near Dorlin was the main exercise center where Commander Viner, a quiet and unassuming man, had built up an excellent assault area. Machine guns nestled in the cliffs overlooking a rocky beach. One of our companies or larger groups would move out to sea in wooden R-boats, sharp-prowed forerunners of the wide-prowed assault craft in use later. Since there was no ramp for exit, the rangers crowding to the front in column on two plank runways along the inner side of the hull jumped into the surf when they neared the beach. Real bullets from the defenses zinged around the craft and cut up spurts of water. Ashore, booby traps with light charges warned us of danger.

We also learned the technique of navigation so that we could handle the boats if the crews were to get lost. As a group we had not been seafaring men; many had never even seen an ocean until our voyage to Ireland in the early part of 1942. But at Dorlin we learned the ways of the tides, the dangers of crosscurrents. We saw naval officers shake their heads ruefully when the waves were dashing against the rocks and heard them state crisply that the swell was too great for landing operations—the assault boats would be broken up on the rocks or swung sideways and wrecked on the beaches. We were to appreciate that in a rough surf heavily equipped troops might be carried under.

Deer were abundant because little hunting had been done since the outbreak of the war, so we were invited to hunt at huge estates near Borrodale and Cripesdale, a pleasant pastime indeed. We found it great sport and the venison a welcome addition to our normal rations. Events moved smoothly for a time until a few of my soldiers began hunting promiscuously. One day a neighboring "laird" demanded payment for a prize bull calf that had been stalked by a deer hunter.

Though it was hard to believe that any Ranger's eyesight was that bad, I ordered an investigation. The medical officer went to exhume the carcass for evidence of American bullets, but it was too decomposed. After some negotiation, the accused Ranger paid the bill and for some time took a good-natured hazing about his bad eyesight.

The major practice landing was made against the Island of Mull where its major city, Tobermory, was to be captured. Lt. Max Schneider, commanding Companies E and F, was sent two days prior to the assault to establish the island's defenses. He was free to enlist the aid of the local police and the home guard. The latter seized the opportunity to test its local defenses.

In the three-day problem my deputy, Major Dammer, was to attack with four Ranger companies within a definite twenty-four-hour period. He was to land, knock out a simulated radio station, and capture the main town. During the planning he asked what would represent the radio station and was shown a tumble-down fort. Hearing that he was free to use any demolitions he wished, Dammer gave the job to Lieutenant Saam, who carried hundreds of pounds of TNT ashore.

Also as part of the plan, one group was to land prior to the main assault to make contact with collaborationists. Then the landing force was to infiltrate into the island toward Tobermory. To add realism, the Rangers on both sides were to use soap for bullets. Leaving the powder charge in the cartridges, they took out the bullets, replacing them with soap and crimping the open edges. They were directed not to fire the soap bullets at less than two hundred yards because at fifty yards they would sting dangerously.

Aboard the R-boats the Dammer Force approached in the dark during a heavy rainstorm. Near shore they ran into two drifters being used as patrol craft by the Schneider Force. A running battle at sea ended with the drifters coming alongside and boarding the R-boats, where they captured Lieutenant Martin and a number of attackers.

The rest of the R-boats made a landing. Saam and his demolitions party struck out for the rock fort while Dammer's main force infiltrated into the island toward Schneider's headquarters. The battle developed. In the excitement one Ranger forgot the instructions for the firing of soap bullets and shot one of the defenders in the face with a wad of soap. Fortunately his injury was slight. The battle raged. Fighting through houses, inns, and fields, the assault force finally drove the American and home guard defenders into Tobermory and surrounded them.

The Dammer Force was successful. Now the 1st Ranger Battalion had to be rounded up. That took one whole day in the rain. Four Rangers holed up in dry spots couldn't be found, so they were left behind.

As the Rangers gathered at the dock, the Scots housewives brought them cakes and sandwiches. A warm demonstration was in progress when the telephone rang in an outside red booth. A distraught Scots woman explained between tears that her house had just caved in. Situated a thousand yards up the draw from the old fort, her home had caught the concussion of Saam's all-out TNT charges. He had leveled the fort, and the blast had caused the plaster to fall and had broken the windows in her house nearby. One of our officers was left to investigate and pay damages.

The next day the four Rangers left on Mull returned to Cripesdale. The same night two of them borrowed a boat and rowed ten miles to Mull. Later they explained they had gone back to see their friends.

After a month at Durlin, we were ordered to move across Scotland to Dundee on the east coast, where we would join a Commando force for joint training. This movement was a nightmare. The troops at Roshven could get out only by boat and were transferred to a train at Loch Ailort. Those at Borrodale could move by truck and then entrain at Glen Finnan. The Cripesdale group were picked up by drifters, or tugboats, for the move to Mull where they were to catch the mail boat to Oban.

The Roshven group was overdue; their old boats had broken down. Some of the Borrodale Rangers' old trucks also broke down, so they resorted to a passenger car which they had to take off its blocks. They thus spent the entire night shuttling their two companies to the train junction. At Cripesdale the drifters anchored at the pier broke loose the night before the move; one was found in the morning at the other side of the loch. The Rangers tried in every way, except one, to get the attention of the boat crew. They shouted. They fired their rifles in the air. Still no answer. Finally they fired across the bow of the drifter, almost creating an international incident of the United States Army firing on the British Navy. Anyhow, they got the drifter's attention.

The collecting of the four Ranger groups had taken at least twenty-four hours. Most of the men had had to spend the whole night attempting to reach the railroad station a scant few miles from their training grounds.

It was during the time the Rangers were at Dorlin that fifty of their comrades made the assault on Dieppe with the Commandos and Canadians. As a combined operation the parent Commando organization had planned a hit-and-run assault on the Pas de Calais area— the most heavily defended coast in France.

Ranger Training, Achnacarry, Scotland

Col. William Darby discusses training of the 1st Ranger Battalion with Lt. Col. M.E. Vaughn, commander of the Commando training center at Achnacarry, Scotland, July 1942.

Rangers cross a stream by toggle rope bridge.

An "opposed landing" exercise in which live ammunition and hand grenades are used to simulate actual war conditions.

A member of the 1st Rangers leaps from a twenty-foot barrier with full pack and rifle.
This was part of the obstacle course at the British Commando training site.

Colonel Darby and his executive officer, Capt. Herman Dammer, talk over the progress of the Ranger training.

Commando-type physical training using a log.

Rangers learned to fire not only their own guns, but those of the enemy. T/Sgt.
James B. Janson of the 1st Ranger Battalion holds a Tommy gun. *Left to right:* 60mm
mortar, antitank rifle (British), M-1 rifle, light machine gun, 03 rifle with grenade,
Browning Automatic rifle, and the 81mm mortar.

Colonel Darby closely observes his Ranger Battalion as the men return from grueling maneuvers in Scotland. October 31, 1942.

Dieppe and
Training at Dundee

AUGUST–OCTOBER 1942

PERSPECTIVE   "Why Dieppe?" is a question that has been asked again and again. The Dieppe raid on the Channel coast of France was carried out on 19 August 1942 under joint British and Canadian command. The force contained seven thousand Canadian troops, one thousand British troops, and fifty U.S. Rangers. The operation was originated in Admiral Mountbatten's Combined Operations Headquarters to test amphibious tactics and techniques in a large-scale operation. The most ambitious attack on the French coast up to that time had been the raid on St. Nazaire in March 1942, which was primarily a hit-and-run commando operation.

Dieppe was planned as a miniature invasion with the aim of seizing a beachhead and taking into account the full use of combined arms and large-scale landings of infantry and armor. Unlike a full-scale invasion, there was no intention of holding the beachhead for an extended period.

There were a number of vital reasons for Dieppe: to test the newly developed LCT (landing craft tank), to determine whether a port could be taken by direct frontal assault, and to see whether the navy could manage a landing fleet of 253 ships and other craft. Also to be determined was whether the air organization could gain supremacy over a landing area while providing support for ground troops.

The Allied Staffs chose Dieppe because it had a harbor used by the Germans as a port of call for their coastal convoys. Putting the port out of commission would hamper the movement of supplies along the French coast. Also at

Dieppe were concentrations of ammunition, gasoline, and food. From the raid, the Allies would learn much at bayonet point on the vulnerability of German defenses.

From an air force standpoint, a daylight attack would bring out Goering's Luftwaffe, which thus far had failed to respond to repeated challenges by raids of the British RAF. Goering obviously had his hands full on the Russian front at that time, and heavy losses in France might compel the move of some of the Luftwaffe from the Russian front, thereby lightening the burden of the Red Army.

Planning the raid on Dieppe was made difficult by both the natural defenses of the coastline and the involved German coastal defenses. From Cape Gris Nez to the River Saane, west of Dieppe, the French seaboard is made up of high, steep cliffs broken here and there by narrow canyons or the mouths of rivers. One of these breaks in the steep cliffs is at the town and harbor of Dieppe where the gap is perhaps a mile wide. Stony cliffs run down to beaches that are difficult for landings because of the rocks and low gradient of the shore.

The Germans backed up these natural obstacles with three batteries of 5.9-inch coastal defense guns which had to be destroyed before ships could approach the shore. Everywhere along the coast the Germans had placed barbed wire; in the water were mines and steel posts to impede landing craft.

¶ FIFTY RANGERS, INCLUDING SIX OFFICERS, WENT to Portsmouth with the Canadians and Commandos for an assault landing across the Channel at Dieppe. Along with other Rangers I had hoped to join the party, but British Brigadier Laycock, in charge of Ranger instruction, insisted that our training must come first.

Captain Roy Murray, in command of this detached group, split them up to gain maximum experience. Forty were assigned to No. 3 Commando, six to No. 4 Commando, and the rest to the Canadians landing at the beaches in front of the town.

Above the convoy of bulky transports leaving England was a quarter moon. The night was dark, the sea calm. Waves lapped gently against the steel hulls, barely audible in the din of shouted commands and roar of an occasional motor torpedo boat.

The Rangers felt alone in this huge expedition since compared to the casual veteran Commandos, they were novices. Around them in the tense darkness shapes hulked. Farther away destroyers of the British fleet protected them. Then lights blinked ahead. A Commando stated laconically, "They're lighted buoys dropped by the mine sweepers to show the path cleared through the mines." Other men were wiggling into their Mae Wests.

Aboard each ship maps were unrolled and the plan explained. Single Commando units—about the size of the Ranger battalion— had the job of taking out the two six-inch gun batteries flanking Dieppe. No. 3 plus other units had the task of knocking out the guns at Berneval, five miles to the east; No. 4 Commando, the gun battery at Varengeville, six miles west of Dieppe. The Canadians were to attack in greatest strength at the city itself. The water shelved gradually to a beach broken by the river Arques. Dieppe lay on the west bank of the stream. The beach in front of the city was approximately a mile long, seventy-five yards in depth. It had a low sea wall which air photos showed to be heavily covered by wire.

The night dragged on. The Rangers were silent, afraid in their uncomfortable life belts. The Channel seemed extraordinarily wide, but as a beam from a lighthouse blinked ahead, the men felt reassured. The German defenders were evidently not aware of their approach. Someone asked, "How much farther?" A sailor answered, "Ten miles."

Rangers with No. 3 Commando gripped their rifles until the perspiration ran. The Channel coast of France was well named "the Iron Coast." Officers briefing them had remarked that the Germans had coastal guns, flame throwers, machine guns in pillboxes, mines—all the deadliest devices of war.

Ships guns suddenly chattered. Blue and red streaks flashed in front of them. Antiaircraft guns barked sharply; their burst high in the sky opened up and then melted away in the darkness. It was 0347 on 19 August 1942. A star shell illuminated some of the landing craft, now seven miles from shore.

An enemy tanker, escorted by several E-boats, was the cause of the fireworks. It was an incalculable incident. The enemy had not been awaiting the landing. Instead, the German tanker was attempting to slip unnoticed through the Channel.

The landing craft of No. 3 Commando were milling around with several boats having been hit. Ranger Charles Grant, a sniper, said he didn't get a chance to hit anything since he didn't get ashore. An E-boat fired on his assault boat, throwing the men into the water. British destroyers, arriving to dispose of the enemy ships, picked him up.

The tanker and most of the E-boats were sunk. The German defenders, thoroughly alerted, shot in and among the craft of No. 3 Commando. The assault force kept straight ahead for shore, but boats were knocked out while trying to regain formation. A few troops got on the beach but, having lost surprise, were not strong enough to knock out the gun battery. Twenty very brave men reached the guns, harrying the crews by sniping but were unable to capture and destroy the battery.

Streaks of daylight, like a stage curtain, opened the coast to view. The steady patter of machine guns, like the opening ruffle of drums, gave way to the crashing of the brass orchestral instruments. The British destroyers opened up with a scheduled fire against every yard of the beach. It was a ten-minute artillery barrage to smother the enemy and blast their weapons. Clouds of white smoke, hiding parts of the cliff for a moment, were whisked away by a breeze. Shell explosions then blanketed other portions of the coast. Douglas Boston planes added their bombs to the general punch at the enemy defenses. Then they too were gone.

The sky was soon cleared of aircraft, but every member of the expedition knew the Luftwaffe would appear. Rumor and report said that the RAF intended to put every fighter in the air on that day. The famous Eagle Squadrons, three in number, were to put on a finale under British colors. The next day they would be part of the American Air Forces in Britain.

Six Rangers touched down on French soil with No. 4 Commando. They hurdled a wall and its barbed wire and went inland rapidly, running and firing. With the Commandos they got into farmhouses, still shooting. Cpl. Franklin Koons, probably the first American soldier to kill a German in this war, said, "We got to a little farm built around a yard. We found a small stable into which we put the wounded . . . and there I found a good spot for sniping. It was over a manger, and I fired through a slit in a brick wall. I had not been there long when I saw the German battery receive a tremendous plastering by shells from the mortars." (Koons was later decorated with the Military Medal by Lord Mountbatten.)

Spitfires came in on a low-level attack, and after a mortar got in a lucky hit on the battery's magazine, the Commandos went in with bayonets. For the next few hours the sky was filled with machine-gun fire. The Luftwaffe, having arrived, were being met head on by the Spits.

No. 4 Commando returned to its ships lying off shore. The six Rangers showed up intact. Sgts. Kenneth Kenyon, Marcell Swank, Kenneth Stempson, and Alex Szima along with Cpls. William Brady and Franklin Koons were dead tired but satisfied. They'd been under fire, but they had found they could do a job. Sergeant Kenyon, a tall blond soldier, spoke of the assault, "It was bad on shore, but, my God, how those Commandos can fight! We were after a six-inch battery, and there was an orchard just before you came to it. Know what those Commandos did? They'd kneel down or lie down and fire, then stand up, grab an apple off a tree, and start firing again."

Sergeant Swank, Kenyon's pal, laughed at a shell-fragment wound in his arm. "I knew nothing could happen to me," he said. "I had a swell mascot with me—a Bible." Then showing a small worn book, he added, "My father carried it all through the last war. And he never got hurt. So when I went away he gave it to me."

When asked about the fighting ashore, his forehead wrinkled. "I'll tell you one thing, though," he said. "In training we used to be made to do a lot of things that seemed silly to us. Well, we know better now. Every bit of ranger training we had came in useful. You got to fight like Indians in this war, I guess. Well, we were trained for it, and any time we weren't sure we just watched our officers—those Commando officers. They're fighting men."

The fight in the town of Dieppe is too well known to require repetition. On the beach the Canadians and British were pinned down by defenses in houses and by guns mounted in caves on the cliffs to each side.

The beach was the worst part of the battle of Dieppe. Tanks were battered and knocked out, many landing craft never got ashore. The troops fought as bravely as had their fathers at Zeebrugge in the last war, but courage was not enough. The tip-off in the Channel had given the Germans time to prepare their defenses. The natural features of the terrain near Dieppe and the ingenuity of the Germans were too much when added to the lack of surprise.

At the town itself, the Canadians got ashore through a terrific barrage of shell and machine-gun fire as well as dive-bombing attacks. The sea wall, however, dammed up with brave men, burned-out tanks, guns, and ammunition.

Dieppe brought on a huge air battle in which the RAF lost ninety-eight planes while shooting down more than that number of German aircraft. The landing and ground battle proved that an invasion of France was possible even though one-third of the ten thousand Allied troops had been lost.

The Rangers' experience cost them seven missing-in-action and seven injured. Four officers and thirty-nine men, reporting their experiences to the Ranger Battalion, infused their knowledge among their untried comrades. Their objective view of the Dieppe operation had its influence on future Ranger amphibious assaults. More training was needed, it was obvious; planning for the assault must be more careful, more detailed; intelligence and reconnaissance must be more complete. This is no reflection on the British Commandos and the Canadian Infantry who fought at Dieppe. They, too, learned these lessons to their advantage.

Subjectively the Rangers at Dieppe learned the meaning of discipline in overcoming fear and in making an assault through flying lead. They felt the first hint of hate against the Germans, for they had lost friends and had seen valiant Commando comrades cut down.

Shortly after the return of our newly battle-tested friends, the 1st Ranger Battalion arrived at Dundee on the east coast of Scotland. Near the city we were to team with No. 1 Commando for joint training in preparation for a landing operation somewhere against the Germans. The main emphasis in the advanced training was on schemes for attacking pillboxes, gun batteries, and coastal defenses.

There were no barracks or camps at Dundee, so the troops had to be billeted in the people's homes. Even on a voluntary basis, this system was unknown among the Rangers. Fresh from the ovation of the Scots on Mull, we were not concerned about living quarters in Dundee. Posters had announced our arrival, but sufficient homes were opened to furnish room and board for only four companies. The other two had to sleep in the city hall the first night.

On the following morning we were prepared to seek a government building for barracks. As we were about to set out in search, an excited group of women swarmed around the city hall. The first night had gone well as the men talked their way into the hearts of their hosts. The word spread rapidly so that by midmorning all my Rangers had homes.

Because of the billeting no mess or recreational facilities were required by the Rangers. The men ate at their respective homes, obtained their recreation in the city and in the family life of the people. Each morning the soldiers lined up for battalion parade, carrying their homemade lunches. If there was a cross-country problem or march, the men carried food for the entire period of the maneuver from their newfound homes.

It was during this time that the cooks, first-aid men, and other administrative personnel generally required to maintain a combat unit became actual members of the Ranger team, equipped and trained for action. The cooks became real fighting men, and oftentimes in later amphibious landings were sent ashore in the first wave as Tommy gunners.

I did my best to exert tight discipline despite this extraordinary billeting arrangement and let every Ranger know just where he stood concerning his personal deportment. I found, as expected, that these men thrown on their responsibility reacted almost perfectly. Furthermore, it was excellent training for the men, since the Rangers later were often to act as independent small groups on their own initiative. While the Rangers were pleasantly excited about this billeting, I found that with this arrangement, they acted as guests with their new families. If any of them were inclined to be rowdy, they didn't have the heart to get drunk and disorderly as might be the case in barracks where, at a late hour, they would only disturb other soldiers. There were only two minor infractions of discipline during the entire month of Dundee. According to the predetermined agreement, their punishment was life in pup tents in a field and only packaged C rations. (C ration is a combat ration consisting of a can of highly concentrated food such as beef stew, a couple of biscuits, a package of cocoa mix which could be eaten whole or made into a hot or cold beverage, a couple of cigarettes, and a packet of toilet tissue.)

During the Dundee phase of training, we acquired a valued member, the only person not an American. Father Albert E. Basil was a captain in the Chaplain Corps of the British Army and at that time assigned to the Special Service Brigade. He first met the Rangers when he conducted a funeral service for one of our members who had inadvertently been killed while traversing a minefield.

After the service Father Basil asked to see all the Catholics. I was a little disturbed at this and said, "That's all right for the Catholics, Father, but how about the rest of us poor damned Christians?"

The Chaplain, taken aback, remarked, "You mean you want me to speak to the Protestants as well?"

"Yes, Father. You see you're our only chaplain. As far as we Americans are concerned you represent the God we worship no matter what our particular creed may be. So if you don't mind, we would appreciate you taking care of all of us."

Though a strange request, Father Basil assented. As long as he was with the Rangers he ministered to Catholic, Protestant, and Jew.

A short time later I asked Brigadier Laycock if he would permit the Rangers' popular adopted Chaplain to remain with us until after we had landed in North Africa. With the Brigadier's assent the Chaplain went with the Rangers. In fact he stayed on with us through the Tunisian campaign until the British Army discovered they had one missing chaplain. After some explanation the matter was cleared up, but, unfortunately for us, Father Basil was then returned to the British Army.

During his nine months with the Rangers, he was a constant source of inspiration and comfort to us. Slight of build, about medium height, with large horn-rimmed spectacles punctuating a very sharp-featured, intelligent, and happy face, he became a familiar sight as his uniform began to look like that of the Rangers. His one unfailing exception to complete Americanization was his insistence on wearing the Commando's green beret and shoulder patch.

At Dundee development of the responsibility of the individual was stressed. On certain problems the officers fell in ranks. They were not allowed to give commands or advice as the noncommissioned officers led the various units.

On one problem I gave the entire battalion the mission of moving twenty-five miles within five hours to the town of Arbroath. The officers were put in ranks, and instructions were given that the various units would get to the destination in any way possible. The usual Ranger rate of march was five miles an hour, so if any of them marched, they should be able to reach the Ferry at the end of five hours without difficulty. The only restriction placed upon their movement was that in no case were they to hire or pay for transportation.

Yankee initiative was therefore challenged. At the destination, toward the close of the fifth hour, the Rangers who had reached Arbroath were convulsed with laughter as each succeeding member or group of Rangers came into sight. They came on horseback, jogging along on plow horses, in horse-drawn buggies, or they hitched rides on trains. They came by automobile and truck, and several made the journey by air. When the hilarity was at its height, the fifth hour struck, and every Ranger was in ranks.

For more than three months, the Rangers had been through as rugged a course of training as had been given to any soldiers in this war. Though volunteers, they had been welded into a close-knit unit able to operate in any kind of warfare. Their bodies were physically hard, wits sharp, hands firm on the trigger, bayonets and knives ready. They were not supermen but highly trained American infantrymen. They were not thugs or cutthroats, as is well proved by their conduct at Dundee. They wore their uniforms correctly, they saluted smartly, and they had confidence in their leaders, who still continued to lead in every problem or maneuver.

Within the unit, we lived by the code of the new American Army as well as by the code expressed so clearly in Major Robert Roger's orders to his scouts and Rangers. The modern Rangers had heeded Roger's orders throughout their training, paying particular attention to his final order. It was, as written in 1761: "Having read the foregoing orders, when all else fails, the thing to do is to forget the above instructions and go ahead."

Eventually our days at Dundee were at an end. Regretfully we left the friendly people who had taken us in as members of their families. On 24 September the 1st Battalion boarded the train for Glasgow, where we were assigned to the II Army Corps and finally attached to the 1st Infantry Division.

Here we met the British crews of the three former ferryboats that were to take us to North Africa. The British sailors and the men at the docks showed us how to stow our equipment and ammunition in the assault landing craft. From 29 September until 13 October, when we took the train for Gourock for a final assault exercise before embarking for North Africa, we continued to train in order to keep ourselves physically fit.

We were a confident group, drawn together by our success in passing the rugged commando course. Held to a rigid standard of discipline and conduct, it became our code that when we got into a scrap we must not come back to our bivouac unless we had won.

So with a jaunty air, we shouldered our packs and on 26 October marched aboard the *Ulster Monarch,* the *Royal Scotsman,* and the *Royal Ulsterman* for the momentous journey to North Africa. Where the trail led, we could not be certain. We only knew that we would acquit ourselves as the best-trained unit in the American Army.

IV

Tunisian Combat

FEBRUARY–MARCH 1943

PERSPECTIVE   In November 1942, when the Allied Forces went into Algiers to pinch off the seaport, they met little resistance because control of the area was held by friendly forces. By good fortune, Admiral Jean François Darlan, commander of the Vichy Armed Forces, was in Algiers and was taken into protective custody. After delicate negotiations, he assumed governmental authority in North Africa and ordered hostilities to cease.

The Allied attack on northwest Africa at Casablanca, Oran, and Algiers had been successful. The problem now was how to get four hundred miles east of Algiers to capture the port of Tunis. The race for Tunisia began on 9 November when, anticipating an Allied occupation of that colony in order to close off Rommel's rear from El Alamein, Hitler began moving troops into Bizerte, the second largest seaport in Tunisia.

On 10 November, as part of the second phase of Operation Torch, the British forces in floating reserve of the Eastern Task Force at Algiers were sent to Bougie as a first step in a rapid advance on Tunisia.

Just ten days previously the British, under General Bernard Montgomery, had won a smashing victory at El Alamein. Now one of the greatest foot and tank races in history began: the effort by the British forces to intercept Rommel's forces before they reached Tunis, some nineteen hundred miles to the west. It was impossible for the Germans to escape by sea across the Mediterranean because the British Navy and Allied Air Forces were in complete command. The Germans had no ships in the Mediterranean, and those the Italians had were insufficient to do the job.

A complicating factor in the Allied race eastward for Tunisia was whether the French would fight on the same side as British and American troops. After the cease-fire by Darlan on 10 November, the American negotiator Maj. Gen. Mark W. Clark was pressured to obtain active French support and French resistance to Axis movements into Tunisia. Darlan, on his part, was hampered because political concessions had to have Marshal Petain's concurrence. Petain, under pressure from Vichy Premier Pierre Laval, withdrew his earlier approval of Darlan's cease-fire, so Darlan revoked the order, thereby confusing the French commanders who now thought that they had to oppose the Allies. On 9 November, Petain had authorized German use of Tunisian airdromes, but Hitler demanded full authority to move large bodies of troops into Tunisia under the pretense of aiding the French in defending against Allied attack. Laval hedged, so Hitler decided to occupy the remainder of France. German and Italian divisions began moving into southern France that night while Italy occupied Corsica.

When the Germans moved into southern France in force, Darlan broke with Vichy, ordering the French in Africa to resist Axis forces. The question of authority among the French troops was still in doubt, however, as some commanders permitted Axis troops to enter Tunisia unopposed. But, the French Army commander in Tunisia, Gen. Georges Barré, withdrew his forces westward into the mountains. Following orders from Algiers, Barré established contact with Allied columns at Bedja on 17 November.

The Allies had originally planned to seize airfields at Bone, Bizerte, and Tunis with airborne and Commando troops. However, the uncertain French reaction caused the Allies to act more conservatively. The force landing at Bougie tried to disembark some troops at a nearby port of Djidjelli but were thrown back because of the heavy surf. Consequently, Bougie's airfield was not in operation for two more days. Meanwhile, lacking any air support, the landing force lost several ships to German air attacks. The commando-paratroop landings at Bone were unopposed. Spearheads were sent across the Tunisian border with orders to contact the French and reconnoiter to the east. At the same time, the main body of the British 78th Division started moving overland from Algiers on 15 November; by 17 November the Allied forces were in close proximity to Axis forces in Northern Tunisia. The race for Tunisia was about to be decided by a clash of arms.

Unfortunately for the Allies, the terrain in Tunisia is easily defended. The Atlas mountains form an inverted V running southwest from the seaport of Tunis. There are few roads and railroads; and in the extreme north, the mountains are cut by rivers and streams, but the valleys are easily blocked.

When the Allied forces—British, American, and French, commanded by Lt. Gen. Sir Kenneth A. N. Anderson—had raced from the landings in Algiers eastward, there seemed every reason to expect a speedy capture of Tunisia. Just before the start of the year optimists thought that the war in North Africa was almost over and all that remained was to drive the scattered Axis forces in Tunisia into the sea and then calmly squeeze the celebrated Rommel from west to east until he submitted.

That was not to be. Just as good luck had contributed to the speedy success of the landings in Morocco and Algiers, bad luck and bad weather dashed Allied hopes of seizing the remainder of Africa quickly and cheaply. By the end of January, Axis forces in Tunisia under the command of Generaloberst Jurgen von Arnim had grown to more than one hundred thousand men; Rommel had seventy thousand men retreating westward in front of Montgomery.

Eisenhower had ordered a continuation of the attack against Tunisia as soon as forward airfields were established and supplies and reinforcements had arrived. After 9 December 1942, when Arnim had assumed control of the Axis forces, now called the 5th Panzer Army, Eisenhower directed Anderson to make one last attempt to take Tunis near a town called Medjec el Bab, but the enemy was too strong. With the coming of winter rains, Eisenhower decided to strengthen the First Army with units from Morocco and switch operations against the Germans to central Tunisia at the towns of Sousse, Sfax, and Gabes.

On 30 January Arnim attacked to secure the pass at Faid. The blow fell on the French; the 1st U.S. Armored Division, which had been planning an attack on Maknassy, moved to reinforce the French, leaving a provisional force to attack Maknassy itself. The 1st Armored Division was repulsed at both places. It was at this time that the 1st Ranger Battalion, on 1 February 1943, was sent to get more information on movements of German and Italian troops retreating from Tripolitania. This was what was known as the Battle of Sened Station.

Despite the rainy season, February was a month of much activity. The Germans were intent on keeping the corridor between Tripoli and Tunis open. To help them, they had a range of mountains called the Eastern Dorsal overlooking the corridor between Arnim's Tunisian forces and Rommel's embattled Afrika Korps in Tripolitania. There were major passes through the mountains at Fondouk, Maknassy, and El Guettar from north to south. Behind the corridor were other passes such as Faid and Pichon. The Afrika Korps was falling back at Tripoli to join Arnim's force in Tunisia. Heavy concentrations east of Gafsa on the Gafsa-Gabes Road were reported on 5 February, indicating an enemy thrust was in preparation to prevent Allied interference with the joining up of the Nazi forces.

¶ AFTER ARZEW, MY RANGERS BEGAN TO CONSIDER themselves a really special unit. We had made an excellent landing, accomplished our missions in jig time, and knocked out the coastal guns to ease the landing of Terry Allen's 1st Infantry Division. Since only the generals knew about the lost communications, the Rangers

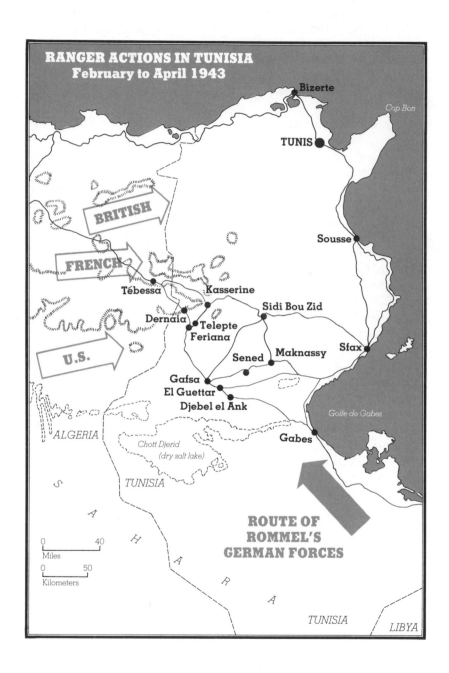

RANGER ACTIONS IN TUNISIA
February to April 1943

Bizerte

Cap Bon

TUNIS

BRITISH

FRENCH

Sousse

Tébessa

Kasserine

Sidi Bou Zid

Dernaia

Telepte

Feriana

U.S.

Sened

Maknassy

Sfax

Gafsa

El Guettar

Djebel el Ank

Golfe de Gabes

ALGERIA

Chott Djerid
(dry salt lake)

Gabes

TUNISIA

S A H A R A

ROUTE OF
ROMMEL'S
GERMAN FORCES

0   40
Miles
0   50
Kilometers

TUNISIA

LIBYA

could impress other soldiers by recounting their deeds in the dark and dawn of 8 November 1942.

After one battle the Rangers considered themselves heroes and experienced soldiers. They looked for a pat on the back, a chance for rest and recreation.

I, however, was of a different mind. For the next two months I marched the men for long distances on short rations, so that the training in Scotland seemed easy in comparison. There were night problems, many of them, and landings were practiced again and again. They replayed the Arzew operation like a phonograph record, changing the needle though by executing it at different times under varied weather conditions and under differing conditions of tide, wind, and swell. Probably years from now old Rangers, if brought back to Arzew, could fall into position without reinstruction. I believe that veteran soldiers, even between campaigns, require continual training to prepare them for new and unusual enemy tactics.

For almost two months we remained at Arzew acting as a demonstration and experimental battalion in what became an army amphibious-assault training center. Towards Christmas there was a rumor that we were to be sent to capture and occupy the Island of la Galite, near Bizerte in the Straits of Sicily. Submarine reconnaissance was made, but an adverse shift in the Allied situation in Tunisia prevented execution of the planned operation.

Meanwhile in Tunisia, General von Arnim's forces were attempting to keep a corridor open along the coast for Rommel's Afrika Korps. The Allied forces in central and southern Tunisia required more information about the movements of German troops retreating from Tripolitania, needing identification of German and Italian divisions. The Allied commanders believed that the 1st Ranger Battalion could obtain the vital information.

On 1 February 1943 we were ordered to stand by. In Tunisia our amphibious assault skill would not be required however. There we could usefully employ our knowledge of night fighting and of hit-and-run tactics. Thirty-two Douglas transport planes, C-47s, taxied into Oran to pick us up. It was a tight squeeze getting all of us aboard with our equipment, but on short order we were flying eastward to the Tunisian battle area. We landed at Youks-Les-Bains Airport near Tébessa, close to the eastern border of Algeria. Symbolic of things to come, the Germans bombed the airfield just as the last truckload of Rangers was leaving for the front.

One didn't have to be a military strategist to understand that the situation across the border in Tunisia was hit-and-miss and that the Tunisian campaign was bogged down. My Rangers moved east of Tébessa to the headquarters of Major General L. R. Fredendall's II Corps. Quickly the general briefed me on the situation, telling me that American troops had had to be withdrawn from south and central Tunisia to oppose the Germans who were then striking westward from Tunis and Bizerte. The Ranger task was a typical one, as we later found out in operations in Italy. This time there was to be no spearheading of strong U.S. formations; rather the opposite. We were to give the impression that Allied strength in central Tunisia was greater than was actually the case. Night missions with fast movement, darting, pinpricking raids, and heavy firing of weapons were to be our job. Secondly we were to capture prisoners for identification of the steady flow of German and Italian troops then moving into Tunisia and Tripolitania. Throughout our operations, the 1st Ranger Battalion, though less than five hundred men, was also to inflict heavy casualities on the enemy. In effect, we could write our own ticket, as long as we did our job.

The Rangers were told that the British Derbyshire Yeomanry was deployed in front of the Allied positions. The Rangers were to campaign behind this reconnaissance screen. In some ways we became a miniature Stonewall Jackson force, operating like the Confederate "foot cavalry" in the Shenandoah Valley during our Civil War.

A series of three raids was planned: one against an enemy position five miles northwest of Sened Station, another against Djebel el Ank, and a third against Medilla. While small Ranger patrols were sent out to gather definite information of enemy action, I took a small group far out towards Sened Station to an observation post of the Derbyshire Yeomanry. High on a mountain top, we slid into the observation post and trained our field glasses on five distant hills which a British corporal pointed out to us.

The little corporal, blonde haired and wearing thick glasses, faced a voluminous book in which he was methodically adding neat penciled notes. In typical American manner I asked the corporal to outline what had happened in the moving panorama spread before him, but firmly, he said that he couldn't do that. We thought it impossible that after two days' observation the corporal did not know the enemy situation. During subsequent action in Tunisia, American observers felt that they weren't doing their jobs unless they gave an easy flowing interpretation in military language of what they had seen or what they thought they had seen from an observation post.

The British corporal steadfastly refused to evaluate what he had seen. He did, however, offer his notebook. In minute penmanship and careful notations the corporal had written somewhat as follows: "Two vehicles came along a road to the right front at 0800 and turned right near the group of trees; six camels came out of a draw in the mountains to the right, walking just off the main road." There was only one concession in the corporal's concise ledger. An artillery piece had fired at a definite moment and was believed to be an anti-tank gun. His method, of course, was right.

Thereafter, I required my Rangers to relate the plain unvarnished truth of what they actually saw without attempting interpretation or evaluation. Stock phrases such as two 88-mm guns at the junction of highway 410 or a machine-gun nest at the left edge of a forest were taboo.

The Yeomanry outpost near Sened Station had identified the Italian Centauro Division and units of the Bersaglieri. These, the best of the Italian troops in North Africa, backed by Rommel's crack German divisions, meant trouble for the rather green U.S. troops.

Half my battalion set out on the first raid on 11 February, each Ranger carrying a C ration, a canteen of water, and a shelter half. From bivouac it was thirty-two miles across valley and mountain to the Sened position on the five hills. The Rangers were transported the first twenty miles by truck and jeep after midnight of 12 February. Then dismounting at a French outpost, we moved in the long Ranger stride over some eight miles of rugged terrain. Before dawn we were less than four miles from our objective. Out came the shelter halves, and the men hid away in the mountains for the day, watching their objective like a cat ready to spring on its prey. We did some reconnaissance during the day and further detailed planning. We heard the zoom of aircraft overhead continually. Too-curious Rangers peeked out from their camouflage, forgetful that the planes were likely German.

Wherever one went in North Africa and no matter how deserted the area might look, a few unkempt Arabs in their baggy burnooses inevitably appeared. Although we had moved with the greatest of stealth, several Arabs wandered into our hiding places and immediately began doing business. They offered oranges as barter for cigarettes, candy, and chewing gum. My soldiers, holed up far inside enemy territory, couldn't afford to take a chance on disclosure of our position to the enemy, so we put the Arabs under guard until after the attack jumped off in darkness.

The Rangers moved forward around midnight, just before the setting of the moon. The desert darkness was complete. No helmets tinkled, no shoes squeaked as we swung across the intervening miles and crawled up the rocky hill where lay the Italian camp. About six hundred yards from our objective, we swung out into a skirmish line. When we got within two hundred yards, the outposted enemy sensed danger and opened fire. Blue tracers crossed our path, but we continued forward on our bellies without firing a shot. At fifty yards we began the assault. For twenty minutes we worked with bayonet, Tommy gun, rifle, and grenade. And then it was over.

The Italians, most of them bedded down for the night, were completely surprised. We went in that last fifty yards making all the noise possible and firing heavily. Italians streamed out of tents, some trying to jump on motorbikes, others realizing they were caught begging for mercy in high-pitched Italian. But some of the Italians reached the 50-mm antitank guns and began dropping shells around my command post.

I called Capt. Roy Murray whose company had the objective in the area of the guns and asked when he was going to reach it.

The captain shouted, "Objective reached, sir."

"Well, when are you going to knock out those blasted guns?" I asked.

Two of Murray's Rangers parked a grenade right on top of the gun at that very moment.

"Fifty millimeters reached and destroyed, sir," said the Captain.

That's the way the raid went. It was clockwork precision and rough going. One Ranger heaved a grenade into a foxhole only to have it thrown back by an Italian. Back it went, this time for a strike.

During the action I called Capt. Max Schneider, another company commander, to find out how many prisoners he had taken.

The captain replied, "I think I have two, sir." The field radio connection was bad, and I asked for a repeat. The two Italians tried to pull a getaway, and the captain fired two quick shots, answering in the same breath, "Well, sir, I had two prisoners."

The six mortar crews in support of the Rangers really waded into the Italian outpost. With a corporal up ahead observing fire, they got their mortars on the Italian camp and then let them have the works.

The results of the raid exceeded all expectations. At least fifty enemy were dead and many others wounded. Eleven enemy soldiers of the 10th Bersaglieri Regiment were captured.

The Italians called the Rangers "Black Death" after the raid that night and every Ranger had his favorite story of Sened.* One remarked, "This was the kind of stuff we loved to do— coming in under fire, which sometimes wasn't a foot and a half over our heads, but knowing damn well those Eyties didn't know where we were, and we could watch their gun flashes when we got close enough."

One Ranger, later a first sergeant, stated, "I remember watching a motor pool, and this Eytie ran out and tried to get away on a motorcycle. We were laying down a mortar concentration on the area, and this guy got the cycle started all right and was about to get out, and just then a 60-mm hits right on top of him, and he just disappeared. There was some pretty rough in-fighting there, but a man doesn't talk about what he does with a bayonet."

Though we had surprised the enemy and demolished the camp, the situation ahead of us was ticklish. We had had one killed and eighteen wounded. There were only two-and-one half hours left before dawn, and the nearest positions of real safety were the mountains twelve miles away. Quickly we formed ourselves into two columns, fast and slow. Retaining the wounded in the slow column I led the troops out of the combat area. The fast column swung out at a killing pace, marching the twelve miles before dawn, reaching the truck column awaiting them. Meanwhile, the medical officer and

---

*After the Sened raid, General Fredendall decorated Darby, four other Ranger officers, and nine enlisted Rangers with the Silver Star for their part in the raid.

first-aid men gave morphine to the badly wounded and sprinkled sulfa drugs on their wounds.

The aid men, as well as the doctor, were as physically hard as the combat troops. The nature of the Ranger hit-and-run raids demanded that every man be able to keep up. Also, as in the code of Roger's Rangers, no member of the unit expected the battalion or the company to wait for him if badly wounded or to be carried to safety if it endangered the lives of other soldiers. My men followed this, but by utilizing modern medicine we were usually able to reduce shock and to evacuate most of our badly wounded comrades.

The slow column marched the twelve miles to the French outpost, where they hid in some hills during the next day. The two seriously wounded men were kept alive during this rough journey while others less seriously wounded did not succumb to shock and were able to move along with minor assistance. Jeeps and trucks sent by the rear headquarters carried the slow column out the next night.

The second raid on our schedule was to be against Djebel el Ank on 14 February. But before that operation was mounted, all troops were directed to leave Gafsa. Forsaking their position in front spearheading attacks, the Rangers were assigned the rear guard, remaining in Gafsa for four hours after the others had left. We set up our defense, put out sentries, and began to feel the chill creepiness of a darkened outpost in the desert. The enemy was approaching, but we were not certain when or in what number. One of the company commanders called the command post and in a shaky voice whispered that the enemy was approaching from the south in three columns. The Rangers had two hours yet to remain in Gafsa and had no wish to be caught in a trap. But orders were orders, and we were there to stay.

Rather than sit still and be overwhelmed, our preference as fighting men was to be on the move. Cautiously I sent one company out to meet the three columns of the enemy. In the pitch darkness, men could hear what sounded like the rumble of muffled vehicles. The men moved forward steadily, hoping for quick action and a chance to see by the flash of gunfire what the enemy looked like. On instruction, no Rangers were to fire without my personal command. Then from the scouts ahead came roars of laughter joined in by the other Rangers when the word was passed around. The approaching

　　　　　　　　　　　　　　　TUNISIAN COMBAT

"enemy" was a herd of two or three hundred camels, kicking rocks as they moved along.

After this "camel" operation, disgruntled Rangers marched out of Gafsa on the long road leading toward Kasserine Pass. The next night while in Feriana we received orders to withdraw to Dernaia Pass. But the orders were four hours late arriving, and by that time we were left well out front all alone. We had no real information of the Axis forces, knowing only that Rommel was thrusting with tanks in our direction. This got the truck drivers excited. Followed by six trucks and several jeeps the column started out across country on foot, leaving the road to the potential enemy.

Time was growing short as the men marched the last ten miles through Telepte, turning westward towards Dernaia Pass and the comparative safety of Allied positions. Heads twisted over shoulders as the Rangers "heard" the telltale clank of enemy tank threads. Sticky bombs, grenades, and antitank ammunition banged against the men's bodies. We were traveling loaded, and as I told them, we intended "to make one hell of a fight" against any enemy tank attack.

Dusty, tired Rangers marched past two deserted American airfields near Telepte. A score or more fighter planes had been set on fire. Evidently the airmen had been unable to get them off the ground because of lack of parts or repairs and had burned them to keep them out of enemy hands. Rangers cursed, for there had been little enough air cover in Tunisia. But a moment later, they shrugged their shoulders for there had been a shortage of troops and proper equipment as well in the Tunisian fighting. America had not gotten into high gear yet in early 1943.

It was 17 February, and the battle of Kasserine Pass was developing. The Germans were threatening by a drive aimed at Tébessa, the main Allied base behind the strategic quadrangle formed by Fais and Maknassy on the east and Sbeitla and Gafsa on the west. The German and Italian troops were thrusting out with their tanks, both to get maneuver room and to strike through the main passes of central Tunisia where they would then be on the flank and rear of the main Allied forces in northern Tunisia. There was no alternative but to stretch the Allied troops in central Tunisia. The Rangers were given the mission of holding Dernaia Pass as a covering force. The road from Gafsa running past Feriana made a junction between Telepte and a height named Djebel Krechem. One road continued north to Kasserine while the other branched westward towards Tébessa. Four miles west of the road junction the Tébessa road snaked tortuously as it went up through Dernaia Pass.

Intelligence officers analyzing the terrain and the enemy's capabilities reckoned that the main attack would come through Dernaia Pass towards Tébessa. The Rangers at the foot of the ridge were stretched out on both sides of the road to cover a minefield. Alongside the road was a wooded draw, or wadi. Four miles of flat desert stretched in front of us, rising to Djebel Krechem on the left of the Dernaia Road and masking our sight of the Telepte-Kasserine Road.

Spread out for two miles across the front of Dernaia Pass, the four hundred-odd Rangers were ordered to hold at all costs. Our job as a covering force was to delay the enemy, forcing him to deploy before moving against French troops of the Constantine Division.

About six miles to the left rear was an engineer battalion; eight miles to the right rear was a battalion of the 26th Regimental Combat Team of the 1st Infantry Division and a combat command of the 1st Armored Division. Directly behind my troops was a battalion of American artillery, two worn-out batteries of French 75s, and the 7th Regiment Tirailleurs Algeriens. The latter unit inducted the Ranger battalion as honorary members of their regiment after the battle. The French were wretchedly armed, having only a few rounds of ammunition available for their obsolete rifles.

Due to the vagaries of war, the Germans and Italians went around Dernaia Pass striking Kasserine to the north. The Axis forces launched their strongest attack on 22 February. The battle there was furious—the 1st Infantry Division bearing almost its full weight. It was nip and tuck for a time with the 16th Regimental Combat Team of the 1st Division compelled to throw in its entire strength, leaving no reserve to oppose a breakthrough. Maj. Gen. Terry Allen called on me for one reinforced "hairy-chested" Ranger company. It was sent, but the rest of my Rangers were not employed in throwing back the high tide of the Axis attack.

The Rangers at Dernaia Pass engaged in no heavy fighting. Their mission of providing a covering position for the 1st Division was simple enough in daylight, when observation across the desert was perfect; but at night both sides resorted to vigorous patrols and infiltration. On one occasion we captured the first men of Rommel's Afrika Korps, burned some enemy vehicles, and killed a few Italians. However Ranger patrols out front at night began "to see things," telling of enemy columns; and the reports, often unfounded, poured in each night via radio.

Eventually, the Rangers discovered a solution—a typical but effective battlefield improvisation. Each night patrols were sent out like the fingers of one's hand on both sides of the road leading out of Dernaia Pass. Each patrol pulled along six light reels of field telephone wire, one-half mile to the reel. Equipped with field telephones hooked in at a central switchboard at the command post, the patrols advanced to the end of their first reel. The patrols, code numbered from one to six from left to right, then reported to headquarters. The switch on the board was kept open so that each patrol could hear the conversations of the others and could crosstalk over the party line. Successively thereafter the patrols worked out a half mile at a time to the three-mile limit. There the six patrols spaced across the front established a protective screen for the Ranger position at the pass.

The patrols remaining out all night gained confidence in each other and became aggressive. On one occasion number three and four patrols were able to ambush a German motorcyclist by coordinating their actions over the hookup. They let him go in toward their lines and then, stretching a rope a few feet above the road of retreat, practically decapitated him when he tried to get away.

On another occasion numbers two and three were able to ambush an Italian patrol. At all times they were able to furnish accurate and timely information. Prior to dawn they would return, using their wire as a certain means of getting back safely.

In addition to furnishing excellent security for the main body, they were able to talk to each other and help each other out. For example, number two would report, "I just heard a machine gun—sounded like it is over on my right near the airfield."

Number five would reply, "Oh no, it is about a mile off to my right front." Thus everyone including my command post knew at all times what was happening.

Two German volkswagens or jeeps came through the lines during daylight another day. Our 37-mm antitank guns blasted one, and the other was left by the fleeing Nazis. Though in good condition the volkswagen lacked a tire, and Lt. Stan Farwell went out that night to investigate the shelled German jeep in search of a good tire. (Farwell, a husky, huge man, had a size 14½ C foot. In Tunisia, far from supply depots, he ran out of shoes early. None were available in Algiers or in Tunisia, so he marched and fought through the campaign in house slippers.) When Farwell went out to look over the battered volkswagen, the command post failed to report his movements to the forward observers at their telephone sets. One patrol, perhaps hearing Farwell, reported that elements of a German bicycle regiment were seen approaching. Initially this caused a belly laugh at my command post since the intelligence reports had been mentioning the possibility of the arrival of a German bicycle regiment for several weeks. Reports kept boiling in from the patrol. They came in *sotto voce,* and soon all the patrols were seeing part of the German bicycle regiment. The mass hypnosis took hold of not only the Ranger patrols but the Rangers on the main-line position. Gradually the enemy bicyclists came nearer. The artillery was called to put down a barrage. Its concussion rocked the still night air and shocked the Rangers back to reality. Suddenly they remembered that Stan Farwell had gone out to obtain a tire for the volkswagen. Firing ceased, and Farwell came lumbering in, his house slippers shuffling in the sand, his huge hand rolling the tire along as if it were a toy hoop.

Father Basil was still with us at Dernaia. He had volunteered for the Sened raid, but for once I had refused to allow him to go. Each day the priest set up his altar in the wooded draw alongside the road and in other front-line positions. One morning about ten o'clock he was halfway through the mass when the enemy artillery from the rear slopes of Djebel Krechem began pounding our positions. The chaplain continued with the service, and the Rangers in attendance kept their eyes on the bursts as they crept closer. Finally the entire group hit the dirt. Fortunately the closest shell was an "over," so no one was injured. Father Basil, turning to his flock, reminded them that the good Lord takes care of His own.

While at Dernaia Pass, Lieutenant Sunshine had some fun with the Germans in Feriana. Carrying a radio, Sunshine would drive a jeep cross country by a circuitous route to a flat-topped hill overlooking the town. Then, from a hidden observation post, he lined the field artillery onto a target. "Shine" was no artilleryman, but his sensing of the shell bursts was clear enough to place the shells directly on target. The Jerries didn't like the situation and must soon have suspected that an observer was watching them from the nearby mountains.

One evening the Rangers were treated to a Wild West show as the lieutenant broke off communication hurriedly. Sunshine's jeep came zigzagging across the desert with shells from two German scout cars falling all around him. The scout cars broke off the chase as his jeep came into our bivouac. Sunshine jumped out of his jeep and in a disgusted voice blamed his carbine for its inadequacy against the enemy. Without another word, he wrapped the carbine around a tree. This gesture was enjoyed by several members of my staff, who had repeatedly tried to get all officers to carry rifles instead of the shorter-ranged carbine.

By now we were becoming real veterans. Any greenness that may have previously clung to us had departed. To our soldiering ability we had added experience in several kinds of warfare. We believed ourselves masters of any situation and were mentally prepared to accept any task.

We remained in our defensive line at Dernaia Pass until the close of the overall battle known as Kasserine Pass when the Axis thrust was withdrawn. On 1 March we went into reserve for rest and refitting at the village of La Kouif. Still close to the front lines, we hid our pup tents and the few larger pyramidal tents we had obtained. I had my tent in a wadi safe from enemy air attack, but nature attacked in a heavy thunderstorm. The wadi filled rapidly during the night awakening me unceremoniously. With the water swirling above my knees, I am sure I presented a spectacle as I shouted for help.

It was chilly in early March at La Kouif so several enterprising Rangers, recalling the airplane equipment at Telepte airfield, made a trip forward. They scavenged several heating elements and blowers used to warm up motors and rigged them up at La Kouif to heat their tents during the last few days there.

V

The Battle of
El Guettar

MARCH 1943

PERSPECTIVE   At Djebel Kouif confidence in General Fredendall had deteriorated and his staff was defending him against mutterings among the troops. The British were fidgeting impatiently over what they termed an unnecessary delay in II Corps planning for its next attack. In Algiers suspicion spread that the Battle at Kasserine Pass had blunted II Corps' spirit—that the American command had become cautious and wary.

Alarmed by the reports of sagging morale in II Corps, Eisenhower visited Tébessa on 5 March. He proposed to place both the French and U.S. Army Corps directly under Field Marshal Alexander on an equal footing with Anderson's Army. Further, Eisenhower decided to replace Fredendall with Maj. Gen. George S. Patton. The news of Patton's coming fell like a bombshell on Djebel Kouif.

In the late morning of 7 March, Patton arrived at Djebel Kouif amid shrieking sirens and a procession of armored staff cars and half-tracks wheeling into the dingy square opposite the schoolhouse headquarters. Even the Arabs plodding through the muddy streets picked up their robes and scurried into the nearest doorways. The armored vehicles bristled with machine guns, and their tall fishpole antennas whipped crazily overhead. Patton stood in the lead car like a charioteer. He was scowling into the wind, his jaw strained against the web strap of his two-starred steel helmet.

Two oversized silver stars designated his command car. On either side of the hood, the car carried a rigid metal flag. One bore two white stars on a field of red. The other was lettered WTF to signify the Western Task Force, Patton's invading command on the Casablanca landing. The following day the WTF plate was replaced with one bearing the blue and white II Corps shield.

On 2 March the headquarters of the British First Army had issued a directive ordering the II Corps to prepare for an offensive to divert enemy reserves from the Mareth sector and to occupy airfields from which air support might be extended to the Eighth Army. They also were to establish a forward maintenance center for First Army, engaged in what clearly was considered the major Allied effort. D–Day for the operation was set for 15 March; Patton took command of the II Corps on 7 March.

To implement the directive, the II Corps was to capture Gafsa and then operate towards Maknassy to threaten the enemy line of communication from Gabes. Performance of this task required that fighter aircraft be stationed on the Telepte Airfield before D-Day, and suitable arrangements were requisite for the defense of the passes between Abiod and Shiba to prevent enemy breakthroughs after the II Corps had committed to action.

General Alexander was convinced that II Corps, because of its poor performance in the Kasserine fighting, needed additional training in battle indoctrination. The above mission given to Patton was a limited one, and he was told that he must be careful to avoid becoming heavily engaged. Patton actually wanted to drive all the way to the coast, but Alexander remained firm.

The II Corps was expanded on 8 March to include the 1st, 9th, and 34th Infantry Divisions, the 1st Armored Division, and the 13th Field Artillery Brigade reinforced by the 5th Armored Field Artillery Group. There were additional units such as tank destroyer groups, antiaircraft, artillery, and air reconnaissance units. Air support was to come from the Twelfth Air Force, with the Rangers included as auxiliary troops.

The Rangers had considered their ten days at Djebel Kouif as days of rest. Darby had gotten sick and was delirious at times, so his executive officer, Herman Dammer, laid the plans for the return to Gafsa. When they pulled out on the night of 13 March, Darby left the hospital and rejoined his unit, but he was still sick and doped with sulpha. After the Rangers got to Gafsa, they moved to El Guettar the next night, and three days later onward to Djebel el Ank.

¶ GAFSA IS ONLY FIFTY MILES FROM DERNAIA PASS. The Rangers joining the 1st Infantry Division in the return by truck were the connecting link between the 16th and 18th Regimental Combat Teams as they rode over the desert to the oasis at Gafsa. Beyond the town is a mountain chain with passes that lead to the coastal plains.

The 1st Infantry Division supported by the 1st Armored Division was preparing for an attack against Gafsa. Creeping forward, they brought up guns and ammunition. The artillery fired a barrage, the infantry advanced on foot, and the light bombers tossed in their bombs, but Gafsa was clear of Germans and Italians. The expected battle turned out to be a dress rehearsal.

It had rained all night before the entry into Gafsa, and we were drenched. Wadis had been flooded, showing us where not to locate a bivouac. The 1st Ranger Battalion turned off the road that wound down through the town. Walls around the palm and olive groves had been ground down by bulldozers in the month since our first arrival there. Selecting a grove just short of the town, we took possession and immediately started digging foxholes. This had now become SOP (standard operating procedure), a new word used by the soldiers for any action requiring no definite orders. After the foxholes were dug, shelter halves were put together for pup tents. While the bivouac was being prepared, sentinels were posted.

More and more units came down the road from Feriana past our encampment, seeking groves for their command posts and camps. The artillery, tank destroyers, engineers, and signal troops attached to the regimental combat teams arrived in Gafsa and crowded into groves until they were chock-a-block.

Soldiers sprawled about, cleaning and oiling their rifles and guns. On the surface the reoccupation of Gafsa on 16 March was peaceful; but underneath, nerves were taut as pressures mounted. Rumors of the battle ahead flew among the troops.

More than three weeks before, Rommel's tanks had been stopped in the Kasserine area. After the American lines had been bent in, they had held and then offensive pressure compelled Rommel to withdraw. The two 1st Divisions—infantry and armor—had reformed and advanced eastward. The fighting had been light until at Gafsa there was none. They had lost contact, but the Germans and Italians were known to be holding the passes a few miles ahead.

Immediately beyond Gafsa to the east there were no natural defenses. In the distance a high rocky mountain, good only for observation, separated two great sweeps of flat land spreading to the east and southeast. The armored division went into the northern battle theater over the rutty track leading to Maknassy. The southern battle theater was left to the infantry division and the Rangers. A macadam

THE BATTLE OF EL GUETTAR

road led into this theater, which was in the shadow of a steep-sided mountain. Beyond El Guettar the road forked, the northern branch going to Sfax and the other to Gabes. East of El Guettar on the road to Sfax was a pass named Djebel el Ank. The enemy was dug in there, its guns concealed on the slopes on both sides of the road.

Along the Gafsa–El Guettar Road the artillery of the 1st Division was emplaced so that it could fire down both the Sfax and Gabes roads. El Guettar, still in the hands of the Germans, had to be cleared before the 1st Division could advance.

We were given the task of determining what was there so that General Allen could decide on his next move. My soldiers got into the harness of their light packs and strode out past the 1st Division troops to the base of the mountain. Climbing up the slope, they found a gorge leading towards their objective. Below them they could hear troops digging foxholes and the buzz of truck tires on the macadam highway. Ammunition was going forward, telephone wires were being laid alongside the road, engineers were probing for enemy mines. It was dark, but the Rangers liked cover for our movements. In two hours we were approaching the town from the mountain side. Not a light showed in El Guettar that night of 18 March. Nevertheless, we had been told that the enemy troops numbered about two thousand; against that overwhelming force the Rangers' five hundred seemed puny. General Allen had instructed us that in taking German and Italian prisoners for identification, we were not to get committed to any fight from which we couldn't extricate ourselves.

Walking warily, our scouts slipped to the edge of the town with other rifles and automatic weapons covering them, but no shots were fired. They reported that El Guettar was empty, the enemy having withdrawn to the heights because of the advance of the American II Corps. We occupied El Guettar, sending word to 1st Division of our good fortune.

With El Guettar in hand, General Allen could develop his plan of attack against the heights to the east and southeast. The pass at Djebel el Ank had to be taken first in order to anchor the division's left flank on the rocky mountain which separated the areas east and southeast of Gafsa into two battle arenas. Assisted by an engineer company, we were ordered to attack the pass as the spearhead for a battalion of the 26th Regimental Combat Team

For the next forty-eight hours, during 19 and 20 March, the 1st Division continued to move guns and ammunition and men forward for the planned attack on 21 March. Ranger patrols scrambled into the mountains overlooking El Guettar, inspecting the face of the steep cliffs for possible flanking routes to Djebel el Ank. Though the maps showed no path through the mountain, we argued that there must be one since an Italian observation patrol was known to have moved to the heights overlooking El Guettar.

After dark of 20 March, we left El Guettar, moving westward on the road toward Gafsa to the rendezvous point. The moon was coming up, and in its cold light we met the other groups in the flanking party underneath a seventy-five-foot cone-shaped hill that stood apart from the mountains in the background. Near the hilly cone the road rose slightly so that down behind us we could see Gafsa.

A few minutes before midnight, two of the 1st Division's combat teams were collected near our jumping-off point. Men were digging emplacements for the 1st Division's artillery in the hard sand. A thousand noises split the night air: the hum of voices, the click of rifle bolts, and the rasping of starting motors. Gun barrels, pointing down the Sfax and Gabes roads, reflected moonbeams.

The 1st Ranger Battalion and our attached engineers and infantry were to have a six-hour head start in our flanking attack. The well-knit Rangers, carrying light packs, were armed with rifles, machine guns, grenades, knives, and infantry mortars. The combat engineers accompanying them carried 81-mm mortars.

In considering the tactics to be employed, a frontal attack on the Djebel el Ank Pass would have been suicide. The narrow road, cut at intervals by stone roadblocks, was crossed by wide belts of mines guarded by thick aprons of barbed wire. Both sides of the pass, shaped like the cross section of a funnel, concealed Italian gun positions dug into the rock. The guns were sighted to fire out across the wire and the mines and could swing in an arc to cover the opposite mountain face. Though the enemy had emplaced machine guns, mortars, and 88-mm guns to make the pass impregnable, they had not made themselves as invulnerable from the north flank.

Ranger patrols scrambling in the mountain during the previous two nights had discovered that the face overlooking the El Guettar–

Gabes road was cut by a succession of gorges and saddles. By following a circuitous twelve-mile route through them, we determined that we could reach the pass, only five miles away as the crow flies. The gorges behind the steep side of the mountain masked the path so that there was no need to expose members of the flanking force on the skyline. In places there were steep-faced rocks where the men had to clamber up or leap down. The gorges were also traps; even a few machine guns could have held them against a force of overwhelming strength. But feeling secure in the pass, the Italians had left their flank unguarded.

Like Rogers' Rangers, my force relied on speed, surprise, and shock. We planned to make a violent attack from the hills while the infantry followed with a frontal attack. The gap would surely fall, thereby anchoring the American left flank for the greater battle to follow.

As the Ranger column was ready to start into the mountain, I asked the captain commanding the attached engineer company only one question, "Do the engineers think they can keep up with the Rangers?" Almost as I spoke the Ranger companies passed by at a dogtrot, leaving the engineers to bring up the tail of the column. There was no tripping or stumbling among the Rangers, and their equipment clung snugly to their bodies.

As we entered a gorge the moon disappeared behind the mountains. The column lengthened out so that each man saw only the two or three in front. Occasionally the swaying antennas of walkie-talkie radios also came into view. Mortar tubes and bases clanked against rocks, but the sound of the 1st Division's motors was gone. Men were breathing hard. No one spoke.

Sometime after 0100 the moon came out, throwing its rays upon the mountains beautifully. The jagged peaks stood out, and the moonlight and shadows danced through the gorges. Occasionally, as the column moved over the saddle of a hill, several hundred yards of the line ahead could be seen winding through the hillside. About three o'clock in the morning I learned that the engineer mortar squads were dropping back because the going was too tough. Their commanding officer asked for instructions so I told him to do the best he could.

The column went forward, stopped, and went forward again.

There was no smoking or talking. On the halts each man dropped where he was. The halts became more frequent and around 0500 the column moved forward a few feet and plumped down again. The trail disappeared in a heavy shadow. There was a cliff ahead—the reason for the hesitation. Down the men went, one by one, passing their equipment from hand to hand. As each man got down he sped away in the darkness, leaving the men behind him with a choked-up feeling—they had to catch up so as to be with friends in the attack.

Farther along a Ranger was standing in a stream bed, whispering to each to climb the little shelf ahead, curve to the left around the base of the hill, and then—at the end of the plateau—go down in the valley to the right. We urged the attached infantry troops to keep as closed up as possible.

Abruptly the tail of the column moved past me as I stood talking to Major Dammer. A soldier carrying a walkie-talkie and another officer were with us. I was in a very good humor and with a broad smile spoke to the others saying, "Do you realize, what we have done, men? Do you realize? We've got five whole columns through!"

Then I directed the men to keep moving very quickly so that they could begin the attack at 0600. Suddenly it was light and nearly time for the attack. The flanking column had reached a spot slightly beyond the Italian positions at Djebel el Ank.

Rifles cracked and machine guns buzzed. My troops were silhouetted against the skyline on an oblong plateau several hundred yards in length and parallel to the road in the pass, behind the enemy's defenses. From behind rocks on the firing line, men were shooting on the enemy in the pass. Then the infantry mortars started in with their belching noise, the shells exploding down in the valley on the other side of the road. As each hit there was a flash, and light grey smoke spread out from it.

From the position in the hills we could look down into the pass with its roadblock and pattern of barbed wire. Off to the south was the other road which led to Gabes, disappearing on its eastward course into the hills. Beyond the road was a salt lake, shimmering in the early morning light.

As if from the balcony of an opera house, we looked out across the plain to the south at black dots which were evidently vehicles of the

1st Division advancing to the east. The guns on the vehicles were firing, and their shells could be seen bursting on the enemy positions farther east of the plain.

Now the German artillery opened up on us, and the explosions rocked the plateau where we lay. They were shooting at our command post, which was silhouetted sharply against the rocks. I sent two Ranger squads down after the 88-mm gun.

Meanwhile the firing of rifles and machine guns kept up as the Rangers fired across the valley. Cpl. Robert Bevan said that he silenced a machine-gun nest at a range of 1,350 yards, using an '03 (Springfield) rifle with telescopic sights. "I ranged in with tracers and then put two shots right into the position. The machine gun was quiet for a couple of minutes and then somebody threw a dirty towel or something over the gun and the crew came out and sat down."

Ranger groups pulled out of their plateau and, running and crouching, went down the mountain to knock out Italian gun positions. A group ran down the hill with their rifles held high, zigzagging and falling down behind rocks and ending with a rush for a sniper.

I used the radio to call: "Darby to C Company, Darby to C Company. We need a little bayonet work. Report to Lieutenant Shunstrom." C Company replied that they were coming. These Rangers had been resting but were on their feet almost in one motion, stretching themselves, pulling the bayonets from their scabbards, and fixing them on their rifles. Down they went to make their charge at a point almost opposite the plateau where the headquarters was located. They charged across the road without cover. From Tommy guns, rifles, and grenades, explosions crackled and roared. I decided at that point to hold them where they were, saying, "Don't go in after them, make them come out after you." The men stopped short in their tracks, waited a minute, and then finished the job.

Attacking up the valley, the Rangers had successively cleaned out many strong points but were stopped at a fortified machine-gun nest. Their own mortars were without ammunition. It was 0800, and I had estimated that the engineers with their mortars would be two hours late: in they came, just at that moment, stumbling across the plateau. Directions were given quickly and the mortars were set up.

There was a terrific wham and a swish. Across the valley stones and sand erupted, but the mortar shell was short. After one correction and then another, the third shell burst right alongside the target, finishing the machine gun. The Rangers' job was done. The 26th Regimental Combat Team came at 1000.

There was mopping up to be done, however, and plenty of shooting and bayonet work ahead as the Rangers scrambled around the rocks. Prisoners were being rounded up—a motley looking group of Italians with long overcoats reaching almost to their ankles. They were taken to the command post where Father Basil in Ranger uniform mingled among them. The Germans had pulled out and left the Italians two days before. In fluent Italian, Father Basil convinced the prisoners that the fight was hopeless and that if they would call to their companions to surrender, their lives would be saved. Not only did they do this but, at the padre's suggestion, willingly lifted the mines from in front of their positions, no doubt saving many unsuspecting American soldiers from injury.

The Rangers fought on, but it was past noon before we had our first casualty. I tried to be as careful as possible, advising the men via radio on the safest routes to get at the enemy. By keeping the battle moving and pressing the enemy, I did my best to protect the men. By 1400 that afternoon, 21 March, I was happy to report to 1st Division that the entire valley was in American hands, and the Rangers had taken two hundred prisoners.

By the time the Rangers and the 26th Infantry Regiment had pinned down the left flank for the American forces, the 1st Division had moved in to hold a ridge of mountains that ran south from Djebel el Ank and then circled westward to Djebel Berda across the road from El Guettar to Gabes. In effect the central part of the commanding heights formed the eastern side of a triangle that included the forked roads meeting at El Guettar to the west. From north to south the 26th, 16th, and 18th Regimental Combat Teams of the 1st Division took over the position. The 18th Infantry was split by the El Guettar–Gabes Road, with one battalion to the north and two battalions on Djebel Berda, five miles to the southwest. The Rangers went in on the right of the 3rd Battalion, just north of the Gabes road.

The Axis forces had evidently not expected to lose the pass at Djebel el Ank. They came wheeling back in a counterattack with three Panzer Grenadier and two Italian infantry divisions. The American II Corps had only the 1st and 9th Infantry and 1st Armored Divisions to stem the attack.

From the heights in our segment, the Rangers looked down on a developing attack of Germans in parade-ground formation. This was the third day (23 March) of the twenty-one day El Guettar battle. The American intelligence had determined that the Germans were going to attack at 1600. There was disbelief about such an accurate forecast of enemy intentions, and to the soldiers' amazement, the time of attack was later corrected to 1645. Excitement rippled through the American forces. When the time neared, every Ranger could see the Germans far below them on the plain, forming for attack. Six battalions—two each of tanks, infantry, and artillery—of the 10th Panzer Division attacked the sector the Rangers were defending. The German general, thinking to awe the rather green American troops, gambled on a frontal attack. The infantry leading was followed by some sixty tanks in what looked like an attack in the American Civil War. The Germans took no cover, seeming not to be aware of the almost certain deathtrap into which they were moving. I was never so wildly excited as when watching this mass of men and vehicles inching toward us. The caterpillar-like force rolled irresistibly forward.

When the Germans were within 1,550 yards, the Yankee artillery boomed one salvo on top of another. The shells were concentrated dead on the enemy troops. Soon the eerie black smoke of the time shells showed that they were bursting above the heads of the Germans. Then a hole would appear in the oncoming carpet of the attack. There was no slowing up by the Germans, but their number was being hacked away by the artillery. A few minutes later the remaining Germans charged the last hundred yards. There was no running, just a relentless forward lurching of bodies. Sputtering gunfire kept up ceaselessly. The Americans did not yield ground, and the attack was broken up. The Germans still on their feet retreated down the mountain while flecks of sand puffed up beside them.

The artillery time shells had been largely responsible for heavy German losses before they came within range of accurate machine-gun and rifle fire. The time shells had just arrived a few days before, but there were no fuze cutters (devices to make time settings) with them. The artillery general, understanding their construction, had visited a blacksmith shop in Gafsa where they fashioned rude but workable devices from scrap metal and horseshoes. The old proverb was thus reversed for "because of a horseshoe, the position was saved."

Meanwhile the two battalions of the 18th Regiment, separated by five miles from the remainder of the 1st Division, were having difficulties in their position on Djebel Berda. On 24 March the Rangers were sent out in broad daylight to assist them. That night at sundown, Company G of the 18th Infantry was overrun by overwhelming numbers of German paratroopers fighting as infantrymen. Watching the battle from Hill 772 on the mountain, the Rangers went down to assist them, leaving Company D alone to hang on to Hill 772 of the Djebel Berda position. One platoon of Company C, led by Lieutenant Shunstrom, was sent around the Germans to attempt the Ranger ruse that had worked so effectively in the past. Undetected behind the enemy, the platoon observed the fire of an 18th Regiment cannon company attached to the Rangers. Each of the six guns plowed six rounds into the Germans. Shunstrom reported back that they "really blew hell out of the Germans."

About 1400 the Jerries discovered the Ranger platoon, which had been reinforced by the remainder of Capt. Jim Lyle's C Company. The German thrust at this far right flank position grew in strength. C Company was drawn from behind the Germans. D Company on Hill 772 had to be withdrawn because they lacked ammunition. The colonel commanding the 18th Regiment asked if the Rangers could hold on. Our answer was a typical "Yes," though we asked for one battalion to assist us. Our small force held off the Germans from the north slopes of Djebel Berda while the two battered battalions of the 18th Infantry pulled back through the Rangers some two or more miles. The situation was still tight. Nevertheless, we stayed out on this right flank, practically cut off for three days but not giving an inch. Then on 27 March we were relieved by elements of the 9th Division.

The Rangers' real work was done, and I was well satisfied. The fighting that the 1st Rangers had done between 16 and 27 March had usually been against overwhelming odds. We had been required to make our long march to Djebel el Ank, a hit-and-run raid, and then a few days later we were asked to stave off a savage counterattack. Through all kinds of combat, my men had fought with skill and cunning, losing only three killed and eighteen wounded.

These American soldiers had shown, as they had learned in training, that lungs and legs and heart get a man to the battlefield and help him fight. The Rangers in their twelve-mile march through the mountain gorges kept closed up in the dark and made the battle the "payoff" for their training.

Our primary task in Tunisia was now completed. The battle of El Guettar continued for some time, but there was not the violent action that the Rangers had experienced. We were now withdrawn for patrolling duties—two companies to Madjene el Fedj, twenty-four miles north of Gafsa, two at Gafsa, and two at Sidi bou Sid. There we remained until the El Guettar battle was written as an Allied victory.

During the battle of El Guettar, I was summoned to General Patton's headquarters, then located in a small public building in Gafsa. The general, now in command of the II Corps, stepped out on his balcony with me and much to his amazement saw a Ranger in a green beret coming down the street. "What in hell is that?" cried Patton, as he spotted this breach of orders requiring the wearing of the helmet.

With a tremor in my voice, I replied, "That is our British chaplain, sir." Then gaining confidence I added, "And about the only man I know who can get away with not wearing a helmet." General Patton swallowed quickly and then laughed hilariously.

It was a sad day among the Rangers when Father Basil left for his own army. He had become known among the Americans in central Tunisia as an interesting and kindly man. Being long out of touch with his own people, his uniform—from the shoes he wore to the combat suit on his back—became American. But never did he relinquish his green beret.

We were soon ordered to march by truck and train to Nemours, near Oran, and arrived there on 17 April. By this time, we were all battle-tested veterans, experienced in mountain and hit-and-run warfare. This, coupled with amphibious experience, made the Rangers all-around infantrymen.

General Terry Allen wrote a letter of glowing commendation of the 1st Ranger Battalion for the actions at El Guettar. A year later this commendation was made the basis for a Presidential Citation, following a similar citation from the president for the excellent fighting at Sorrento on the left flank at Salerno.

The Rangers in North Africa

Aboard troopship enroute to the attack at Arzew, Algeria, members of the 1st Ranger Battalion practice loading into assault landing craft. November 6, 1942.

Rangers capture a big gun position at Arzew. The photograph was taken at dawn, November 8, after a night of fighting.

Rangers force open the door of a questionable building during early stage of the fighting at Arzew.

Ranger sharpshooters aim at enemy positions during early morning attack on Arzew. November 12, 1942.

Darby directs beach landing exercise at Arzew. December 1942.

Maneuvers at Arzew, January 20, 1943. *Top:* Speed march across hilly terrain. *Bottom:* Darby and his officers reviewing the 1st Ranger Battalion.

Lt. Ralph Ingersoll, Engineer officer accompanying the Rangers, and Sgt. Phil Stern, Ranger photographer, at El Guettar, Tunisia; captured enemy troops on the right. Stern was wounded a few days later.

El Guettar, Tunisia, April 1943. *Top:* Colonel Darby watches the parade of Italian prisoners march by after the 1st Ranger Battalion captured the strategic height of Djebel el Ank near El Guettar. *Bottom:* Italian prisoners of war carry their wounded. The Rangers won a Presidential Citation and Colonel Darby was awarded a Distinguished Service Medal for this action, which opened the pass at Djebel el Ank and enabled the Eighth Army and General Patton's II Corps to join forces and advance.

First anniversary of the 1st Ranger Battalion is celebrated at Zeralda, Algeria, in June 1943. *Left to right:* Colonel Darby; Capt. Roy Murray, commanding officer of the 4th Ranger Battalion; and Maj. Gen. Terry Allen, commanding general, 1st Infantry Division.

VI

Landings in Sicily

JULY 1943

PERSPECTIVE   After El Guettar there was still a great deal of fighting to be done by the British and American troops against the enemy in Tunisia. Patton was ordered back to Algiers by Eisenhower to retake command of the I Armored Corps. At that time General Omar Bradley was placed in command of the II Corps in Tunisia. The news of the command change was closely guarded until the day Patton left II Corps. Even then it was censored from the news dispatches until after the capture of Bizerte, for had Patton been publicly withdrawn from the Tunisian fighting front, his departure would have provoked enemy speculation on the next Allied move. Eisenhower was anxious not to reveal his further intentions in the Mediterranean area.

Hard fighting went on in the Tunisian campaign with many casualties in American and British forces as well as in enemy ranks. The Allied forces kept inching closer and closer to Bizerte and Tunis, the major seaports in Tunisia. Eventually the Afrika Korps came to an end: on 7 May Bizerte and Tunis fell; the final surrender was made on 9 May. There were 275,000 German and Italian prisoners including all their generals. The Italian Navy, much to the Royal Navy's disappointment, made no attempt to evacuate the Axis forces.

The 1st Ranger Battalion had returned to bivouac a month before the final surrender at Tunis to expand into three battalions. This was done to permit enough time for training before the attack on Sicily.

The decision for the assualt on Sicily had been developed at the Casablanca

Conference when Churchill and Roosevelt agreed on how the war would be prosecuted from that point forward. They settled on the operation against Sicily for July 1943 with Eisenhower continuing in overall command.

In the strategy discussion before the directive was prepared, there was continuing divergence of American and British viewpoints. The Americans were still hoping for a cross-Channel invasion of France in 1943 and wanted to reduce Allied requirements in the Mediterranean in favor of continuing the build-up in England. The British concluded that a Channel crossing in 1943 was premature, wanting to exploit the North African success with operations aimed at weakening Italy. Both groups of planners agreed that the Tunisian campaign was not likely to be concluded before late spring. Consequently, troops and shipping could not be concentrated in England before September, and even then would not have reached parity with German strength in France. Prospects of a 1943 Channel crossing had practically disappeared.

British planners urged that pressure be maintained in the Mediterranean in order to weaken German forces. General Marshall, wary of British methods, feared the creation of a Mediterranean vacuum that would eat up the resources for the cross-Channel operation. If a landing in France were not possible in 1943, he argued along with Admiral King, then some Allied resources should be diverted to the Pacific to enable the Allies, and particularly the Americans, to retain the initiative there. The ultimate outcome was a compromise, with limited operations being authorized in both the Mediterranean and the Pacific.

The Americans insisted that Operation Husky (code name for the invasion of Sicily) be an end in itself and not a stepping stone to further operations in the Mediterranean. Its express purpose was to secure the Mediterranean line of communications, divert German divisions from Russia, apply pressure on Italy, and create a situation in which Turkey could be enlisted as an active ally.

At the May 1943 Trident Conference, following Casablanca, Churchill obtained American approval for Eisenhower to plan for the exploitation of Husky with the object of eliminating Italy from the war. Eisenhower, however, was not to have additional forces; in fact, some units would be withdrawn to England. As part of the Husky plan, there was to be early seizure of ports and rapid capture of airfields, to be used for close support missions of the troops.

After some other planning ideas which did not have total Allied agreement, it was decided that Montgomery's Eighth Army would attack at the southeastern coast of Sicily and that Patton's Seventh Army would attack to the west, adjoining the Eighth Army, at Gela and Licata.

The plan included naval diversions designed to pin down Axis forces in western Sicily and to threaten western Greece. These deception efforts were supposed to confuse the enemy. However, Axis commanders had generally pinpointed Sicily as the next Allied target after Tunisia.

Sicily is about the size of the state of Vermont. Largely mountainous, movement is confined to main roads. Near Catania there is a sizable plain which merges into Mount Etna, over ten thousand feet in height to the north. Mount Etna restricts movement between Catania and Messina to a narrow coastal strip. The main mountain range runs along the northern coast with spurs emanating from it towards the south. Rivers and streams, many of which dry up in the hot July climate, are not major obstacles. Messina, at the northeastern tip of the island, is just two miles from the "toe" of Italy proper.

Patton's Seventh Army was assembled, trained, and staged in North Africa, from Bizerte all the way west to Algiers, while Montgomery's Eighth Army used ports in Tunisia. Most of the units had seen previous action in North Africa, but some had just arrived from the United States or the United Kingdom. On 10 July Axis forces on the island of Sicily totaled between 300,000 and 365,000; the Allied invasion force numbered 478,000.

As planned by Gen. Omar Bradley, commander of II Corps, the strong right arm of Patton's army—II Corps—would attack in the Gulf of Gela and force three simultaneous landings across the twenty-mile strip of the island's soft, hummocked beaches. While two battalions of Rangers slipped into the port of Gela itself, the 1st Infantry Division would land east of that village, push inland across the rolling plains, and seize the airport at Ponte Olivo by daylight of D-plus-one. Six miles farther east, two regiments of the inexperienced 45th Division would break a path to the Biscari Airfield by dark of D-plus-two. On the right the remaining regiment of the 45th Division would push into the hills to seize the airfield at Comiso by daylight of D-plus-two. This regiment would also establish contact with Montgomery's forces near the cliff-like city of Ragusa.

After securing the key airports, II Corps would then advance twenty miles into the southeast sector of Sicily to gain the arterial highway linking that corner with Caltanisetta. This city was the hub of a network or roads radiating to the three corners and intervening sides of Sicily. Because of the bold mountainous character of the island, it was apparent from the start that the campaign would become a struggle for these roads.

In addition to the landing forces of II Corps (including the 1st Infantry Division, the Rangers, and the 45th Division), there was to be a landing at Licata, a seaport to the west, by General Truscott's 3rd Division and a combat command of the 2nd Armored Division. Also, airborne troops would be dropped from 220 C-47 aircraft. They included four battalions of infantry and a battalion of pack howitzers, all under the command of Patton's Seventh Army. These troops were to land in the high ground behind Gela to the north where they could protect the beach from counterattack by any enemy reserves waiting farther inland. The parachutists would come in under darkness at midnight approximately three hours before the amphibious landing.

¶ WHILE AT NEMOURS I WAS CALLED TO ALLIED Headquarters at Algiers to learn of the next Ranger task, that of tak-

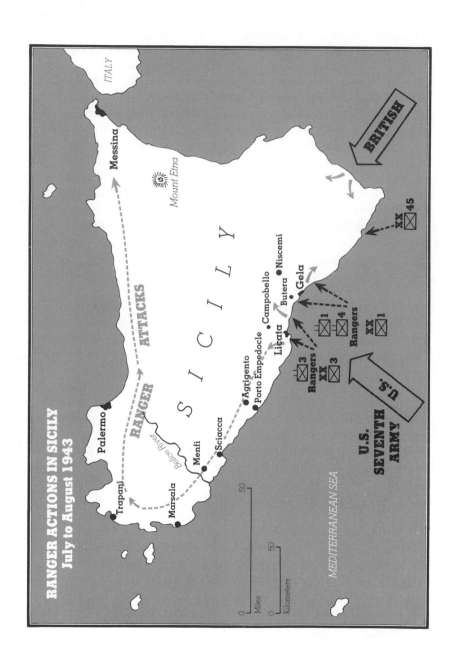

RANGER ACTIONS IN SICILY
July to August 1943

ITALY

Messina

Mount Etna

SICILY

Palermo

Trapani

Marsala

Menfi

Sciacca

Belice River

RANGER → ATTACKS

Agrigento

Porto Empedocle

Campobello

Licata

Butera

Niscemi

Gela

BRITISH

XX ☒ 45

Rangers XX ☒ 3
☒ 3

☒ 1
☒ 4
Rangers XX ☒ 1

U.S.

U.S.
SEVENTH
ARMY

MEDITERRANEAN SEA

Miles

Kilometers

ing Palermo. When asked how many battalions were required to take out the coastal defenses of the port, I answered "Fifteen." This was not the answer desired, for the staff appeared to expect that only a few Ranger battalions could do the job. At the meeting I was asked to expand my single battalion to three and was given six weeks to find the men and train them.

When I applied for men, I found the infantry in North Africa had first priority. Since there was no alternative, I took a few assistants and made a recruiting drive around Oran. We circularized the town—putting up posters in recreation centers in an appeal to red-blooded Americans, made stump speeches, and "impressed" soldiers found in the local hot spots. I made fifteen or twenty speeches elaborating on the exacting discipline and the less glamorous sides of Ranger life. When I spoke to one thousand men, I got one hundred volunteers; when I spoke to two thousand, I got two hundred. Meanwhile Capt. Roy Murray and his Rangers were scanning the soldiers at bars and recreation centers. They sized up prospects from a distance and then offered them the rugged life of a Ranger. Fortunately Allied Headquarters required units to release volunteers for the Rangers, although that didn't increase the popularity of the Ranger recruiting party.

I had obtained the men for the 1st Ranger battalion by selecting from a volunteer group. Although most of the men turned out well, there were sufficient cases of misfits to cause me to doubt the advisability of depending on volunteers. Instead I proceeded to select the men I needed because I believed that the best men don't always volunteer. Among my original Rangers were a number of men who had volunteered, as they thought, to get out of work. Another misconception was that membership in a unit like the Commandos or the Rangers meant that men could live an undisciplined life where they wouldn't have to shave, bathe, or train. Now, I put the emphasis on searching for men who were young, usually of medium size, and rugged looking.

As the recruits rolled in I selected and sent them in small groups to Nemours, where Major Dammer had set up a replica of the Commando Depot. The training program was a combination of what we had learned from the Commandos and of combat experience at

Arzew and in Tunisia. First a rigid campaign of physical conditioning was put into effect. One of the ways of testing a man's courage
was to send him down a nearly vertical cliff slide of some six hundred
feet to a beach below. There was no path except off to the side, and
loose gravel slipped under the feet of the fully equipped soldiers. The
men were also put through weapons-training and battle-
preparedness courses.

We staged a number of "opposed" landings north of Nemours.
The new Rangers and the navy seamen working with them were
green, but they leaped at the opportunity to be shot at while making
night landings. Together they spent night after night making landings on the coast at a beach similar to that at Gela, where revised
plans called for a landing. Machine guns were fired out to sea over
the heads of the incoming troops, making it as realistic as possible,
and the beaches were mined with TNT charges. A few bullet holes
were put through the boats.

An experienced Ranger was shot in the back, though not seriously, by one of the jittery recruits who failed to keep the safety catch of
his rifle engaged. Soon the training period was over. The Rangers—
now the 1st, 3rd and 4th Battalions—moved forward to embarkation
points. A 2nd Ranger Battalion was at that time training in the United States under the direction of several former Rangers who had
been found physically unfit for combat.

Under my direct command the 1st and 4th Battalions went to
Algiers, where they were to be attached to their old friends, the 1st
Infantry Division. By this time Terry Allen's "Famous First" had
come to think of my Rangers as their own special spearhead troops.
Likewise, we referred to ourselves as the "point" force since we were
out ahead all the time. The 3rd Rangers, under the command of Major Herman Dammer, were dispatched to the vicinity of Bizerte to
join the 3rd Division, an organization which had not previously seen
the Rangers in action.

At dawn of 9 July, a huge amphibious force put to sea. One hundred and thirty warships were included in the gigantic ship concentration, while 324 vessels were employed for the transportation of the
assault troops and their equipment. The ships rendezvoused in the
Tunisian channel and then moved eastward toward Sicily via Cape
Bon, south of Pantelleria.

As the first convoys moved out of the harbors, General Patton issued his first order of the day addressed to the "soldiers of the Seventh Army." He exhorted the Americans to feel pride in their selection to fight by the side of the famous British Eighth Army and pointed out, "in landing operations, retreat is impossible. We must retain this tremendous advantage by always attacking, rapidly, ruthlessly, viciously, and without rest."

The 1st and 4th Ranger Battalions aboard the U.S.S. *Dickman* and H.M.S. *Albert* and *Charles* were to land alongside the 1st Division on the Gela beachhead. Accompanying them were two engineer battalions for clearing mines and for doughboy fighting when necessary; a chemical mortar battalion armed with the new 4.2-inch rifled mortars was to give the fast-moving Rangers close artillery support.

The town of Gela is on a hill about 150 feet above the coast. Off to the left or western flank was a fort at a height of about 200 feet. The town was sprawled close to the shore and at its exact center a pier jutted out into the water some 2,000 feet.

My plan was to have the 1st Battalion take the beachhead to the left of the pier while the 4th Battalion, landing simultaneously at H-hour, would go in on its right. At H-plus-thirty minutes the 1st Battalion, 39th Engineers, to be used as infantrymen, would move in behind the 1st Ranger Battalion. Following the engineers, the chemical mortar battalion and a battalion of shore engineers would land at H-plus-sixty and H-plus-ninety respectively. Once ashore the 1st Ranger Battalion would swing out to the left toward the fort while the 4th Battalion would go to the right to take out other coast defenses. The engineers would then take the center.

The beach at Gela was heavily mined and defended by three shore batteries, one battery of 77-mm field artillery, two mortar companies, and twenty-five machine-gun nests. The air photographs showed concrete pillboxes camouflaged with vines and brush or concealed in huts.

Throughout the planning for the assault, it was intended that the amphibious units would be met by two guide boats that would lead them ashore. Shortly after midnight of 10 July, we got off in the transport area, looked around for our guide boats but couldn't find them. I was on an LCS with a navy four-striper from the *Dickman*, who commanded the combined Anglo-American boat flotilla. There were some forty-eight boats in all; and because of the rough sea off Gela, the boats began milling around in the water. Everyone was expecting to find the guide boat flashing its signal light, but it wasn't there. Orders were shouted back and forth: "Follow me! Over here!" Sorting out the landing craft was a difficult job while the storm was still in progress and forty-mile winds were whipping up the waves.

When the boats were almost collected, the guide boat appeared. I called to its skipper, "Are you on course?"

The answer came back, "Sure, I'm on course."

That was all I wanted to know, so we followed the guide boat towards the beach. As we got closer, six searchlights on shore turned on us and, as one of the Rangers later said, "The Jerries on the flanks began to tune up, and the show was on."

Many men in the boats had been seasick on the packed ships. En route to the flaming shore they became sicker than ever. Holding their heads in their hands, they moaned, they vomited. A searchlight picked out one of the boats showing several pale green faces. One of the men growled, "Why don't they shoot out that goddamned searchlight?" Blue streaks of fire flew toward and among the boats. The Italians on shore had depressed their ack-ack guns.

Near shore the gunboat guides showed their lights and hailed the first assault wave, shouting: "Straight ahead. Go straight ahead. You'll see the light on your right. Look out for mines ashore. Good luck."

Going towards shore we could see blue tracers cutting across the beach. The LCS leading us carried twelve rockets in two banks, about the size of 105-mm shells. It looked as if nobody could possibly live through all the stuff the Italians were shooting out across the edge of the beach, but the rocket boat rode onto the beach behind a wave firing six rockets, three from each bank. I was aboard the rocket boat and thought that it was a tremendous feeling. When the rockets went off, it seemed as if the boat had blown up. The rockets hit an ammunition dump in the town, blowing everything sky high and knocking out the defenses on that side of the beach. An entire block and a half of buildings was leveled. It was a lucky hit.

The Rangers were now close to the pier jutting out from the center of Gela. The division's intelligence officer had warned us that the pier was set to blow up as we were about to land. He was right. As the Rangers' boats ran parallel to it, the whole center section exploded, but without injury.

Off the beach we came under mortar fire but, being well dispersed, lost only one craft. Searchlights spotlighted the men as they jumped out of their boats; but as the ships out at sea ranged on them, the lights went out one by one. Twenty-eight craft hit the beach at the same time. Red and blue streaks of fire plunged across their path. Naval guns spouting black smoke and bursts of flame made direct hits on an annoying battery of guns.

The flotilla commander had boasted that he would put my boat high and dry on the beach, which he did. Many of the boats were sticking on a sandbar several hundred yards off shore. We splashed through a few yards of surf, went rapidly across the beach, and hugged the sea wall. The town was dead ahead. Behind us the 83rd Chemical Mortar Battalion swung ashore in LCIs (landing craft, infantry), landing just to the right of the pier.

Ashore, I looked back out to sea and saw the LCIs coming in. Two of them hit the sandbar and stuck, but the center boat leaped over the bar and closed on the beach. A man aboard had been shot and fell off the bridge, hitting the telegraph key. The accidental signal sounded like full speed ahead, and the boat got the extra surge of power needed to hurdle the sandbar.

This lone LCI became the object of converging fire from all the enemy guns. But, their hard luck was a break for the Rangers. The firing on the beach dropped off considerably, allowing us to advance into the town with our own mortars in support.

Sergeant Randall Harris got an abdomen wound in a blast of gunfire that also killed his captain. Covering the wound with his hand, he led his men up the beaches and helped them take their next objective. A lieutenant finally persuaded him to go back to a first-aid station for treatment.

"Hell, I'm not helpless yet," said the sergeant. "Get me some prisoners to guard—or something." Harris was promoted to second lieutenant on the battlefield for his bravery.

In town the 1st Ranger Battalion swung to the left and the 4th Battalion to the right, leaving the center to the engineer battalion. Warily men hugged the buildings. The pop of a gun would hold them up for an instant. Each Ranger covered a buddy in approaching snipers' nests. Pins were pulled from grenades and the potato-like objects were held ready to be thrown into buildings. It was dark, but the Rangers were able to clear streets quickly against light resistance. In each battalion one soldier in three carried a flashlight and was prepared to signal upon challenge. The lights were distinctive: red, amber, and black. A squad rounding a corner in Gela would flash the code "dot-dash-dot." If the correct answer came back, they would move on. Sometimes the answer was a burst of rifle fire.

The last hours of darkness passed swiftly. The 1st Ranger Battalion had worked through the streets westward to the vicinity of the fort on the town's flank. Their first glimpse of the rows of barbed wire, pillboxes, and guns mounted inside was enough to deter the lightly armed Rangers from attempting an immediate attack. The prearranged plan of attack provided for naval gunfire on call of the army commanders ashore. Through an accompanying naval officer, I asked for fire on the fort from the United States cruiser *Savannah*. In a few minutes a salvo of big shells landed on the fort, throwing up debris. Hitting in a steady stream, the shells silenced many of the guns. My men ran forward at the first lull in the defenders' fire, asking the cruiser to lift fire. Just as we got close to the fort's walls, several projectiles hit inside the fort. The concussion was terrifying, and the fort surrendered. Naval gunfire had given us a convincing demonstration.

Originally we had planned to assault the fort directly from the beaches; but last-minute reconnaissance showed fishing boats using the beach in front of the town, revealing the unmined and relatively undefended nature of the beach there. After we captured the fort, we took a hasty glance at the pillboxes, minefields, and barbed-wire defenses. "Phew" was all we could say.

I next decided on a frontal assault of Gela, estimating that it would be less hazardous than conventional attacks on the heavily gunned and defended flanks. We retraced our steps to the landing beach near the pier. Up and down the beaches officers were marshalling their men. Ammunition and food were being piled on the sand. DUKWs, those seagoing self-propelled trucks, were plying between ships and the shore, landing antitank guns and artillery pieces. Engineers were probing for mines. A DUKW riding over an exploding mine rose in the air, but no one was hurt. A huge, lumbering robot mine detector being unloaded was dropped on the beach. It touched off a mine, and the explosion smashed its delicate parts into a twisted steel wreck.

As we reformed at the edge of town, we heard the drone of German planes. Twenty of them dived on the beach, their machine guns chattering nervously. In an instant they were out to sea, still strafing. Then they were over the ships and gaining altitude in a wide circle to return to the landing area.

One of my fabulous Rangers, Sergeant Legg, claims that he shot down one of the ME-110s with a Browning automatic rifle. When the plane came in low from the sea he ducked behind a wall. He tossed his BAR to his shoulder and fired a few shots, but missed. When the plane made another run he held the trigger for a long burst and saw flames spurt from one of its fuel tanks.

About 0700 six Italian tanks came into town, and, according to Sergeant Rada, "We thought we'd have to grab the lifeboats. The tanks came right in the town, blasting away. We worked up to the rooftops, tossing sticky grenades on them. We had a 37-mm that shuttled from one target to another, going from one street corner to the next, taking pot shots at the tanks as they came in." In the buildings other Rangers were firing their rocket launchers at point-blank range. Capt. Jack Street and Sgt. Shirley Jacobs, their grenades gone, carried fifteen-pound blocks of TNT to the top of a building and dropped them on the tanks.

Going up a street in my jeep, I saw one of the Italian tanks coming up the main street towards the city square. My driver swerved the jeep into an alley and backed out just enough to clear the machine gun for firing. When the tank was within rock-throwing distance I squeezed off an entire belt of ammunition at it. The rounds ricocheted off the sides of the tank like water hitting a wall. Unharmed, the tank turned up a side street to avoid drawing abreast of my position. Swinging the jeep down the main street, we went in search of the 37-mm antitank gun being used by Captain Shunstrom, hooked it on the rear of the jeep, and returned to the square. We wheeled it into position and on the third shot saw the tank flame up.

The rest of D-day morning was hectic. There were still snipers and enemy-held pillboxes in town. About noon, eighteen huge German Tiger tanks lumbered into Gela for the second counterattack. For a time it looked bad. I called for the 4.2-inch rifled chemical mortars and for cruiser fire. The chemical mortar troops plopped their twenty-five pound shells against the tanks in the streets. Captain Shunstrum turned a captured 77-mm against them too. Twelve tanks were blasted out of action.

On top of the German tank attack, the enemy sent a battalion of Italian infantry against the town. As I was massing my mortars to meet the new thrust, I encountered General Patton who had come ashore an hour before. The general, arriving fresh on the town, asked me to point out the enemy counterattack. In the hurry of preparations I inquired, "Which one do you want to see, General Patton?"

The Italian infantrymen approached in mass formation. Our mortars, holding fire until they were about two thousand yards away, laid down several hundred 4.2 shells in a minute's concentrated firing. The Italian thrust disintegrated.

By late afternoon Gela quieted. The Ranger command post was set up in a restaurant where we found a supply of cognac and champagne, but a visiting staff officer from a higher headquarters commandeered our site. Though the Rangers were ordered out, they figured their cache of spirits hadn't been requisitioned, so they took it with them.

Two days after the landing, on 12 July, we were ordered to advance against San Nicola, four miles away. Although the enemy had been thrown out of Gela, they were not through. The spearheading Rangers and the 1st Division faced fifty sleepless hours of bombing, tank, and artillery attacks, and one of the hardest fights we had encountered.

We were now on the Gela plain — the only level ground in that part of Sicily. The road from Gela led northwest toward San Nicola, the left of twin peaks guarding a pass. The ground did not incline steadily to the mountains: "The peaks just rose out of nothing," was the way one Ranger described it. We could make out through our field glasses the heavily fortified and wired-in area on the left peak miles ahead. Closer down the road was a small knob where a farmhouse stood among cactus.

On the Rangers' right flank the 1st Division advanced against German tanks. The 2nd Battalion of the 16th Regimental Combat Team held the right flank of the division on a hill between Gela and the inland town of Niscemi. Without antitank guns, that battalion was forced to retreat from hill to hill towards the sea. Forty-five soldiers and a young captain refused to give up, however, and held onto Hill 41 with a bazooka* and one self-propelled gun. With these weapons, they charged the top of the hill toward the tanks and drove them off. The battalion regrouped, advanced, and seized Niscemi.

Attached to the Rangers for the attack on San Nicola was a regiment of armored infantry and the engineers and mortar troops that had landed with us. After dark the 1st and 4th Ranger Battalions attacked the peak on the right of the road while the armored infantry went against the San Nicola fortress. Accustomed to night fighting, my raiders went up the steep sides of the mountain, cut through barbed wire, and captured our objective in an hour. The infantry troops, untrained in night fighting, lost their way in the advance. The streaks of gunfire and explosion of enemy shells from the batteries just behind the twin peaks confused them. They wandered off course and began milling around, but there was nothing wrong with their guts or willingness. When morning came they were caught in the open while the Rangers were sweating it out atop the right peak. The enemy batteries—five of them—opened on the split forces. The dread of every commander had occurred. With one group in the air and one pinned to the ground, we had lost initiative, were off balance, and were unable to support one another. The Rangers on the mountain had no artillery and were taking a heavy pasting from the enemy.

After an hour or so the enemy artillery lifted its fire and started working on the 1st Division farther to the right. This gave me a moment to regroup and gather ourselves for an attack. Up front was Ranger Captain Colby. Though not an artilleryman, he could describe where the friendly artillery and mortars were striking. He also was able to pick out the five enemy batteries, three of them in a draw behind San Nicola and the other two on a mountain peak farther to the north toward the fortress of Butera.

Back on the plain the Ranger staff and the forward naval observer,

---

*Slang term for a shoulder-fired antitank rocket launcher, so named because it bore some resemblance to a home-made musical instrument of the American comedian Bob Burns.

a young lieutenant, had been flat on their faces during the bombardment. Now they got up. I quickly requested the cruiser *Savannah* to stand by for action. Then, calling to the commanding officer of the Engineers, I ordered an attack on San Nicola. These engineers were real fighting infantrymen, and with them I had the armored infantry. We had picked up five tanks somewhere which I sent with the assault force.

Off Gela the *Savannah* was moving back and forth on course between two fixed points. It was a very calm day. My only experience with naval gunfire had been in the capture of the Gela fort so I had a few misgivings about the use of naval artillery for support so far inland. The range was at least seven miles. Being an artillery officer by training, I wondered if the rolling ship's platform might not cause the shells to strike off target, endangering my men. But it was worth a try, so I called for fire.

Captain Colby up forward called the hits for the first few rounds. Then when one shell exploded near the fort, he requested a concentration. The *Savannah's* big guns each spoke three times as fast as one could say "Boom! Boom! Boom!" The shells swished through the air, forty-five rounds in one minute. The Rangers up forward later said it was beautiful to watch. Rubble, guns, and wire splashed into the air. The attacking force followed up after the ship ceased to fire, capturing the fort quickly.

The ship had fired so fast they missed putting the fuze in one shell. A Ranger found the projectile sticking in a wall and couldn't wait to tell the naval gunnery officer about it. Inspection of the enemy batteries showed direct hits on a number of their guns.

There were many local battles for towns and airdromes around Gela. Though dismissed with a sentence or two or unmentioned altogether in the communiqués, they were hard, bitter battles for us. One such engagement was a battle for the town of Butera, eight miles inland from Gela. As we left San Nicola, still on the fringe of the Gela plain, we looked up and up at Butera perched four thousand feet high on a hill behind deep and well-gunned passages. One Ranger said of the citadel, "It looked like a castle sitting up there."

The planning for this operation especially involved two of my captains, James Lyle and Charles Shunstrom. I picked up a field telephone in my command post on a hill overlooking the plain of Gela for a conversation with Lyle.

"Jim," I said, "we're going to attack. We're going into Butera. Now, listen, I'm sending up some assault guns. I'm going to put four self-propelled 75s in your position. So find a spot for them.

"I'm sending in one company. If it is fired on we'll blast the hell out of the enemy. I want you to shoot anything that moves while we're getting our stuff up. O.K.?"

"Roger," came Lyle's reply.

Putting the telephone back on the hook, I next called Shunstrom, who stepped from the group of soldiers lounging near the command post.

"Chuck, you're the leadoff man. I know your boys are tired. They've fought hard and they need a rest, but they are the best for this job. You understand?"

"Yes, sir."

Chuck moved off down the hill.

I pulled out a bottle of cognac from a bag. "I found this after we drove the Italians off this hill," I said. "That's when I knew they left in a hurry. You don't leave cognac behind unless you're in a hurry."

There was only a swallow around—a toast to the success of the night operation.

Below us was Gela, spread out like a toy village. Invasion transports lay in the harbor beyond it with small craft shuttling their cargoes to the beach. Several miles ahead the road ran around the base of the Butera fortress, wound up towards the top, and then went north. Rugged mountains were on both sides of the inverted ice cream cone of a fort.

Shadows were blackening the valleys. American artillery was firing. The puffs would show at the guns and a few seconds later the sound of the explosions could be heard. From the sea the cruiser was also plastering the fortress.

Lieutenant Clifton Roe, tank platoon commander, reported to me. "I want you to put your tanks by that stone house you see on the ridge," I said. "I may use you as supporting artillery. We are going into something we know nothing about, but we're going to face it out. We may take this place without a fight. We may walk into a trap, but we can't tell. So get in position."

I crouched over a map with my company commanders and studied it by the faint glow from a flashlight. There were no written orders and no paperwork for this attack. The instructions were simple and direct.

"You'll move in exactly twenty minutes," I told them. "If you are not fired upon, do not fire. One mile from the town, Shunstrom, you will hold on the town. If you get in trouble, fire a steady stream of red rockets: that will be the signal for our artillery. If you're successful, shoot two green flares: that will be the signal for all the Rangers to move on the town.

"Gentlemen, the best of luck, and we'll see you tomorrow morning."

Shunstrom gathered his platoon commanders about him and gave these orders. "I want fifteen yards interval between each man. March at a slow pace. We go in alone and with fixed bayonets. Be sure to keep plenty of distance. We don't want to be caught bunched in an ambush." The Rangers went off in single file.

A few minutes after midnight the column reached the top of a ridge where they looked out across the valley on Butera capping the cone-shaped peak. It was formidable against the starlit sky.

Shunstrom called me on the radio, telling me that they were going upward for the attack. For three hours they climbed towards the fortress until it was just above them. Then one platoon was sent forward for a flank approach.

Meanwhile back at my command post requests had gone out for artillery fire to be ready on call to shoot at Butera.

Up ahead the flanking platoon advanced closer. Machine-gun and rifle fire crashed. The Rangers hit the dirt, rifles ready. Sgt. Francis P. Padrucco, acting as platoon sergeant, had twenty men who were part of the outfit that went straight up the road to the citadel itself.

"We got to a bend in the road," he explained, "and a machine gunner opened up on us at a range of about twenty feet. He wounded my lieutenant and the radio operator. But our scout with a Tommy gun let go with a whole drum of ammunition; he got seven."
lieutenant and the radio operator. But our scout with a Tommy gun let go with a whole drum of ammunition; he got seven."

Shunstrom talked to his flanking party, telling the sergeant to pull his men out. "We'll shell the damned place," he added.

"You mean you don't want us to go on?"

"Do you think you can?"

"We'd like to try it."

"Okay, but don't take too many chances."

This caused consternation at my headquarters. Hearing of Shunstrom's difficulty, the artillery was prepared to fire. They were awaiting the withdrawal of Shunstrom's company so the way would be clear. Then the attacking platoon, having decided to make the assault, started in. When Shunstrom relayed back word of the new development, I frantically called the artillery positions to tell the artillery men, "Cease-firing." I held my breath as one battery after another was called. Luckily, we were successful.

Close to the citadel Tommy guns and carbines poured fire into the defenders. Pvts. John See and John Constantine crept within earshot of the garrison whose soldiers were lolling and chatting beside their guns and trucks at the top of the high pass. Constantine, one of the many Italian-speaking soldiers, called on them to surrender. The few German officers with them tried to make the Italians fight, but after a few halfhearted shots they refused. The Germans escaped, and the town fell to the Rangers.

A little later Shunstrom's company was ordered to the crest of the slope again. Just as it neared the entrance of the city, the green victory flares arched across the skies. Butera had fallen to two platoons of Rangers—a fortress that could have been held against a division.

The Rangers moved through the cobbled streets of the town. There was no sign of life until daybreak when the half-starved, emaciated residents came out of their homes to cheer the Americans. Other families poured out of their miserable caves below the city. After taking four hundred prisoners, my men opened the enemy food supply caches and distributed almonds, wheat, olive oil, and other foodstuffs to the wild crowd, a situation which almost got beyond control.

Butera was one tough position to capture. If we hadn't had help from that cruiser, we couldn't have taken it. We laid salvo after salvo on these positions, and the Italians went streaming out. We had to knock out some machine guns, but it was the shelling that did the trick.

While the 1st and 4th Rangers were fighting for Gela and Butera, the 3rd Battalion, led by Major Herman Dammer, had landed three miles west of Licata and marched around Agrigento where they swung back to the shore to capture Porto Empedocle. (They had left Nemours earlier than the 1st and 4th. After training for a time at El Alia near Bizerte, they had been loaded along with an infantry division on 4 July.)

There was no enemy fire to oppose Dammer's men until after they had landed on the beach near Licata at 0400 on 10 July. Machine guns and 47-mm guns opened on them from the mass of rocks overlooking the beach. Men scrambled toward the guns, capturing them one by one. When an infantry battalion landed behind them, the Rangers had cleared out the defenders. Then pressing eastward along the ridge running into Licata, they ran into other small enemy groups armed with machine guns and rifles.

While the infantry advanced eastward, the 3rd Rangers remained in Licata to hold the town. The next morning German dive bombers strafed the port area, wounding one of the Rangers. Eight others were wounded as the result of an explosion of an antiaircraft shell that had been fired from a ship outside the harbor and landed in a doorway of a building occupied by the Rangers.

The 3rd Rangers then went into bivouac for two days, but early on the morning of 12 July they marched to Campobello to the north, remaining there until the evening of the same day. Trucks picked them up and carried them on to the town of Naro where the big church was gutted with shellfire. They then went west on foot to the town of Favara, which they entered and occupied on the next morning. The townspeople came out to welcome them, and a few who spoke English told the Rangers proudly of the numbers of "troops" they had furnished gangster Al Capone.

Up to this time the Dammer Force had met very little resistance. Marching out of Favara down the winding road to the west, they approached Agrigento where there were sizable numbers of Italian troops. About three miles out of Favara enemy artillery opened on the Rangers. Without heavy guns or air support, they felt naked before the Italian guns emplaced high on the hills ahead of them. One regiment of the 3rd Division was to capture Agrigento while the Rangers out front were swinging around it counterclockwise for a return to the coast.

The country ahead looked as if some giant hand had dropped handfuls of sand to form peaks and valleys. Two miles west of the Ranger position was a road junction, from which four roads ran like the legs of a bug. They were approaching westward up one leg, another was to their right on the same side of the junction, two others went out the far side. The head of the bug as it faced south toward the coast was the town of Agrigento perched high on a mountain. Behind the bug's head the road junction lay in a valley from which rose another mountain to form the back of the bug. The two legs on the other side of the road junction pointed at two peaks, the one to the north named Montaperto. Another road ran through a valley between the peaks. Artillery on Montaperto could fire eastward on the road junction and down the road to Favara, could cover Agrigento, and also the peak to its south. It was truly an artilleryman's dream.

The Italian roadblock at the junction was the immediate concern of Dammer's 3rd Rangers. Continuing forward on the easternmost road, they were met by small-arms fire about midnight from the roadblock. The Rangers deployed, and while one force kept the Italians occupied from the front, the rest slid around and surrounded the defenders. For a few minutes the firing was intense; then the Italians surrendered. In the skirmish lasting one hour, 165 prisoners were captured.

The Rangers started out towards Montaperto on the morning of 16 July. Poorly directed enemy artillery fire was dropping around them, but they continued their advance. Then suddenly out of Agrigento three tracked vehicles bearing guns headed toward them. The Rangers left the road, climbing up into the mountain that formed the back of the bug to their right. Believing for some reason they were being surrounded by the Ranger battalion, Italian soldiers came streaming out of Agrigento. "The scene was much like a Keystone comedy," the Rangers said later. At least six Italian soldiers were clutching precariously to each of the fast moving trucks, motorcycles, and sidecars. Ranger Whitehead earned the Silver Star here by submachine gunning these motorcyclists as they veered around a curve in the road.

Major Dammer's 3rd Battalion went on ahead to Montaperto, where four Italian batteries of 100-mm Skoda guns were echeloned to fire down the valley past Agrigento. Sensing the danger, he moved his troops against Montaperto, meeting no rifle or gunfire as they scrambled up the hill. Their greatest difficulty was the sheer effort of crawling upward so that they could observe the fire of their 60-mm mortars on the enemy. They got these handy infantry weapons firing effectively and drove the Italians away from the gun batteries. A lucky hit then landed among the ammunition, and the enemy artillery position and weapons went up in one great explosion.

South of Montaperto on another peak was the Italian command and observation post for all the guns in the valley. If this spot could be cleaned out, their artillery would lose most of its usefulness. Approaching the enemy post in plain sight, Dammer's men were challenged by Italians who said they'd fire if the Rangers didn't get off the hill. While the Rangers were looking for cover, the Italians chose to give up.

From there Major Dammer and the battalion went south over the hill to Porto Empedocle. For a three-mile stretch, row upon row of vineyards sloped gracefully towards the sea. The battalion paused for rest in an almond grove about two thousand yards north of Porto Empedocle.

At 1430 the attack on the town was made in a line of companies, three attacking east of a draw running north and south out of the town and three attacking west of it. Intent on reaching the port, Dammer's men did not stop to mop up the numerous snipers. Dammer did not meet any determined defense on the left flank of his approach to the sea, but on the right flank Captain Miller ran into the crews of a battery of dual-purpose coastal guns. After a short scrap Miller rounded up 91 German and 675 Italian prisoners. The battle was over by 1600.

The Rangers, having gotten far ahead of the divisional troops, had lost contact with the main body following. Also they were out of food, having had only one meal in the previous twenty-four hours. Though rifle ammunition was still available, there were no more 60-mm mortar shells—their heaviest weapons.

The Rangers let out a cheer when they saw the white star on a United States Navy spotting plane flying above the port. But it was one of those mean situations when communications were needed in a hurry in order to avert trouble. The navy pilot, thinking they were enemy troops, would undoubtedly train the cruiser's guns on them. The small radios carried by the Rangers couldn't get through to higher headquarters; also they had no vehicles to send information back.

Fortunately, all Allied forces had definite instructions to attempt to save the ports of southern Sicily from destruction, as they would be badly needed for supply purposes. At the time, though, the Rangers didn't know that the navy had the same instructions. The navy plane dropped leaflets with an ultimatum declaring that the Allied forces didn't want to knock out the port, but unless it surrendered, they would destroy it. Down at a wharf in the harbor, the Rangers found many oil barrels and, guiding these through the water, they spelled out the words "Yank" and "U.S. Army." On reading these signals the Navy plane came down on the sea, picked up Major Dammer, and flew him to the cruiser *Philadelphia*. The navy relayed news of the capture of the port to the 3rd Division, while the Ranger leader then asked for food for his men. Immediately the navy fed the army, giving them salted crackers, meat, and cigarettes. For another day the ship cared for the Rangers, feeding them, supporting them, and acting as liaison with the division.

Traveling the next night with a reconnaissance troop along the Agrigento–Porto Empedocle road, a radio patrol of three Rangers was overtaken and attacked by a column of fifteen enemy light tanks bearing the "Death's Head" insignia. A Ranger sergeant thrust a grenade into an open port of the leading tank, sending it over an embankment to destruction below. That was the last fighting by the 3rd Battalion in the first phase of the Sicilian campaign. It had been only seven days since their landing.

The 3rd Battalion went into bivouac just below Montaperto late 17 July and remained there until the next day when they moved to the vicinity of Raffadali for about a week. Then rejoining, they fought their way through the mountains to Messina.

The success achieved by my men in the landings in Sicily showed that the expansion of the 1st Ranger Battalion into three had not watered down our fighting spirit. After making a difficult and successful assault at Gela, the 1st and 4th Battalions had fought off powerful counterattacks, opening the way for the follow-up troops and supplies to come ashore. Similarly, the 3rd Battalion had captured Licata intact and had also cleared out the hills nearby. New laurels were added to the name of the Rangers as they fulfilled General Patton's assault order to the letter.

After the fight at Gela, General Patton awarded me a Distinguished Service Cross. I declined the offer of a full colonelcy, however, and the command of an infantry combat team in the 45th Division. I was not yet ready to leave my Rangers. This had happened twice before in the Tunisian campaign. I felt that I could do more good with my Ranger boys than I could with a regiment in a division.

VII

To Messina

JULY–AUGUST 1943

PERSPECTIVE The Allied leaders, Roosevelt, Churchill, and Stalin, all had reason to be pleased with worldwide gains in the summer of 1943, including the landings in Sicily. In the Pacific, the Americans were pinching off the last of the Solomon Islands and were moving on in strength into New Guinea. Naval battles had been successful, and American forces were about to continue their island hopping northward to Japan. On the Russian front after Stalingrad, there was a strong move westward all along the line from the Black Sea to the Baltic. Stalingrad had been a long, difficult, and decisive battle. In winning it, the Soviets found they had the ability to counter the previously invulnerable Nazi tank-air force team.

After the landings at Sicily on 9 July 1943, both Montgomery's Eighth and Patton's Seventh Army had struggled to expand the beachheads and to capture ports for needed troop supply. Between 12 and 15 July the Allies had joined their beachheads, established a continuous line, and advanced northward against spirited resistance, capturing several key airfields. By the fifteenth, Patton had the 2nd Armored and 82nd Airborne Divisions in reserve near Gela, while the 9th Division was still in Africa. Montgomery was meeting stiffer resistance as he moved toward Catania, a major seaport on the eastern shore of Sicily.

On 15 July, Field Marshal Alexander outlined his plan for securing Sicily. With Messina as its ultimate objective, the Eighth Army was to advance northward on either side of Mount Etna. Patton's Seventh Army would protect Montgomery's flank as he pivoted northeastward and would push a force north to the coast to cut the island in two. The two armies would then eventually mop up Sicily.

On 17 July, Patton had seized Agrigento and the port facilities at Porto Empedocle; he also sent II Corps northward to Villa Rosa. He then obtained Alexander's approval for an immediate push toward Palermo on the northwest coast. The following day Patton created a provisional corps under Maj. Gen. Geoffrey Keyes and assigned to it the 2nd Armored, 3rd Infantry, 83rd Airborne Divisions, and Darby's Rangers, telling Keyes he expected him to overrun western Sicily. This was to be an easy task, for the Italian General Guzzoni's mobile forces had largely evacuated that part of the island.

In a march reminiscent of the foot cavalry in our Civil War—and despite the rugged country and skillful rearguard action by Guzzoni's withdrawing mobile forces—Truscott's 3rd Division made the hundred-mile advance to Palermo in four days. The shattered city, having been bombed heavily by the Allied air forces, surrendered on 22 July.

While the Americans were having faster going on the west and north of the island, the Eighth Army—moving northward along the eastern shore of Sicily—encountered stiff opposition. General Guzzoni had shifted his better divisions to that front, so Montgomery was unable to expand his bridgehead and get to Catania as soon as he had hoped.

Aware of Montgomery's difficulties in the costly frontal attack along the coast, Alexander again modified his strategy on 20 July. He ordered Patton to change fronts and drive eastward along the north coast of Sicily toward Messina. There were only two feasible routes of advance through the difficult mountainous terrain: one along the coast and the other on the Gangi-Nicosia-Randazzo road. Patton turned the 1st, 3rd, and 45th Divisions eastward and by 23 July had moved halfway across northern Sicily. Meanwhile, Germany's General Kesselring had moved the 29th Panzer Grenadier Division and two regiments of the 1st Parachute Division to Sicily.

By 2 August the 1st and 45th Divisions had reached a point where Axis resistance was stiffening. The 3rd Division relieved the 45th and prepared to assault the Nazi position at San Fratello, while the 1st Division, now reinforced with a combat team from the 9th Division, made plans for the capture of Troina.

Patton made every effort to support Bradley's II Corps. Additional artillery was provided, and the remainder of the 9th Division unloaded at Palermo on 1 August and prepared for movement to the 1st Division sector. Ships were also enlisted to follow the operations and give all possible naval gunfire support.

The Eighth Army was having a tough time but moved forward enough to force the Germans back. With their key positions threatened, the Germans began to pull back to the Catania position, and General Guzzoni decided to evacuate the Italian troops to the mainland. The Germans had selected five positions on which to delay while the evacuation was in progress.

On 3 August, the 1st and 3rd Divisions launched attacks in their respective areas: the 1st Division in the mountains at Troina and the 3rd Division along the northern coast. The 3rd Division was stopped after they crossed the Furiano River, and in spite of overwhelming artillery and air support at Troina, the 1st Division was unable to crack the German defense.

On 5 August, the 9th Division attacked through the mountains toward Cesaro, forcing the outflanked Germans to evacuate Troina that night. From that point on, Patton made three end-run amphibious operations along the north coast.

¶ WITHIN A WEEK OF LANDING IN SICILY, AMERICAN and British forces had carved out a series of half-moon beachheads around several southern ports. A concerted drive was then begun to compress the enemy. On the eastern side of the island, General Montgomery's British troops were attacking frontally. To their left, and fifty miles from the eastern coast of Sicily, an American force attacked north from Gela in an enveloping maneuver. Finally the western sector, some eighty to one hundred miles from east to west and forty to fifty miles on its north-south axis, had to be cleared of masses of Italian troops. Crisscrossed by winding, narrow roads that climbed tortuously up and down mountains, this portion of Sicily was defended mainly in the cities and by roadblocks at junctions and in defiles.

A provisional corps of American infantry, airborne and armored troops was to send out striking columns towards Castelvetrano, Marsala, Trapani, and finally Palermo. I was in command of one of these columns, X Force. On paper, X Force comprised the 39th Regimental Combat Team, a battalion of "Long Tom" artillery guns (155 mm), and my three Ranger battalions. However, events had moved so swiftly in the first week of invasion that units were split up and out of communication with their major headquarters. Though I had a command, no one could tell me where all my troops were bivouacked. Answers to my queries invariably suggested that the troops were somewhere "up ahead" along the coastal road.

At nine o'clock on the night of 20 July, X Force was ordered to advance along the coastal road to capture Castelvetrano and Marsala. Leaving the three Ranger battalions near Ribera where the corps headquarters was located, I took several of my staff, jumped in jeeps, and drove west. The natives had withdrawn into their homes, leaving the main roads for troop movements. I rode along at fair speed, my rifle across my knees ready for action. Another Ranger's fist was closed around the butt of the machine gun, his trigger finger cocked. Shadows flickered in the mountains to our right while the sea, a few hundred feet below and to the left, was black. Not a light appeared on the water, although destroyers were undoubtedly on patrol.

At midnight my party was in Sciacca, a coastal city, deathly still and forbidding. Other troops were on the road, but none of them had any knowledge of the 39th Regimental Combat Team. Beyond Sciacca the road curving inland crossed stream after stream over undamaged bridges. The enemy had obviously decamped. At every bridge we passed I would poke my head underneath and shout, "Hey, what outfit is this?" Sleepy retorts drifted back, but none of the units had heard of the elements assigned to X Force.

About 0300 near the town of Menfi, a tired voice came from under a bridge to indicate that, at last, the 39th RCT had been found. The sleepy voice came to life when I announced myself. Out from under the structure tumbled the tall, broad-shouldered regimental commander, Col. John A. Toffey, Jr., who explained that the Italian troops were only a few miles west.

I remarked that X Force was to destroy the enemy, but we would first capture Castelvetrano and then advance on Marsala on the western tip of Sicily. We conversed for a few minutes, exchanging information. I admitted that I had no plans and asked whether the regimental commander had any.

"No, I haven't," the latter stated, "but let's have a cup of coffee and get some sleep before we attack."

Two hours later we were up and moving toward Castelvetrano. At 0900 we came to the Belice River. In the midst of crossing, one of the battalions was caught by an unexpected enemy attack. The action was sharp, but a well-executed envelopment caught the Italians on the flank. They threw down their arms.

Castelvetrano fell almost as easily, on the twenty-second; the same day, another column entered Palermo.

Among the Ranger recruits at Nemours, I had found a curly-headed, red-faced private who became my bodyguard. Private Riley had a rugged husky frame and was an all-around good soldier, quick on the trigger, and indefatigable on the march or in bivouac. A former racetrack bookie, Riley had an engaging manner and quick mind. In clipped phrases replete with simile and metaphor, he found dealing with the natives of Sicily no different than dealing with racing fans at home. Human nature was the same everywhere, and Riley capitalized on his understanding of it.

In enemy country where people were half starved and emaciated from lack of food, Riley was always able to find food and drink for us. At Castelvetrano, X Force pulled into a grove for a night bivouac. Within an hour Riley came bursting into camp with several bottles of what looked like whiskey or wine, attractively wrapped in lead foil. My staff and I prepared for a party. Pouring healthy drinks, we rose to toast the president, the king of England, and others. The first drink went off with a few wry faces; after the second, even the avid Ranger thirsts were stopped while they checked the bottles. They couldn't translate the small Italian printing on the label but in large print across the foil were the words *Vermi Fuggia*—Worm Medicine.

Two days later the task force, including two battalions of Rangers, arrived in Marsala where they were joined by the 82nd Airborne Division. They took Trapani and then turned eastward to San Guiseppe, south of Palermo. X Force, the flank guard for the 2nd Armored Division, saw that division wheel by in a cloud of dust.

X Force and the 82nd Airborne Division were encumbered with 12,500 prisoners. Our supply base was forty miles away at Sciacca on the south coast of Sicily. The prisoners were a strange lot laden down with blankets and overcoats, not to mention each man's jealously guarded cache of pillaged souvenirs. It was doubtful that there were enough vehicles in all Sicily to carry these Italian prisoners and their huge bundles of equipment. There was only an occasional truck, and like ants, fifty to sixty of them would clamber on the truck, as many as twenty on the trailer, and even another ten standing on the hitch between the trailer and truck. The few trucks were grossly overloaded, but they were able to go on.

Anxious to be rid of the prisoners, I ordered a Ranger detachment to march the straggling group to the prisoner-of-war collection center immediately. As they entered each town the Rangers would move ahead and with fixed bayonets prevent the prisoners from sitting down in the streets. In the heat, blankets, overcoats, and souvenirs were discarded by the wayside. As the prisoners moved down towards the coast, the number of Italian civilians following like locusts became larger and larger. Justice was done in some measure, for the civilians were able to recover articles to replace those stolen from them by the Axis troops.

While the Ranger detachment was escorting the prisoners to Sciacca, X Force advanced to Palermo where it was disbanded. The provisional corps, however, remained to police western Sicily. The 1st and 4th Ranger Battalions, having completed their Sicilian fighting, were sent to Corleone just south of Palermo for rest and refitting. In two weeks time we had made the landing at Gela, captured San Nicola and Butera, and marched and fought another hundred miles. We were now to prepare for a landing in Italy after Sicily was in Allied hands.

Having remained in reserve at Menfi during the campaign in western Sicily, the 3rd Ranger Battalion was now ordered to join the 3rd Infantry Division which was advancing eastward to take Messina. At that time the division had reached San Agata, on the north coast fifty-five miles west of Messina, after having won the bloody battle of San Fratello where they had taken an enemy ridge by a combined land and sea assault.

The German line extending from the north coast through San Fratello and over the mountain ridge to Troina had collapsed on the day the 3rd Rangers joined the 3rd Division. The campaign became a deadly serious race by the Germans to protect their withdrawal into the Messinian peninsula until they could ferry most of their forces to the Italian mainland.

Nature dictated the fighting in northern Sicily. A ridge named Monti Nebrodi separated the fighting in northeastern Sicily into two theaters. South of it the British Eighth Army and part of the American Seventh Army were applying a squeeze, while the remainder of the Seventh Army pushed from the west. Three to four thousand feet high and paralleling the north coast about ten miles inland, the ridgeline extended directly into the city of Messina. The mountains fell off steeply to a plain on the north, but ridges guarded rivulets spaced every four or five miles. Because of this broken terrain, no roads crisscrossed the plain, and movement was restricted to the single coastal road. As a result, American troops were forced to fight determined rearguard German and Italian units for successive

TO MESSINA

ridges along the coastal road. It was slow, costly fighting that came when the Allies were battling to gain time and cut off enemy troops in Sicily.

To assist forces on the road, the American commander (Patton) sent amphibious end runs to get behind the enemy. This approach left pockets of enemy resistance on the mountain slopes. So despite its experience in amphibious assaults, the Ranger battalion was given the task of making coordinated attacks from the mountains in end runs "a la mule."

I decided to accompany the 3rd Battalion with one company of the 1st Battalion. Mules had been requisitioned and sixty were received, along with eighteen horses. I offered to take over the mule transport and run the supplies, mainly because I was the only one in the area who had had experience with mules. In my field artillery duties prior to the war I had commanded a pack artillery battery. Looking for excitement and some fun, I rode proudly across northern Sicily on a rotund mule affectionately known as "Rosebud." Although I admit that this mule was gentle, he still bit me in the seat every time I tried to mount him.

When the 3rd Ranger Battalion joined the 3rd Division we were attached to the 7th Regimental Combat Team and immediately ordered to secure the commanding heights at Popo di Marco, four miles southwest of Capo D'Orlando. Under enemy bombardment we moved into position in daylight, 12 August. Some mules and radio equipment were lost but there were no casualties. The battalion advanced up the hill and took Popo di Marco under heavy artillery fire. Later in the day, we came out of the hills to assist the frontal attack of the 7th Regimental Combat Team on the road between Naso and Capo D'Orlando.

The next town on the timetable was Patti, thirty-five miles from Messina. The 3rd Division planned a nutcracker attack, striking the town by end runs from both the sea and the mountains. Now shifted to the 15th Regiment of the 3rd Division, the 3rd Rangers moved by truck to San Angelo di Brolo in the mountains. There the mule train joined us. We moved down towards Patti and coordinated with the assault landing from the sea, capturing two hundred Italian prisoners.

The pressure was on. The night following the capture of Patti, the

Rangers proceeded to Monteforte where we were joined by pack howitzers for a march into the mountains. About midnight the mules and the artillery were brought together. It was dark and men were stumbling about and cursing. Fortunately there were native guides available, or it would have been impossible to cross the unknown ridges. The artillerymen knew nothing of how to pack their guns on mules. I did know how to break the howitzers into loads but had never had to improvise as we were compelled to do that night.

The battery commander stood close as I prepared to demonstrate in the darkness how to break the gun into proper weight loads and put them aboard the mules. Six hundred yards of rope had been ordered, and the supply officers furnished hawser, four inches thick. A knot in the hawser would have made a noose through which most any part of the howitzers could have fallen. We unraveled the hawser into its strands painstakingly and rolled them with telephone wire. With much pushing, grunting, and explosive language, we fumbled around until one gun was in parts and loaded on a mule. Then calling the battery commander, I indicated the black object in front of us and stated very positively "You've seen how it's done. Carry on." To the credit of the young officer, the job got done sometime during the night, although every saddle had the load strapped on it in a different way. The rigs for the mules were as varied as the saddle ads in a Sears Roebuck catalog.

Up in the mountains, we started to meet strong enemy resistance. When we reached the town of Monteforte, the townspeople told us they had seen two Germans. Looking closely, soldiers came across the unmistakable treadmarks of the tires of a German motorcycle or Volkswagen. Cautiously we pushed forward by foot and mule, exclaiming in wonderment at the ingenuity of the Germans in getting motor vehicles into an area where it seemed none could operate. On meeting an Italian civilian we pointed to the prints on the road and asked if he had seen the Germans ride by. The Italian rocked with laughter and nodding his head said yes, he had seen two Germans go by. On being questioned whether they rode on a motorcycle or in a jeep, the Italian roared with further laughs, explaining that the Germans, lacking shoe leather, had cut up rubber tires and attached the pieces to their shoes.

At daylight on 16 August we moved southeast into the mountains to the town of Sanbruca, about four miles west of Messina. The Straits of Messina were visible through the haze below, as were portions of the coastal road running into Messina. The pack howitzers fired on ships in the straits but accurate observation of the results was impossible through the mist. A patrol was sent in during the night, entering the largely evacuated city at dawn on 17 August. The Sicilian campaign had been completed in thirty-eight days.

The night Messina fell my Rangers bivouacked in a cemetery there. German batteries across the straits were blasting the city, some shells hitting the cemetery and knocking caskets out of the walls. Skeletons were all around, and the smell of death curled the hairs of the Rangers' nostrils, but the exhausted 3rd Battalion slept on.

Dammer and I had just fallen asleep when a motorcycle messenger buzzed up to the cemetery. A young officer jumped off and handed us a message. We were to hasten to Palermo for final preparations for an assault somewhere in Italy. I looked from Colonel Dammer to the messenger. I'm afraid my eyes said clearly that I would like to throw him into one of the empty caskets and seal it in the wall.

The tired, dusty 3rd Battalion was gathered together and hurried back to join the 1st and 4th Rangers. Our clothes were in tatters, shoes worn thin, and most equipment was ready for salvage. Only our weapons were in tiptop shape. We would need them in Italy.

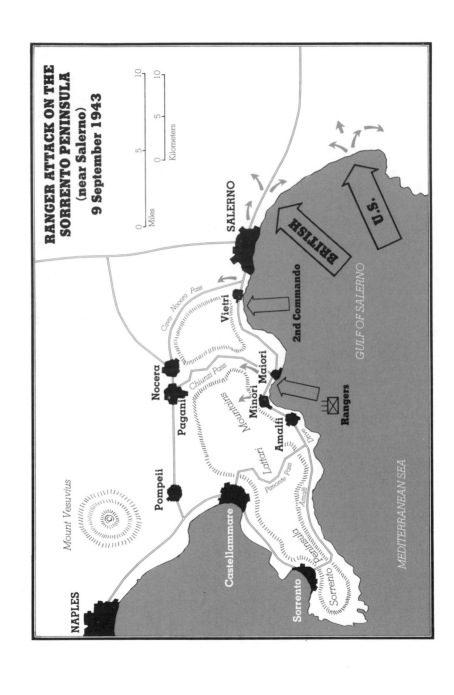

RANGER ATTACK ON THE
SORRENTO PENINSULA
(near Salerno)
9 September 1943

Miles
0   5   5   10

0   5   10
Kilometers

NAPLES

Mount Vesuvius

Pompeii

Castellammare

Pagani

Nocera

Sorrento

Sorrento Peninsula

Chiunzi Pass

Lattari

Pimonte Pass

Monticano

Cava- Nocera Pass

Vietri

Minori Maiori

Amalfi

Amalfi Drive

2nd Commando

Rangers

SALERNO

BRITISH

U.S.

GULF OF SALERNO

MEDITERRANEAN SEA

VIII

Sorrento—
Salerno's Left Flank

SEPTEMBER 1943

PERSPECTIVE   On 24–25 July 1943, while the Sicilian campaign was still being fought, the Italians—weary of war—revolted and overthrew Mussolini. His successor, Marshal Pietro Badoglio, pledged that Italy would continue the war, but he soon began secret negotiations with the Allies. Surprised by Mussolini's sudden fall, Hitler ordered German troops to prepare for withdrawal from Sicily back into Italy and ordered German divisions then in Italy to seize control and disarm Italian forces there. In addition, he placed a strong reserve force in northern Italy since it was feared that the Italians would attempt to block the Alpine passes and cut off German troops in Italy.

Among the Allies there were different strategic objectives. The British, having had a traditional interest in the Mediterranean, urged that past Allied successes be exploited by an invasion of Italy or the Balkans. General Marshall, on the other hand, wanted to withdraw maximum forces from the Mediterranean to speed the build-up for the projected invasion of northern France. The United States Navy, having its primary interests in the war in the Pacific, demanded the transfer of scarce amphibious shipping to the Far East.

Finally, as a result of the Trident and Quadrant Conferences in May and August 1943, the Combined Chiefs of Staff agreed on the major European operations for 1944. The Normandy invasion, code named Overlord, would be the primary American-British effort in Europe and would command priority in men and supplies. Operations in the Mediterranean were to be designed to help Overlord succeed by immobilizing a great number of German divisions. This could best be accomplished by forcing Italy out of the war and by threatening Germany's southern frontier with an invasion of Italy. Possession of Italian airfields would enable Allied bombers to strike industrial areas in southern Germany and southeast Europe which had previously been out of range of bomber forces.

Lt. Gen. Mark Clark, commanding the American Fifth Army, was directed on 27 July 1943 to prepare plans for the capture of Naples as a base for future offensive operations in Italy. The invasion of Salerno, south of Naples, was to be preceeded by intense Allied air bombardments, and a naval task force was to carry out a diversionary attack in the Gulf of Gaeta.

Italy signed a secret armistice on 3 September; at 0430 on the same day, two British divisions from the Eighth Army made an assault crossing of the Straits of Messina and moved inland against negligible resistance on the toe of Italy. From 3 September to the seventh, convoys carrying the Fifth Army prepared for a rendezvous late on 8 September, preparatory to the amphibious assault in the Salerno area early on the ninth.

The bulk of the German troops had successfully withdrawn from Sicily across the Straits of Messina. Of the sixteen German divisions in Italy, eight were in the north under Rommel, two near Rome, and six farther south under Kesselring. Although the Allies could not gather a force equal in strength to that of the Germans, the British and the Americans had command of sea and air, as well as the initiative. A daring assault was planned. It was hoped to gain the ports of Naples and Taranto and capture several airfields. The airfields near Rome were as yet beyond the Allies' reach, but there was an important group at Foggia which could be adapted for heavy bombers.

As the Allied armada was approaching the Salerno beaches, an announcement was made of the Italian surrender. Keyed up for battle, the news came as a shock to the men; it relaxed the tension but had an unfortunate and negative psychological effect. Many of the men now thought that their task on the next day would be easy.

Covered by a strong British fleet, the assault convoys entered the Gulf of Salerno with only minor enemy air attacks. The enemy apparently could not tell exactly where the assault was to be made.

The Fifth Army landing was to begin at dawn, 9 September, the major assault to be delivered by the U.S. VI and British X Corps, with British commandos and Darby's Rangers on the northern flank.

¶ AFTER SICILY WAS OCCUPIED, THE BRITISH EIGHTH Army had crossed the Straits of Messina, landed on the toe of Italy and advanced up the peninsula. The Fifth Army, mainly American in composition, was now preparing to land on the west coast below Salerno. The objective was Naples with its excellent harbor, but the

SORRENTO—SOLERNO'S LEFT FLANK

landing could not be made so far north because it was out of range of effective air support from Sicily.

The main Allied landing was scheduled for the beaches some fifteen miles below Salerno and forty-five miles south of Naples. If we were to make a swift advance on Naples, the routes north from Salerno had to be kept open. A force on the Sorrento Peninsula could provide for this and in addition could observe German movements in the plain of Naples.

Given the assignment of capturing and holding the Sorrento Peninsula, a mixed force of American and British troops was placed under my command for the landing. There were British Commandos, American paratroopers, glider-borne artillery, and a force of tank units, engineers, medical personnel, and the Rangers' trusty chemical mortar battalion. In all, there were probably eight thousand highly trained troops, as rugged a group as could be found among the Allied forces in Europe.

Our job was a D-day assault against the Sorrento Peninsula west of Salerno. The Italian coast running southeast from Naples swung west out around the Sorrento Peninsula, which divided the Gulfs of Naples and Salerno, and then returned to its general southeast line below the city of Salerno. Sorrento was a scenic, mountainous area, tailor made for battle. Running across the center of the twenty-mile peninsula, a humpbacked ridge three to four thousand feet high shut off Salerno and the main Allied landing from the Naples plain. At its western tip it sloped to the sea where lay the Isle of Capri. Climbing in winding paths around the peninsula was the famed Amalfi Coastal Drive. Three passes cut through this ridge, and whoever dominated them held the key to the battle of Salerno. Nearest Salerno was the Cava-Nocera Pass, through which ran Highway No. 18; about five miles west was Chiunzi Pass; and near Pimonte was a tunneled pass that led across to Castellammare on the Gulf of Naples.

A fourth method of getting to the northern side of the peninsula was over the Amalfi Drive.

Intelligence indicated that much of the German artillery, tanks, and reserves were in the Naples plain. From the Sorrento heights, the Allies would be assured a bird's-eye view of the German concentrations and an opportunity for some excellent shooting, particularly by the navy. Actually, the navy wouldn't be able to see its targets—

but we Rangers were rubbing our hands at the chance to pull another stunt of forward observing as we had done in Sicily.

By this time I had to have a staff to coordinate my plans. Under the direction of General Clark, I formed a Ranger force headquarters, employing several British officers. My first mission was to destroy the coast defenses in the area of Capo D'Orso, near Maiori. In addition we were to clear the road leading from Maiori through Chiunzi Pass. Then, after seizing the passes at Nocera and Chiunzi, I was to hang on in defense while preparing to operate against the rear of any enemy holding up the advance of the British X Corps landing south of Salerno. The entire job of the Rangers and accompanying units was to ease the way for British and American forces when they came rolling up through Salerno and Nocera.

About eight miles due west of Salerno and about one-third of the distance out on the Sorrento Peninsula lay the town of Maiori. There was no headland to point out the exact beach. As we had done before, we found a "scramble" beach, exactly one thousand yards in length. The gradient or slope into the water was so steep that if a battleship backed up to it, men could go down the gangplank without getting their feet wet. It was a beautiful beach, but like all perfect landing beaches, it had to be found in the dark.

The navigational difficulties of moving a small boat into a beach area are immense. The finest compass in the world swings back and forth when thirty-five steel-helmeted soldiers carrying rifles are aboard. The troops never sit still, and their constant movements cause the compass to deflect. No fine-hair accuracy is possible. A large ship knows no such handicaps, and with its finer instruments can tell just where she is by taking fixes on various geographical points. My headquarters had been concerned about finding the small beach at Maiori, and we were tremendously relieved when arrangements were made to have a Hunt class destroyer guide us.

We were aboard three LSIs (landing ship, infantry) and some LCIs. Since there were only sufficient landing craft to float one battalion at a time, the initial wave was placed in the larger craft, the LCIs; the small LCAs carried on the davits of the LSIs were to be used for shuttling back and forth to shore with succeeding waves of assault troops.

The 4th Ranger Battalion was selected to point the way in the assault, followed successively by the 1st and 3rd Rangers, the 83rd Chemical Mortar Battalion, and the engineers. After the 4th secured a beachhead, they would become a blocking unit so that the 1st and 3rd battalions could move up the road to capture Chiunzi Pass.

The small boats carrying the Rangers rendezvoused off the destroyer on 9 September. The captain shouted from the bridge, "I say, are you there?"

I answered, "I'm here."

The captain then said, "Off we go." The LCAs lined up in column behind the destroyer, very much like a mother duck and her brood.

In going towards Maiori the destroyer moved out, changed course a couple of times, and finally swung into the lane from which the small boats had only to continue straight ahead. The captain leaned over the rail with a farewell, "You are now on course." The flotilla leader of the small boats blinked his rear light on, saying in effect, "No matter what happens, from now on you're on course. Don't change it even if your compass is pointing in reverse direction from what it ought to be."

In the darkness only the mountains of the Sorrento Peninsula could be seen in the distance, so we did not sight the small beach until the flotilla boat was about two hundred yards offshore. When the first assault craft hit the beach, it was exactly in the center of the thousand-foot landing strip. This landing was a complete surprise to the enemy. We broke radio silence when we hit the beach, telling the navy in code that we had landed.

Passing quickly through the beachhead held by the 4th Battalion, the 1st and 3rd Rangers headed north up the highway into the mountains toward Chiunzi Pass. With scouts ahead, the men marched in single file on the edges of the road, advancing swiftly. It was pitch dark and the only sounds were the shuffle of combat shoes and the singing of crickets. An occasional toad jumped out on the road.

Suddenly the main party of Rangers came upon a parked car that the scouts had overlooked in the intense darkness. A not-unfriendly German voice hailed them. Guns whipped around, and after a few shots the enemy surrendered. A group of fourteen Germans had been laying mines on the road. Several of their number had gone off for a few hours, and when the Rangers approached, they thought their missing members were returning.

By 0800 in the morning we had established ourselves in the high mountains on both sides of the Chiunzi Pass road. There on the peaks we dug in for defense. The 1st and 3rd Battalions were on the right or eastern side of the road, and a parachute regiment was on the left at Mt. Ceretto, almost four thousand feet in height. The Rangers on the right held Mt. St. Angelo di Cava, more than three thousand feet high, and Mt. di Chiunzi, about twenty-six hundred feet in elevation.

Meanwhile two British Commando units, each the size of a Ranger battalion, had landed between Maiori and Salerno at Vietri sul Mare. The object of their attack was to seize and hold the Cava-Nocera Pass on Highway No. 18 leading northward from Salerno to Naples. With this main route in possession of the Allies, the British 46th Division below Salerno on the left flank of the main landing could swing north towards Naples.

It would have been a feasible mission if the main Allied forces had arrived on schedule, but it took them some twenty-one days before they came through on the road to Naples. My troops landing at Maiori got caught in the area west of Salerno and were out on a limb for those twenty-one days. All my soldiers were rugged raiders, but we lacked enough artillery for a full-scale defense. We were equipped to hit and run but not to stick it out in a slugging match against forces armed with medium and heavy artillery and outnumbering us at least eight to one.

From their positions on the main passes near Nocera and Chiunzi, Allied troops controlled all movement on the Naples plain to the north. Our guns were sited on Highway 18, denying it to the Germans and compelling them to use Highway No. 88, which swung eastward and southward into Salerno. Holding their reserves in the Naples plain some five miles to the north, they could be observed clearly by the Rangers.

While the 1st and 3rd Rangers were in position at the heights near Chiunzi Pass, they were able to employ naval gunfire to assist themselves and to harry the Germans in the Naples plain. Looking down to their rear in the Gulf of Salerno, the Rangers had the thrill of seeing the combined British-American battle fleet pulled in close toward Salerno for their support.

Naval gunfire played a tremendous part in the defense of the left flank on Sorrento. Two officers, Thompson and Tophew, were on Mt. St. Angelo and Chiunzi Pass, and a Ranger officer was aboard one of the ships in the harbor of Salerno. Hooking in as they had done at Gela, the officer on the observation post could report back to Ranger Force Headquarters, and we in turn relayed the information to the ships. In addition to a British battleship there were two cruisers and a monitor—a two-gun, flat-bottomed boat that looked like its Civil War namesake. The Rangers will never forget the battleship's firing. She would toss a salvo from her big guns, and the shells would ricochet many miles.

The Germans were denied Chiunzi Pass simply because one observer was up there with a radio and could talk to the navy to direct their gunfire support. As the navy warmed to their task, they moved their ships right into the hollow of the coast near Amalfi. Most of the ships cocked their guns like howitzers into the air in order to clear the mountain. The battleship, not being able to elevate its guns as high, used the pass at Chiunzi like a bowling alley. One Ranger, not knowing the naval guns were in support, heard the first fifteen-inch shells coming through the pass. He said that it sounded like a freight train with the caboose wobbling from side to side.

The forward observer, at a place nicknamed Schuster's Mansion (named for Capt. Emil Schuster, a medical officer of the 3rd Ranger Battalion), said the spot was hot and noisy during the firing. Once when a shell came closer than usual, its concussion blew out all the windows. On another occasion the observer, spotting the Germans in a park near Nocera issuing ammunition to their troops, thought he would issue Allied ammunition as well. The fifteen-inch guns of the British battleship let one salvo fly directly into the park. It touched off the ammunition dump and obliterated the park in a series of huge explosions. Needled by the naval gunfire, the Germans attacked the Rangers, but the strong natural position guarded by veteran troops was practically impregnable from a head-on attack.

Meanwhile, the 4th Rangers moved along the Amalfi Drive to the city of Amalfi and westward on a road reminiscent of the Storm King Highway on the Hudson in the vicinity of West Point and Newburgh, New York. They then swept across the peninsula and through the Pimonte Pass to Castellammare, on the Gulf of Naples.

On D-plus-three, the 1st and 3rd Battalions were on the heights near Chiunzi Pass, and the 4th Battalion at Castellammare. The three battalions thus commanded the passes and could continue to hold them in the face of very strong resistance as long as they had the ammunition. That was the rub: the ammunition supply was down at the main Allied beachhead below Salerno. Frantically the Rangers flagged down a motor torpedo boat that was going by in a hurry. The supply officer went aboard and had a fast ride down past German-held Salerno to the main landing where the beach master listened to his tale and ordered that he be given the ammunition. An LST (landing ship, tank) was loaded with 4.2-inch ammunition. Four thousand rounds were supplied to the Rangers, but unfortunately it was British and without rifling, so it was useless in our mortars. This difficulty had occurred through a number of mischances. The Rangers were an American force attached to the British. I had submitted the requisition for additional mortar ammunition from Palermo to the Allied staff in Algiers.

The Rangers eventually got the additional American ammunition, but we had to scramble for several days. If it hadn't been for our standard operating procedure of carrying extra mortar shells ashore in the assault boats, we might well have lost our hold on the Sorrento Peninsula. We had made no effort to take in rations or water on the first assault wave but instead stowed three days' supply of ammunition. Going to the harbor beforehand, we sought the craft assigned to us and, over a number of objections, got permission from the navy to preload them. In each boat we placed one clover leaf, or sixteen rounds of 60-mm mortar shells, and also one case of small arms ammunition, either machine gun or eight-round clips for the M1 (Garand) rifle. In some of the boats we stowed white phosphorus shells and grenades.

For the Sorrento Peninsula and its mountain fighting, there was an evident need for extra mortar ammunition, so each Ranger carried one round of 60-mm ashore with him on the landing. The first men to leave the boats were unencumbered with heavy equipment. Each carried one extra bandolier of ammunition around his neck; as soon as he hit the beach he threw it off above the high watermark. The last four men out of the boat carried the cases of mortar and small-arms ammunition. When they passed the high watermark on the beach, they simply dropped their loads and kept going. The beach naturally looked like a junk yard when morning came, but the second wave's supply officer straightened it out.

Even with all the extra ammunition the Rangers had carried, we were reasonably safe for only three days. Luckily the supply of mortar shells got straightened out, and the beach dumps soon began to fill up.

Operating in mountains that rose sharply as high as several thousand feet, the mortar battalion had to improvise or find means of carrying their ammunition. The Chemical Warfare Service had built a small cart exactly fitting the ramp on an LCI. These carts, loaded with ammunition, were pulled ashore down the ramps of the boats. A German half-track and a German command car we had captured the first night were used to pull the carts to the dumps on the beach. Nine jeeps were brought ashore within two hours of the landing, and they, too, were used to tow the carts.

Groups of curious Italians came down to look at the Rangers. These natives were hungry looking and emaciated but were able to help us in carrying supplies. Every time they delivered a load to the troops on the mountain, each was given a C ration. It was a wonderful business and seemingly satisfactory to both parties until an officer from one of the higher headquarters began paying them with money. Then the Italians spent much of their time lining up for pay and began to demand certain rates and limited hours of work.

After the landing at Maiori part of the Ranger staff occupied the hotel at the beach. It had been untouched in the landing and was clear of all vacationers so our soldiers lived in comfort. The owner seemed pleased to have us as guests and was naturally happy that the war had passed by, leaving him unscathed. Price was never mentioned; but when we prepared to depart, we were presented with a whopping bill for seven hundred dollars.

We moved up into the mountains the first night after establishing our beachhead and knocking out the coast defenses in the area of Capo D'Orso. The 4th Battalion did this job and then organized a roadblock on the left and rear of the force.

The 1st Ranger Battalion cleared the road to Vaccaro and took over the high ground overlooking Route No. 18 so that they could observe all the way from Cava to Nocera. The 3rd Ranger Battalion followed the 1st Battalion, took position on the left on Mount di Chiunzi, and prepared to attack Pagani. The 4.2-inch mortars followed the 3rd Battalion and went into position so that they could lay their massed fire on Pagani and Nocera. The antitank platoon proceeded north from the landing to cut off the road leading to the western edge of the peninsula towards the town of Sorrento. We kept contact with the Commandos on the right, between the British and the city of Salerno. Again we used our flashlights, showing red and blue lights in "dot-dash-dot" recognition signal between elements of the Ranger force.

On the Gulf of Naples the 4th Battalion was forced out of Castellammare and went west along Amalfi Drive to the area of Vico Equensa. In the withdrawal they blew up bridges and trestles along the coastal drive, putting in roadblocks and developing defenses.

Here again, by the Rangers' clever use of terrain, the Germans were prevented for more than two weeks from getting into the Sorrento Peninsula, much as they needed it strategically. The British Commandos were along the Nocera Pass on Highway No. 18 at the base of the peninsula. To their left on the commanding heights of Chiunzi Pass, my Ranger force and additional troops were holding the high ground in the mountains and were able to fire upon any of the enemy attempting to attack the Commandos in the Naples plain below. We also looked down on Castellammare and had our guns sited to prevent the enemy effort from surrounding the Allied forces by following Amalfi Drive entirely around the peninsula. After two weeks, the strengthened German force finally pushed the 4th Rangers out of their positions at Vico Equensa, so they swung along Amalfi Drive around the edge of the humpbacked peninsula to the south coast.

There was one other pass—at Pimonte—that the Germans might cross to get in behind the Allied troops at Chiunzi and above Cava. The 4th Battalion cut the highway which ensured that the Germans could only follow Amalfi Drive to the Rangers' sector. They then went back into the mountains south of Pimonte. There to the left of Ranger positions on Mt. Cerreto, they set up a defensive position at the entrance and above a half-mile long highway tunnel. It was the finest defensive location imaginable. The battalion dug in for the attack they knew was coming. Having no choice but to move on the road, the Germans tried to force the tunnel. But at the mouth was a self-propelled cannon, a 75-mm gun on a half-track chassis.

"It was like shooting ducks," said one Ranger. Up in the caves and behind rocks above the entrance of the tunnel we had the road in our sights and poured a tornado of small-arms fire and mortar shells into the Germans. It was too much for the calculating Germans, who knew the odds and withdrew.

The positions held by the Rangers were vital not only for the security of the forces below Salerno, but also for observation of the German supply lines. Because of the small number of men and the large area to defend, we stretched ourselves thin, as we had done at the Dernaia Pass in Tunisia. The terrain was in our favor, and we quickly developed strong points, covering the gaps with machine-gun fire. Seven German counterattacks strongly supported by automatic weapons, mortars, and grenades were repelled during this period.

Day by day the Germans kept hammering at the position, realizing fully the value of the Sorrento Peninsula. It was a long, hard fight, but the Rangers hung on, trusting that one day soon the American and British forces below Salerno would break out of their beachhead and drive north towards Naples.

It was fortunate that the troops had had a rugged training course. We needed endurance, fighting without rest or relief and always short of food and water. Worse than that, there was the continuous threat that overwhelming forces might sweep aside our thinly held lines and knock out the Allied left flank. It's no wonder the 1st and 3rd Ranger Battalions received Presidential Unit Citations.

Husbanding our strength, the Ranger force, Commandos, and parachute troops held the three main passes and the Amalfi Drive behind them, cutting it off at the eastern flank near Vietri sul Mare and at the western flank about two miles west of the town of Amalfi. The tip of the Sorrento Peninsula leading to the Isle of Capri was left to the mountain goats and any Germans who wanted to act like them.

Finally, twenty-one days after the landings, the forces in the main beachhead south of Salerno began to break out. As they came storming up Highway No. 18 toward Salerno, my force rushed down the mountains toward Pagani, directly ahead, and to Castellammare, off to the west on the coast. We pushed out the Germans and then swung past Pompeii and Vesuvius in a fast marching advance. The Germans had made up their minds to leave this area and left the roads as far as Naples practically clear. Off the coast the naval ships followed them, firing broadsides at the meager German resistance.

The Rangers kept on the move, following the paratroopers into Naples by a few hours. The first night the entire group slept in the botanical gardens, lying down under palms and curling up in comfortable grassy plots. An enterprising Ranger found a restaurant for the officers' mess and another for the men. As at Gela, there was food and drink aplenty.

As soon as the initial occupational matters in Naples were attended to, my staff and I figured that we had earned a little rest and recreation and settled down to a session of beer drinking and enjoyment.

While a cadet at West Point, I had enjoyed infrequent visits to New York, spending an occasional evening at one of upper Manhattan's better known German beer gardens. Invariably the master of ceremonies would light upon me as the man he needed for his stooge with "Ach du lieber" and other songs appreciated by the audience. Lt. Col. Herman Dammer, the executive officer of the Ranger force and a New Yorker, also knew the beer-hall routine. Here he was master of ceremonies and again the finger was pointed at me when they swung into various old German songs.

Just as we were lifting our beer glasses in an enthusiastic flourish and the singing was at its height, there was a tremendous crash. A group of American paratroopers burst in through the splintered door with Tommy guns poised and hand grenades ready. They believed that they had accomplished the dream of every paratrooper—the capture of a German headquarters complete.

I looked up at the intruders, and to my further disgust saw that the commander of the paratrooper battalion was an old familiar face from West Point, a man who had been overly serious and conscientious. The humor of the situation didn't appeal to this man and his paratroopers until long after everyone else in the room was bent over in loud guffaws. We, of course, invited our visitors in for a beer.

We had moved into the Sorrento Peninsula on the morning of 9 September. It was now mid-October and getting colder, though we were comfortable as long as we stayed close to the shore near Naples. We went into bivouac for a short time; and just as we were beginning to enjoy our rest, we were ordered into the mountains where we were to fight to the east of Cassino, near a town called Venafro.

PERSPECTIVE   When the Allied troops landed at Salerno on 9 September, the German troops had reacted immediately. Disarming the Italians, they took over the whole defense themselves. The Rangers ran into heavy enemy pressure in the crucial Sorrento position, and the matter was brought to the attention of General Clark. He sent an observer to Darby's headquarters, who assessed the situation on the afternoon of 10 September and recommended the Rangers be reinforced with motorized infantry. So the 1st Battalion, 143rd Infantry, and Battery A, 133rd Field Artillery Battalion were added along with Company B, 751st Medium Tank Battalion, and Company A, 2nd Motorized Chemical Battalion. Along with these reinforcements came Company H, 36th Combat Engineers, and a company of the 601st Tank Destroyer Battalion.

By the eleventh, Allied troops had gone about ten miles inland. The airfield at Montecorvino was taken, but it remained under enemy fire and could not be used. The Nazis had by this time moved the greater part of three divisions from the north and a regiment of parachutists from the east. With German troop dispositions improved, Kesselring decided to try to destroy the Salerno beachhead before British Eighth Army units could advance up the boot of Italy to join forces. But his plan failed.

The Allies pushed ahead, and on 16 September the leading elements of the British 5th Division made contact with Fifth Army patrols forty miles southeast of Salerno. Two days later, Kesselring began a deliberate disengagement and withdrawal from the Salerno area, falling back from one delaying position to another through mountainous terrain ideally suited for such tactics. The Allies moved into Naples.

The 1st and 3rd Ranger Battalions were awarded Distinguished Unit Citations for their performance in this action. (It was the 1st Ranger Battalion's second such award—the first had been for El Guettar.) The cost had been high, however. The 1st Ranger Battalion had lost thirteen men killed and twenty-one seriously wounded. The 3rd Ranger Battalion lost seven killed, one missing, and fourteen wounded. The 4th Battalion lost eight killed, eight missing, and twenty-one wounded. Most of these casualties were suffered during the fighting following the seizure of Chiunzi Pass.

Since their combat roles were finished, the Ranger force and the 82nd Airborne Division, along with their attached units, were relieved from attachment to the British X Corps on 3 October and brought under control of the Fifth Army. Three days later Darby was directed to have two of his battalions ready for combat by the end of the month.

IX

Up The "Boot" to Venafro

OCTOBER–DECEMBER 1943

PERSPECTIVE   By early October the Allies had achieved their first objectives: Italy had surrendered, the Germans had evacuated Sardinia and Corsica, the Port of Naples was in Allied hands, and the seizure of the Foggia airfields gave the Allied air forces excellent bases for raids against northern Italy. Allied troops in Italy had established a line from the Volturno River on the west shore to Termoli on the east shore. This was the winter line for German Field Marshal Kesselring. It was certain that from there north the going would be tough for the Allies because of the mountainous terrain and the difficulty of dislodging the German defenders during the winter months.

On the Russian front in the period from July to December 1943, there had been almost continuous attacks by the Russians on the entire western front stretching from the Black Sea to the Baltic, with gains in some places of as much as two hundred miles westward. Pacific operations still continued at Bougainville, in the Solomon Islands, and on the whole of northeast New Guinea. On 21 November American forces moved against Tarawa in the Gilbert Islands and soon after island hopped in the central Pacific to the Marshall Islands where American forces won a great victory at Kwajalein.

During the late fall, Allied leaders were discussing possible strategic moves. Stalin, Churchill, and Roosevelt arranged a meeting at Teheran, Iran, in early December 1943; subsequently Churchill and Roosevelt met in Cairo with Chiang Kai Shek to discuss the war on the mainland of China.

At Teheran Stalin wanted to know when Operation Overlord, the invasion of Normandy, would occur. Secondly, he insisted that the commander be named so that there would be one man responsible to get the job done. This caused still more debate. While the British had pretty much agreed that the overall commander would be an American, they thought it should be General Marshall. Roosevelt was urged to make him available, but on 5 December said he could not spare Marshall from the chief of staff position in Washington. The alternate suggestion was that Eisenhower be the supreme commander of the Allied Expeditionary Force. Eisenhower was accepted, but public announcement was withheld until 1 January.

There were many compelling reasons for a continued Allied advance northward in Italy. The first was that the Allies had knowledge of the original German plan to withdraw into northern Italy; some pressure might hurry this movement along. Furthermore, Rome was a very important political objective, and its liberation would mean prestige for the Allies and consequent loss of face for the Germans. Capture of the numerous airfields around Rome would increase the range of the Allied air forces. In early October it became very plain that the Germans proposed to fight between Naples and Rome, and this action would draw large numbers of German troops into Italy.

There were also forceful arguments against the idea of a continued advance. From the Volturno River north to Rome was over one hundred miles of mountains cut by swift streams usually running across the Allied line of advance. The countryside was naturally designed for delaying actions, especially because the Allies had so few troops trained for mountain warfare.

Navy control of the Mediterranean was assured for the Allies, but the continuing shortage of assault shipping severely limited possible exploitation of the Allies' superiority for future amphibious envelopments of German positions.

On balance, the responsible military leaders agreed the best decision was to move forward.

Kesselring had ordered the Volturno River line held until 15 October in order to gain time for the construction of winter positions to the north in Italy. The Allies looked for good crossing sites, and on the night of 12 October the Fifth Army opened its offensive across the Volturno, each of its two corps attacking simultaneously with three divisions abreast. In bitter fighting, five of the six divisions finally won bridgeheads, but German artillery fire held up the construction of bridges until 14 and 15 October.

As the Germans fell back from one natural strong point to another, they carried out very effective delaying actions. From mid-October until mid-November Allied ground forces were exhausted by the struggle with the constant rains, the washed-out temporary bridges, and the demolition mines and booby traps left by the withdrawing Germans. In a month of extremely difficult fighting, the greatest advance along the line was forty miles, and the shortest, twenty.

A directive issued 8 November by Gen. Sir Harold Alexander called for a three-phase offensive. The Eighth Army was to attack first, driving north to

Pescara, then wheeling along the good east road toward Avezzano. When this attack was well under way, the Fifth Army, with Darby's Rangers attached, was to attack up the Liri and Sacco valleys to Frosinone. An amphibious force of approximately two divisions of the Fifth Army was to land south of Rome and advance inland to seize the famous Alban Hills.

Shortage of troops and shipping made it difficult for Alexander to implement his plan. Seven veteran divisions were being transferred from the Mediterranean to the United Kingdom for Overlord; the French units that were to replace them were still being trained in North Africa. The usual lack of shipping was made worse by the supply needs of the Allied air forces, mostly heavy bombers, that were to operate from the captured airfields. Worse yet, most of the assault shipping in the Mediterranean was scheduled for immediate transfer to England. Enough amphibious assault ships for one planned amphibious assault were left, but they were to be removed by 15 January 1944, according to the directive of the Combined Chiefs of Staff.

The Eighth Army launched its offensive on 20 November and succeeded in establishing some small footholds on the north bank of the Sangro River, but an outbreak of torrential rains stalled the attack until the twenty-seventh. By early December the whole Eighth Army was across the Sangro, but the weather and German resistance grew steadily worse. Tanks bogged down, ammunition resupply became difficult, and the casualty rate became serious. The Fifth Army attacked on 1 December, but it, too, could make only limited gains in a series of heavy actions that would last until 15 January. The planned amphibious operation to the south of Rome had to be postponed and eventually eliminated.

¶ AFTER A FEW DAYS OF LEAVE IN NAPLES, MY RANGer force of three battalions retraced its course southward past Vesuvius, Pompeii, Castellammare, and across the Sorrento Peninsula past Pimonte and the tunnel where the 4th Battalion had put up its successful defense against the German attacks. Beyond the southern entrance of the tunnel and overlooking the coast, we selected a campsite at San Lazzaro for retraining and rest.

We had two wonderful weeks at San Lazzaro. As in similar situations, I did not allow discipline to be relaxed, requiring the men to keep busy drawing new clothing and weapons and preparing their equipment for coming campaigns.

Each morning the reveille gun boomed out to sea, awakening the Rangers to the day's schedule of physical conditioning and weapons training. All the Rangers joined in discussions about past battles. Behind us stretched almost a year of hard fighting: Arzew; then Gafsa, Sened Station, Dernaia Pass, El Guettar, Djebel el Ank and Djebel Berda in Tunisia; Gela, Butera, Licata, Porto Empedocle, Castelvetrano, Marsala, Trapani, Patti, Brolo, and Messina in Sicily; and Sorrento's Chiunzi Pass in Italy. What lay ahead, we did not know. The road was long, and it was best to look only to the next bend. We could look forward only to fighting up the "boot" of Italy.

The 4th Battalion, now commanded by Lt. Col. Roy Murray, left San Lazzaro first. Their path took them through Naples to the battle area on the south bank of the Volturno River. It was 1 November and cold in the mountains of Italy. Up they went among peaks of the Apennine chain, two to four thousand feet high.

The 4th stopped behind the 3rd Infantry Division, which was exploring the crossing of the Volturno River. Then, thrown into the advance party, they forced a crossing of the river and fought their way to the heights to the northwest during the next two weeks.

The front was then about forty miles above Naples where the Fifth Army, to which we were attached, was encountering strong opposition after crossing the Volturno River and its plain to the north. In front of us were a series of peaks, over two thousand feet in elevation, where the fighting was bitter. We had to gain those peaks, but the Germans—fighting desperate rearguard actions—were holding the high ground; when forced to withdraw, they simply went back to the next peak. It was heartbreaking combat.

At this time the line of attack in Italy ran almost north and south. From the Gulf of Gaeta up toward Cassino and Venafro, the American Fifth Army and the French were fighting. Farther to the northeast the Eighth Army front was anchored on the Adriatic near Termoli.

In the sector where the Rangers were to spend from five to seven weeks in combat, the American 3rd and 45th Infantry Divisions were in the front lines. The 4th Ranger Battalion was attached to the 3rd Division; the 1st and later the 3rd Battalion to the 45th Division. The 3rd Battalion, which had been pretty badly used up at Sorrento, had been left behind at first to refit and to train its replacements.

At 2230 on 8 November the 1st Rangers loaded in trucks for the thirty-mile run to Venafro. It was a year and a day to the hour since the night we made our first assault landing at Arzew. There had been a lot of fighting in between. Now instead of making an amphibious landing, we were en route to relieve a regimental combat team in the mountains northwest of Venafro.

At 0130 in the morning we arrived in the Venafro area. In the moonlight we could see the towering mountains to the north and west. Venafro was a small city tucked in the shadow of Mountains San Croce and Corno, both over three thousand feet high. Off to the east, the plain of the Volturno River stretched down to the water's edge two and a half miles away. The river angled to the west there, and the roads from the north and south paralleled its course, so that they ran into Venafro, the corner of a triangle. West of Venafro the mountain steepness blocked road building, except for one narrow macadam road running southwest through the village of Ceppagna and the town of San Pietro Infine, where it joined the main highway leading north to Cassino.

It was the same old hill story all over again. As at Djebel el Ank and on the Sorrento Peninsula, the Rangers wasted no time in sweeping up into position, relieving various infantry companies of the 45th Division. We moved into our locations on the heights during daylight of 9 November. Later that day the 83rd Chemical Mortar Battalion, which had fought through Sicily and Sorrento with us, was attached to the battalion.

The same day, the Ranger force cannon company and its 75-mm guns mounted on half-tracks arrived to complete the tactical formation. This unit was assigned the task of guarding the flanks. The mountains prevented any large German forces from coming into the Venafro area without attacking over Mt. Corno or swinging around the flanks along the road through Ceppagna on the southwest or from the north over a very poor road leading into Venafro.

Thus began the thirty-five days of intense activity with the action confined to the battle area around Mt. Corno. The Ranger fighting was the kind understated in the communiques as "active patrolling in the Venafro sector." On the afternoon of 10 November we lost our first men. Three were killed and one wounded by German rifle and machine-gun fire. A few minutes later six ME-109s dropped bombs on us in a diving attack, but we suffered no casualties. Two of the planes were shot down by the supporting artillery of the 45th Division. An hour later six more ME-109s dive-bombed us, but again there was no damage.

For two days the 1st Rangers had been in position on the two mountains of Croce and Corno. The battalion consequently was split in two, its headquarters in a "cave" between the peaks. It was a niggardly force for holding the important observation posts—the only ones that overlooked the Volturno plain. My request for reinforcements brought the 509th Parachute Battalion. It was sent to the northern peak of San Croce, while the 1st Rangers took over the task of holding Corno.

By midnight of 10 November, when the casualties were counted again, there were three more killed. There was no spirited or desperate fighting, just hide-and-seek action. The Germans, on a part of Mt. Corno near a huge rock that perched above the remainder of the peak, were facing the Rangers at a distance of less than two hundred yards. In between was a chasm that dropped sheer for perhaps one thousand feet. The only link was a narrow ridge at right angles to the front lines. Defended by both forces with obstacles, barbed wire, mines, and guns laid to fire down its length, this ridge was practically impassable.

It was apparent that the German headquarters was in the town of Concacasalle in a valley some twelve hundred feet below the Rangers to the north. The Germans had only one path to their positions on the western rim of Mt. Corno. They had to climb from the town up a hogback ridge right under the eyes of the Americans.

The first mission of the 83rd Chemical Mortar Battalion on arriving at Venafro was to move into position on the eastern slopes of the mountains behind the Rangers and sight their tubes on this hogback. Rangers were observing this route to the German positions constantly. As soon as anyone moved out of Concacasalle, Ranger headquarters and the mortar unit below were warned. The Germans would be allowed to get well onto the ridge; then the mortars would lay down concentrated fire. During the thirty-five days in this sector, they used thirty-eight thousand 4.2-inch mortar shells weighing twenty-five pounds each. By firing all their mortars rapid fire, they could lay down twelve tons a minute—and this they did on many occasions.

On 11 November the 509th Parachute Battalion was given the job of taking the ridge joining the two mountains of San Croce and Corno. Supported by the chemical mortars firing smoke shells and by the Ranger cannon company, they captured the ridge. Our right flank, Company A, made physical contact with the paratroopers' E Company. The position was now secure, and I felt that I was in readiness for any German counterattacks, particularly when my leading three companies pressed farther forward on the ridge near Mt. Corno. During this day, the first German prisoner was taken, and the first escaped Allied prisoner came through German lines to safety.

I now turned my attention from the combat front to my supply problems. The men needed hot food and water. I sent orders back to the Rangers remaining at San Lazzaro to send up all the 1st Battalion men who were now out of the hospital or who for other reasons had been left behind. Mules were brought to carry ammunition and food up to the men. The kitchens were moved up close, and hot food was cooked for my soldiers.

On the ridge that the paratroopers and Rangers had taken, it was evident that the Germans had departed in great haste, leaving behind their dead, rifles, and ammunition in quantity, and mines that had been laid too hastily to be well concealed. Another prisoner brought in this day explained that his unit had orders not to retreat under any circumstances.

Concacasalle, a sleepy little village of perhaps twenty-five buildings, appears frequently in the dispatches of the Rangers. For five weeks we looked down at it, seeing Germans slink into doorways. We requested the artillery to shoot into the town and saw cement and wood thrown up by the explosions. Every day or so we sent a night patrol down into the vicinity of the town. We usually caught one or more German prisoners and from them got a running flow of information as to the numbers of Germans in the town and behind it.

During succeeding weeks the Ranger force was in constant movement. Companies in the front line were replaced as often as possible to relieve them from the constant harassing fire of the enemy. I also brought the 4th Ranger Battalion up to join the 1st Battalion. Relieved by Rangers, a regiment of the 45th Division went into the front line to the south of my troops. This was an indication that the Fifth Army was regrouping and rearranging its troops. The 45th Division took over the front of the 3rd Infantry Division, which displaced farther south toward the Cassino area.

In mid-November the weather turned colder with heavy rainfall. The mountains were miserable, and we heartily desired movement and new action. Static warfare broken only by patrol action was nerve racking. The enemy brought up heavier artillery, shelling the Rangers continually. Visibility got poorer; fog and waiting increased the tension. Clouds that covered the peaks were used by both sides as cover for moving in patrols or for attacks. On a small scale it was similar to the naval actions in the Pacific Ocean where the fleets moved forward and retreated under the protection of bad weather fronts.

The fighting continued to take its toll of my men. Late in November three men were wounded by antipersonnel mines while laying wire in front of their position. A lieutenant entered the field to assist the wounded and was in turn injured by another mine that he set off. The next day two patrols met in a fight, and one Ranger was wounded by a hand grenade. Another Ranger patrol was hit by mortar fire and four men were wounded. The account ran steadily like this for many days.

The Rangers were giving more than they received, however. Prisoners continued to be captured by the patrols, and evidence piled up that the Germans in Concacasalle were losing many men in the continual pounding of that village. American artillery and mortars would keep active by firing on the town with several rounds every ten minutes during the day and night. Then varying their time interval, they would increase or decrease the amount of fire. It was steady and must have annoyed the Germans equally as much as their counter-fire stirred the Rangers.

On 19 November the Germans put on their first attack in strength. Late in the afternoon, several companies of Germans struck us via the ridge leading to our position on Mt. Corno. Companies C and D fought all afternoon and evening, supported by 4.2-inch and 60-mm mortar fire. Company B came up to assist them as a reserve, but it, too, had to be committed to action as the Germans kept attacking, despite their heavy losses in the restricted battle front.

The second day saw no letup in the German attack. In midmorning D Company dislodged a five-man German patrol two hundred yards from their lines, killing two. That night A Company went up to the hill position along with the engineers who were to clear mines in front of D Company. Sniping continued throughout the day, and at dark the enemy was still hanging on in the rocks below the high point of the Ranger position. At first light of the next morning we poured mortar fire on the Germans still in the rocks below, but we were unable to dislodge them despite direct hits on the rocks.

A lieutenant colonel visiting at Venafro refused to believe the stories of the strange fighting at grenade-throwing range. The Rangers took him up to see the rock where the Germans were in position, since he wasn't impressed by the stories of the battles for it. He went out to the top of the rock and looked over. Sitting a few feet away, a Heinie with his machine pistol cocked, looked up at the visitor and said in perfect English: "You're new around here." The inspector's retreat would have done credit to a champion sprinter.

I moved the 4th Rangers into the line to give the 1st Battalion a rest. Immediately a section of Company B attacked with an attempt to drop Molotov cocktails into a cave occupied by the enemy, but they were driven back by artillery and automatic-weapons fire. Company E, meanwhile, made a sweep from the right to get in behind the enemy where they destroyed two machine-gun emplacements and killed four Germans at a loss of six wounded. Upon the return of the company, a patrol retraced their steps but found no enemy. They ran into booby traps, however, one of which was a machine gun fixed to fire on the tripping of a wire.

Company B tried its attack again the next morning, 22 November. One of the attached engineers, aptly named Private Nervy, dropped two Bangalore torpedoes into an enemy dugout; despite this, the group was again driven back by enemy fire. Company E pulled the same stunt of dropping a "pole charge," as we called the Bangalore torpedo, into an enemy dugout, killing one German. Two others running from the position were shot, but enemy machine guns again prevented the Rangers from occupying the position. The enemy attempted to return to the dugout a few hours later, but four of them were shot. The Germans, however, were determined to regain the few yards lost. A Ranger patrol saw forty Germans moving into a skirmish line opposite the left center and digging in.

At my headquarters the radio spoke all day. One of the communication sergeants took down the information that came in and was sent out. This log shows more clearly than any description a day of battle in small-scale action, such as that at Venafro where the Ranger force was gradually whittled down by injured, killed, and sick.

Time	23 November
0925	Captain Shunstrom reports that E Company has captured two prisoners, one of whom was shot trying to escape.
0958	Muleskinner killed by shellfire, and mule hit in leg—mule destroyed.
1002	Enemy small-arms fire heard.
1004	Company E suffered casualties by heavy shellfire, wounding four, one missing, and one known dead.
1007	Enemy shot green flare on left flank: meaning enemy (the Rangers) has broken through, according to a prisoner.
1008	Enemy shell has hit own position—a cave under a rock.
1015	Prisoner says they have had quite a few casualties in last few days. Is now carrying papers of lost comrades. New replacements coming in daily.
1023	Enemy machine-gun fire heard.
1024	Enemy attacking right flank of Company E. Call for mortar fire on forward slope.
1026	Section sent out on forward slope towards Company C's position in counterattack.
1028	Captain Shunstrom ordered Company D of the paratroopers to slide over to support our counter-counterattack.
1032	Captain Shunstrom moving Company D paratroopers over to the pass and using half of them in attack.
1035	Running low on grenades.
1040	Water, grenades, and three cases of "frags" (fragmentation bombs), one case of .30 caliber 8-round clips, and one case of offensive grenades required in addition to those sent at 0700.
1045	Our guns have started firing.
1047	Captain Shunstrom reports counterattack repelled momentarily. Moving back downhill to right in front of OP No. 1. OP No. 1 alerted.
1057	Have 60-mm fire concentrated in middle of enemy company.
1058	Emergency line (telephone) still out between Company C's CP and Force CP.
1059	Captain Shunstrom requests same concentration from fourteen guns as he had on previous day—seven smoke and seven HE shells.
1104	Enemy machine gun heard.

1107	Own 4.2 coming in very well.
1109	Colonel Darby returned. He is sending two tracks to fire on enemy positions. Will fire solid shot and as they shift to left will use HE and then on extreme left will use time shots.
1118	Increase counterfirepower!
1119	Enemy attacking again. Colonel Darby orders paratroops to use Company D to start counterattack.
1123	4.2 mortars, go right one hundred yards. Pour it on!
1124	Paratroops coming through OP No. 1.
1126	Shellfire coming from left of Concacasalle.
1128	Enemy mortar fire coming in.
1133	Enemy tried to break through C Company's position but failed to do so.
1135	Cannon Company is about in position. Will fire five to ten minutes after order given.
1137	Send runner to notify mortars to stop firing when paratroopers are sighted.
1138	High-velocity gun firing into slope, coming from angle left of Concacasalle. May be 88- or 105-mm caliber.
1141	Paratroopers now crossing in front of OP No. 1. Light mortars, cease-firing!
1142	We are making attack. High-velocity and small-arms fire still coming in.
1145	Paratroopers moving toward where 4.2s are falling.
1146	Have mortars fire smoke only.
1147	Paratroopers report no contact as yet.
1148	Cease-firing, all mortars! Stand by with plenty of smoke! Stay laid on same targets. Will call!
1150	Captain Shunstrom requests all available litters be sent up hill to cave.
1152	All available headquarters men and volunteers from D Company will start up hill to contact litter bearers—relieve same coming down with loads.
1155	E Company can see paratroops moving below their position.
1158	Open all 4.2s with smoke on same targets!
1200	Lieutenant Miller says, "We knocked hell out of 'em. Dead Heinies all over the place."
1214	Increase rate of counterfire!
1216	Send paratroopers light machine-gun ammo to OP No. 2.
1219	Put down concentration at point to left and rear of Concacasalle, two hundred yards left and rear of town.
1231	4.2s increase range one hundred yards and use smoke.
1235	Enemy shelling bypass. Cannon Company cannot return. His

position being shelled. Reconnoiter for new position. Enemy has dug-in mortar positions. Paratroopers pinned down.

1236   Paratroops skirmishing with enemy. One platoon ran into mines and a couple of dug-in enemy positions. There are a few casualties.

1237   Colonel left to go up the hill.

1251   Six rounds of WP landed on ridge between OP No. 1 and high point. No one hurt.

1253   Few enemy still on rock. Very little firing. A few paratroopers are back to the top of the hill.

1303   Miller (Mortar Company) reports no activity.

1310   Paratroopers crossed in front of A Company's position. A Company alerted to be ready to support paratroopers' withdrawal. Paratroopers into minefields. Suffered three casualties, all wounded. Paratroop attack seemed to be deciding factor in stopping counterattack. Paratroop company now on ridge to our left.

1326   Colonel Darby—to assistant division commander via Captain Snom: W. have received two heavy counterattacks today by about two hundred men following very close behind artillery screen. All were beaten off, but to do so we countered with our last reserve. We are not yet calling on a battalion of 180th. We think enemy are stopped, but situation is not good. Must have counterbattery fire. Assistant division commander promised fire.

1400   Message to division commander. Same message as to assistant commander with following additions. We have suffered heavy casualties. Another enemy attack in force will lose big hill for us. Artillery cannot be used until wounded are out. If we could get company of 180th to hold where we made attack from, it would save big hill. 45th Division's Artillery alerted for counterbattery fire. A Company of 180th to be used as colonel sees fit.

1410   4th Rangers ordered to put OP with telephone in Le Noci.

1415   Lieutenant and three enlisted men (paratroopers) wounded.

1418   D Company of paratroopers move over to reinforce E Rangers.

1419   E Company has thirty-one men left; F has twenty-five.

1430   C Company ordered to sit tight by Shunstrom.

1452   Platoon B Company has five enlisted men left.

1455   Mortar shoot clearance granted colonel by companies.

1522   Shelling of road by Cannon Company is on.

1530   More counterbattery.

1550   Division phoned that company of 180th under way to join us.

1555   Place artillery shells on all concentrations fired on this morning.

1600   Cease all artillery fire. Falling near own troops.

1612	Cease-fire, all mortars!
1619	Enemy attacking.
1628	All mortar fire cease. Head wind blowing mortar smoke back towards own positions.
1752	Shunstrom reported to CP from hill.
1800	Fire 4.2-inch white phosphorous (WP) shells at one-minute intervals.
1815	One gun ready to fire. One round WP—on the way.
1830	Company B, 180th Infantry reported in.
1853	MG fire coming from "hogback."
1900	Observer relaying by voice fired on by enemy machine gun.
1909	Start counterbattery fire.
2000	Lieutenant Avedon and three enlisted men wounded by 88-mm shellfire while stringing wire in Venafro.

T. Sgt. Robert O. Johnson was one of those blasted by an 88-mm shell at Venafro. It knocked him down as he and his lieutenant were carrying a wounded man to shelter. Communications maintenance had become a matter of survival. Only three of twenty-two members of the battalion communications section remained at the end, the others being knocked out by mortar or artillery fire.

"I almost got it good," said Sergeant Johnson. "I had to go for two miles up to Mt. Corno checking telephones, and the whole way I had mortar fire right in my hip pocket. I don't know which was worse— that or the time at Anzio a little later when artillery blew the top off our CP."

We were living through a period of constant attack and counterattack. There was rain and some snow, and the mountain was bitterly cold, particularly at night. On 24 November the attacks and counterattacks were still coming thick and fast. At 1615 I called back to my command post: "We are receiving heavy counterattack on left flank. Rush infantry company up to me immediately. I am at the 'Cave.' Get 4.2 and artillery busy, and for God's sake get somebody on the wire. Hurry."

All through these days Concacasalle and the hogback leading up to the German position were under constant observation. On the 24th an Italian girl entered the Ranger position to tell us that there were no Jerries in the town. She asked the Yanks to stop shelling the town. The report was obviously untrue since Germans were seen practically every hour of daylight running from doorway to doorway.

The Germans were full of tricks. One day they sent up a white flag as cover for an attack, but the Rangers—being wary—didn't bite on that old ruse. The next day the enemy, reinforced by its own paratroops and firing-machine pistols, followed a rain cloud into our position, but their rush was thrown back. Twice during another day the Germans used rainclouds for cover as they swung through in counterattacks.

We celebrated Thanksgiving with turkey dinner at about noon, eating hastily while preparing to stave off German attacks. We, too, were making our strength felt and just after Thanksgiving dinner took ten prisoners, Lieutenant Buck rounding up nine of them. One of the prisoners said that they had been in position for just four days and under our heavy mortar fire had been cut from eighty to forty men in that time.

The activity around Concacasalle continued as we sent patrols down to grab some prisoners. After they had returned, forty Germans were seen moving up to position on the hogback. The mortars were ready to cut loose as soon as the enemy was in a favorable position. When the mortars and artillery were not hitting the town, Allied planes came over in dive-bombing attacks, knocking hell out of it.

A patrol report by two officers and seven enlisted men on 28 November provided the following information:

The patrol left the Ranger observation post in the direction of Concacasalle at 1500, arriving an hour and a half later on a road about five hundred yards behind the town. An enemy soldier approached Concacasalle, followed by two other foot soldiers leading two mules. The mules were loaded with what appeared to be large boxes of goods. As they continued down the trail to the town, four other Germans appeared, following the mules. All were in full kit, and one was carrying a light machine gun. The entire group reached the north end of the town and made their way through it by running from doorway to doorway under cover. Meanwhile, two more German soldiers came into town from the east fork road. The first group continued through the town, came on through to a part of the town nearest our front lines, and turned right on a trail leading to the vicinity of the hogback. The men appeared to be in very good spirits as they were laughing and shouting back and forth to each other. The two men who had come in from the right fork entered a building in the west center part of the town, coming out at the double in a short period of time and going back the way they had come. One was carrying a briefcase or package of some sort. Another soldier in overcoat, boots, and full kit moved from the center to the eastern part of the town where the buildings thin out toward the fields. He was carrying a similar package or briefcase and seemed to disappear in the fields. On the road on which the pack train had entered the town, a German sentry stood at a gate at what appeared to be the position of "parade rest." On the left, from the direction of the hogback, there was a sound of digging and cutting of wood. Three of four buildings had smoke coming from them. The sounds from the buildings gave the suggestion that they were butchering.

Appended to the patrol's report was the brief remark of the Ranger Force Headquarters, "Will request bombing mission on the basis of this report."

On 29 November we developed an idea of blasting the Germans out of their hill position. We sent for eight hundred pounds of TNT, three hundred feet of cord, five hundred feet of wire, safety fuzes, friction tape, a long rope, electric and nonelectric caps, firing reel, an exploder, twelve bags of sand, cap crimpers, and fuze lighters. It was a rush job.

The next day at 1530 preparations were made to blow up the rock that sat on top of the mountain. We planned to make an attack following the explosion. The explosion went off, and at the same time, from another direction, the Germans started an attack. Shelling by the Germans also commenced, and there was a lot of noise for a long time. The melee went on for the next two or three hours, and when it was all over, the situation stood about as it had before.

We had several more ideas for getting at the enemy. One was to drop a booby-trapped ration box from an airplane. Another was to put up a loudspeaker at night close to the German position, surrounding it with mines, and sighting all the Ranger weapons on the area so that they could kill anyone who tried to remove the speaker.

On 30 November we received the first word in some time of the 3rd Battalion. It had not moved into the battle area until late November and had been fighting with the 36th Division in an effort to take Mt. Rotondo and the town of San Pietro, about four miles southwest of the other Ranger positions and along highway No. 6 leading to Cassino. The 3rd Rangers had fought their way to within eight hundred yards of San Pietro but were driven back by mortar and machine-gun fire from the heights. They had then withdrawn to the town of Ceppagna close to the 1st and 4th Rangers.

The heavy attacks on Mt. Corno let up during early December. Patrols continued to observe Concacasalle, and snipers were sent out day and night to whittle away the German force. The enemy also sent out squads to put in mines and particularly trip wires hooked to charges of TNT. Their losses were terrific because each time they came up at night close to the Ranger positions, the outposts fired mortars and machine guns on them.

During these days the Germans were still up to tricks. A German would shout for help in English from behind some rock or at the bottom of the hill near the Ranger positions, expecting a Ranger to show himself. Another time they dressed as women, and on 7 December they even disguised themselves as monks and nuns.

The last entries in the Ranger diary at the Venafro position refer to an evening broadcast of Viennese music and a propaganda talk using a loudspeaker. No Germans tried to get through the mines to reach the loudspeaker. The final entry was about my promotion. I had been down to the headquarters at Caserta where Lt. Gen. Mark Clark promoted me and told me of the next job for the Rangers. It was to be a landing somewhere up the Italian coast, either at Gaeta or at Anzio.

The 1st Ranger Battalion and the 4th left Venafro on 14 December to return to the vicinity of Naples. The 3rd Battalion remained there until the twentieth.

Altogether the Ranger force had spent some five weeks in the mountains at altitudes of two to three thousand feet. It was close-in fighting, and the lines were sometimes as little as twenty to forty feet apart. This was a new type of fighting for us and very costly because of the large-scale use of grenades and artillery. We now had to rest, replace the 40 percent of our number who had been wounded or killed on the mountain, and prepare for our next amphibious landing.

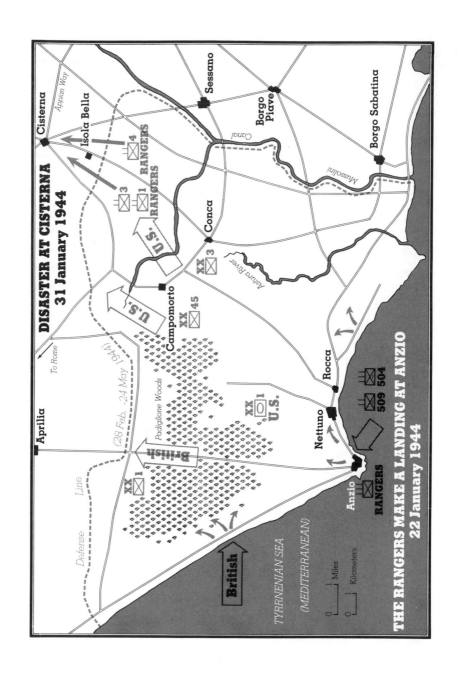

DISASTER AT CISTERNA
31 January 1944

THE RANGERS MAKE A LANDING AT ANZIO
22 January 1944

Landing at Anzio

22 JANUARY 1944

PERSPECTIVE The decision on 8 January to launch the Anzio operation brought jubilation to the Fifth Army. A successful landing at Anzio, believed entirely attainable, would dissolve the Gustav Line defenses, enabling General Clark to move quickly into Rome and pursue the Germans into northern Italy and beyond.

Commanders and planners began to solve the complex problems attending Operation Shingle, the launching of an amphibious operation at Anzio. General Clark expressed his desire to remain in command of his Fifth Army rather than take command of the Seventh Army that was to invade southern France some time during the summer of 1944. When General Alexander arrived at the Fifth Army Command Post on 9 January to confer with Clark on the Anzio operation, he brought a letter from Prime Minister Churchill urging the speedy capture of Rome.

"Without Rome," Churchill had written to Clark, "the campaign in Italy will have 'petered out' ingloriously."

In reply, Clark assured Churchill that he was delighted with the opportunity of launching Operation Shingle, saying "I have felt for a long time that it was the decisive way to approach Rome."

General Alexander's intelligence officers judged correctly that the Germans had about two divisions in reserve near Rome able to move at once against a VI Corps landing. With Allied air attacks to hinder the movement of these divisions, as well as reinforcements to the beachhead, they thought that the Germans would be unsuccessful in opposing the landings. As Alexander saw the operation, the Anzio force was to cut the enemy's main communications in the Alban Hills southeast of Rome and threaten the German rear. He felt that the landing would enable the Fifth Army to sneak through German defenses and make quick contact with the beachhead.

Clark's intelligence officers were not as optimistic. They, too, estimated that the Germans had a corps headquarters and two divisions plus contingents of paratroopers and armored forces near Rome. But they believed that a landing would constitute so serious a threat that the Germans would have to react violently. The Anzio operation, they felt, would be seen as an emergency to be met by all the resources and strength available to the German High Command in Italy. As soon as the Germans understood the magnitude of the landing and realized the impossibility of other attacks along the coast, they could bring a ruthless concentration of forces against the beachhead to prevent movement to the Alban Hills; otherwise their withdrawal from southern Italy would become necessary. Clark's staff estimated that the Germans could bring in an additional division from the Adriatic front and have it near Rome by the third day of the operation; then they could call upon two more divisions in northern Italy which could arrive during the following two weeks.

Some have surmised that General Clark deliberately issued an ambiguous order to VI Corps. He directed them: " a) to seize and secure a beachhead in the vicinity of Anzio, b) advance on Colli Laziali [Alban Hills]." But the decision was left to the VI Corps commander, General Lucas, whether he was to dig in and go on the defensive after he got ashore or whether he should strike out into the Alban Hills. In Lucas's diary he said that General Alexander told him, "We have every confidence in you . . . . That is why you were picked."

Lucas was not reassured. To him, "This whole affair had a strong odor of Gallipoli and apparently the same amateur was still on the coach's bench."

¶ WHEN THE RANGER FORCE CAME DOWN OUT OF the mountains at Venafro, we assembled at Lucrino Station near Naples for the Christmas season of 1943. The soft blue water and warm sun at Pozzuoli Bay was a pleasurable contrast to the cold, miserable dampness of Mount Corno. We were weary and tired of the day-to-day patrols. Homesickness overwhelmed the men, many of whom had been overseas for the better part of two years.

With two assault landings, hard marching, and mountain fighting under their belts, the men of the three Ranger battalions had seen about everything in the fighting line. They were confident, experienced soldiers who had earned the right to cock their helmets over

142   LANDING AT ANZIO

their ears, if they so chose. Though in trim physical shape, their skin was drawn taut over cheeks and eyes were sunken.

Their food had been the C ration varied by hot meals when the cooks could get it to them. Occasionally they had eaten off the country, but Italian food had lost its appeal. Many of them had seen the tomato paste mixed in the open where flies and dust added to its consistency.

I had been directed to prepare for the next landing at the end of January at Anzio. Aware of my soldiers' exhaustion, I decided that Christmas was to be a season of rest and recreation. Though the Rangers were physically rugged, their spirits needed a lift. The Mediterranean sun warmed the men. We had dances, moving pictures, and, for one of the few times in the war, we got far enough away from the front-line action to attend the USO shows.

The holidays were fun. Riley, my irrepressible bodyguard, put on his best smile and sallied out into the countryside to barter and bargain for chickens, whiskey, and wine. Wine was plentiful, but whiskey—a green-tasting Scotch-type—had to be the result of a long search.

In green beret and attired in a complete commando uniform, Father Basil turned up unexpectedly one day. He had been with the British Eighth Army but couldn't remain away from his adopted flock. Long into the night stories were swapped of the doings of the Rangers and of the priest since their parting in Tunisia.

On Sunday many of the Rangers attended the mass said by Father Basil. Unable to spend much of their money, the Rangers poured out their goodwill in the collection plate. The Chaplain's eyes bulged with astonishment and disbelief as the Rangers outdid themselves in offering bills of large denomination. To Father Basil's concern about their generosity, I replied, "I know of nothing better they could do with their money. This is only an indication of what a walloping success you will make if you ever visit us in America."

The holidays were soon past. Intensive training, patterned on that at Achnacarry and Nemours, began at the start of the new year on a beach and landing area at Pozzuoli, which was almost an exact replica of that at Anzio. The numerous recruits trained in assault landings were also able to have the invaluable contact with the navy crews so essential to the success of an amphibious operation.

The boat crews were working all day carrying ammunition and goods to the troops north of Naples, but night after night a number of them were assigned for landing exercises with us. Most of the navy coxswains, like the new Rangers, got a kick out of carrying out the problems with the live ammunition zipping over their heads.

Planning for the assault landing at Anzio had actually begun while the Rangers were fighting at Venafro. My staff had spent part of its time at Caserta discussing the details of the proposed amphibious "end run." The completed plan was simple and similar to those which had gone before. As at Arzew and Gela, the Rangers were to land directly in front of Anzio, burst into the town, and sweep out to occupy a half-moon of beachhead territory limited in extent by a "phase line."

The three Ranger battalions, Company H, 36th Engineer Regiment, and the old standby, the 83rd Chemical Mortar Battalion, comprised a veteran assault force skilled in working together. In addition, the 509th Parachute Infantry Battalion, in picturesque high boots and tucked-in trousers, was accompanying us ashore in the assault boats.

Anzio, a coastal city on the edge of a flat plain, had been selected for the landing largely because it was within striking distance of Rome and yet within range of Allied fighter aircraft operating from fields below Naples. It was not a big chunk of enemy territory to bite off seemingly, but the Ranger force appreciated the magnitude of its task in gaining a solid foothold so as to draw German divisions from the main Allied front. In this way they hoped to break the static battle being fought at Cassino, Venafro, and elsewhere on the front.

We developed our plan carefully. Unfortunately there were not sufficient landing craft to float the entire force at the same time. Units like the veteran mortar battalion had to come in on a later landing. That's a tricky thing in war. It is all right to turn around for supplies and supporting troops, but it is a comforting feeling to have the initial assault troops all afloat at the same time. We had to take a chance that we would not need artillery support during the initial phase of the battle.

Again the Rangers were given the difficult assignment of landing in the harbor and fanning out to occupy both Anzio and Nettuno. Then after putting in roadblocks on the coastal road to the north and south, we expected to contact the 1st British Division and the 3rd American Division which were landing simultaneously north of Anzio and south of Nettuno, respectively.

In studying the air photographs of the landing area through a magnifying glass, we found a stretch of beach in front of the town of Anzio. In its exact center was a showy white casino. The waves breaking in long rollers corroborated the information on the hydrographic maps that it was a shallow beach—the dread of all assault forces—sloping only one foot in each 130 feet. This meant a hundred yard march in water ranging from shoulder high to knee deep. As a result we weren't looking forward to the landing, knowing that it would be slow and dangerous going because no training in the world can keep men from being hit while thus exposed.

The plan called for landing two battalions abreast, the 1st on the left and the 4th on the right, at **H** hour. The 3rd Rangers and the paratroopers were to come ashore in succeeding waves using the same landing craft as the first echelon.

The navy would take us in from the transport area some miles out to sea by using guide boats mounting recognition lights. We had visions of another Gela where we had milled around until we located the guide boats and thus were dubious. However, we were assuaged when informed that there would be many brave sailors in tiny boats waiting to guide the landing force ashore.

The town of Anzio was strung out along the coast and ran down to a harbor at the end of a peninsula. Less than one mile south of Anzio was the town of Nettuno; in between was the estate of Prince Borghese. A railroad ran parallel to the coast. In front of the Villa Borghese were cliffs that dropped down to a sea littered with rocks. Just south of the Anzio harbor and directly in front of the town was the beach. It was rather narrow, backed by a sea wall three and a half to seven feet high with barbed-wire protection. The built-up part of the town was hardly more than two blocks wide, behind which the railroad ran through a cut. Over this railroad were a number of overpasses and footbridges. A half mile farther inland was the main road and railroad to Rome, closely paralleling each other.

The Ranger force loaded at Baia on 20 January 1944. There on the broad Pozzuoli Bay, they beheld a familiar sight—the ex-Glasgow ferryboat, H.M.S. *Royal Ulsterman*. It was an omen of good fortune, for it had been one of the ships at their first landing at Arzew. In addition the *Princess Beatrix,* the *Winchester Castle,* two LCTs and one LST were at anchor awaiting the assault troops.

We went through the motions of loading with an old familiarity. Having learned at Sorrento the importance of having extra bandoliers of rifle ammunition, grenades, and mortar shells, we stowed ammunition in every corner of the mixed British and American landing craft and ships.

The voyage past enemy-held territory above Naples was uneventful. At midnight on 22 January the British ships swung the LCAs from their davits and put two Ranger battalions down for the first landing group. The boats churned around in the darkness for a few moments and then picked up the guide boats. Disembarking with the 3rd Division directly off the latter's landing beaches south of Nettuno, the Rangers were compelled to swing out on a dogleg to get to their own beach. We were under way quickly with the two LCIs moving forward with us for about one mile. Ashore, lights weaved in and out, evidently those of automobiles following the main road.

After picking up the first guide light, the first wave of the Rangers continued ahead towards the next light. Then we spied the Anzio pier and, near it, a guide boat bobbing up and down. Its crew waved the Rangers to shore.

About ten minutes before the Rangers hit the sand at Anzio, a rocket ship—a monstrosity loaded with hundreds of rockets the size of six-inch shells—was supposed to fire for one single minute. On the way in, the whoosh of rockets on the 3rd Division beaches could be heard; but for some reason the Rangers' rocket ship failed to follow suit. The Rangers held their breath while they were off the pier at Anzio; their rocket ship had not fired. The first group touched down at 0200 in an unopposed landing, exactly on schedule. In Ranger style, the troops ran aggressively across the beach, moving inland to gain their initial beachhead where they would reorganize.

Still the rocket ship didn't fire. The Rangers were trying to pull their heads through their shoulders, since no one ashore knew what might happen. Luckily the ship's commander used his head and held his fire when he realized that he was off course and the time schedule was mixed up.

We had insisted that we be landed exactly on the correct beach. I had laughingly said that when I got out of my boat in the center of the flotilla, I wanted to be at the front door of the casino. The navy put me down on the exact spot.

The failure of the rockets probably assisted in the complete surprise attained by the Rangers. One German soldier challenged us, but he was shot quickly. Another coming out to investigate the firing got the same dose. We met no further resistance until we were in the center of Anzio.

Even then I was not completely happy. It was the first time that I didn't have a strong assault force ashore in the first wave. The landing craft made a turnaround to pick up the remainder of my initial assault troops. The men kept coming ashore and fanning out through the town of Anzio. Some went right toward Nettuno. My command post was established appropriately enough in the Anzio casino, and communications were set up out to the Ranger representative on board the *Royal Ulsterman*.

Resistance was very light and scattered, giving the Rangers the remaining hours of darkness to get set for a possible counterattack. In the 1st Battalion area on the right a wheeled personnel carrier was captured just before dawn and its two occupants killed in the fracas.

An hour after the 1st and 4th Rangers had made it ashore, some of the mortar and engineer troops moved from an LST to a number of DUKWs for probably the first such use of these boat trucks in a tactical landing. They brought three 57-mm antitank guns with them as added artillery support to meet expected enemy tank attacks over the flat terrain near Anzio.

One of the DUKWs shipped so much water in its run to the beach that it had to be abandoned. An assault landing craft later towed it ashore so that the Rangers could get the antitank guns and put them into position. The guns had to be towed by hand, and they were so heavy that a roadblock at the eastern end of the beach had to be demolished before they could be moved into the town.

In the port of Anzio the main quay was bristling with wires leading to heavy mines. Engineers worked deftly once they had located the mine, pushing a pin into the charging device so that it would not explode. When the mines were cleared, the port was ready for the larger landing craft and ships.

The engineers were handy men to have along. They proved themselves not only experts in engineering tasks like lifting mines on the beaches, cutting the wire, and repairing bridges, but they could fight like infantrymen—and did.

During the hours of darkness the assault landing craft had returned with the 3rd Ranger Battalion and later some of the paratroopers and the remaining engineers. Meanwhile stocks of ammunition and baggage kept coming ashore and, just after six o'clock in the morning, the second wave of DUKWs brought in additional personnel of the 83rd Chemical Mortar Battalion and some more ammunition. This time we were not going to be caught short as we had been at the Sorrento Peninsula.

As in all other landings, we had the mission of taking out enemy coast defense guns. The 3rd Battalion overran and knocked out a battery of four 100-mm guns at the west end of Anzio, while the 4th Battalion had little difficulty clearing out light enemy resistance at a footbridge on the north side of the railroad.

My troops, fighting against scattered resistance, searched for the defense pattern of the enemy but could locate only small parties in the woods nearby. However, the Germans were near, for they shelled Anzio through the remainder of the night.

By dawn the Rangers had thrown up a roadblock at the northern end of Anzio and carved out for themselves a very good beachhead. Rapidly we pushed inland on schedule, reaching the second-phase line beyond the beach area by 0800.

The 509th Parachute Battalion moved out in a long snake-like column toward Nettuno early in the morning. As they marched close to the shore past the Villa Borghese, they could look back on the port of Anzio where enemy artillery shells were falling. By midmorning the paratroopers had occupied Nettuno, routing small enemy parties hidden in buildings. By noon they had made contact on their right with a regiment of the 3rd Division, killing forty Germans in the process. A few prisoners began to stream back, and thirty-two Germans were counted by noon. Eighteen other prisoners, who claimed to be Russians, were put to work as stevedores helping the Ranger force at the docks.

All day of 22 January we consolidated our position while holding a thin strip of beach. On the left the 3rd Battalion had shaken hands with the Scots Guards of the 1st British Infantry Division. The various landing craft, carrying vehicles and supplies, poured into the port throughout the afternoon and night. By evening, patrols seeking to probe the enemy strength returned with negative reports.

On D-plus-one we moved inland, keeping contact with the Scots Guards on our left. The beachhead widened out, the 509th Parachute Battalion moving in on the right of my Rangers and filling the gap between us and the 3rd Division.

The ground of the beachhead area was uncommonly flat and bare for some distance inland. Along the roads there were little groups of houses of stucco or stone construction. Fifteen miles inland was the main highway from Naples to Rome, the famed Appian Way. To the right of the beachhead beyond the 3rd Division were the Mussolini Canal and the Pontine Marshes. Several miles to the left was the last high ground between the beachhead and Rome. Across the Appian Way was the Colli Laziali, a mountainous ridge backed by other ranges from two to four thousand feet high. Nestled within these surrounding features of hills and marsh was a billiard-table battlefield. The Allied forces were going to learn every inch of it during the coming months.

For the next week the Ranger sector was a flat surface of the Anzio plain between two roads, one running due north from Anzio to Carroceto ten miles away, the other running due north from Nettuno the same distance to the vicinity of Spaccasassi. Colli Laziali, the Alban Hills, rose up eight miles beyond the far edge of this four-sided terrain segment, the last barrier between the Rangers and Rome. The sun's rays were reflected from the red-tiled roofs of Velletri and Genzano on the heights.

The Germans entrenched in the hills had observation of every move of the Rangers in the plain. Their artillery hidden in emplacements fired downhill against our foxholes, seeming to look into every one of them. Ack-ack on the hillside came to life when Allied aircraft appeared, stabbing into the sky from camouflaged positions. Dirty cream-colored German jeeps unconcernedly swept up and down the Velletri-Rome highway.

On the Anzio side of the highway both the German and American battle areas were flat and marshy. Sparse woods thinned out a few miles in from the coast. Farther inland, the ground was cut by occasional ditches and drainage canals, most of them less than three feet deep. A fringe of bush grew along their banks. The tile-roofed concrete farmhouses among haystacks and outbuildings hugged the roads. At each road junction a few houses were gathered together into the semblance of a village.

The Ranger force had moved several miles out of Anzio, keeping our position between the British on the left and our own parachute battalion on the right. From the Padiglione woods the Rangers looked north across several miles of flat terrain to a network of small streams. On the left along the main highway from Anzio was the town of Carroceto, a cluster of red-tiled buildings. To the right front the miniature village of Padiglione nestled near a bridge over a small brook.

All during the day of 24 January enemy artillery fire drove us to the protection of our foxholes. Enemy patrols could be seen scurrying from one drainage ditch to another. A patrol of Company A, 1st Ranger Battalion, sent out to Carroceto, reported on its return that the village was occupied by an estimated reinforced company with three or four tanks. Other tanks or self-propelled guns were moving along the road north of Carroceto. Another patrol working forward on the Ranger right flank, through the continuation of the thin woods, found the bridge at Padiglione had been blown up. A mile north of the town a group of Germans could be seen laying mines. The Ranger patrol advancing in the stream bed towards Padiglione came within a few feet of an enemy patrol of fifteen slinking around the six or seven muddy white farmhouses. After a few shots both patrols withdrew.

At my command post a report was received that the enemy was dropping parachutists in their sector, but investigation proved that it was the crew of a German plane that had been hit over Anzio by American antiaircraft guns.

Orders had arrived during the night that we would move forward at daylight to protect the flank of the British 1st Division during its advance on Carroceto. My 4th Battalion and the paratroop battalion awakened soon after midnight to move forward in column towards the network of drainage ditches several miles ahead. In the ditch they strung out from Carroceto in a southeasterly direction through Padiglione, a boundary point between the Rangers and the paratroopers. At dawn they jumped off in attack, drawing a sputtering of machine-gun and rifle fire from several houses just beyond Padiglione. A platoon of tank destroyers was directly behind them, and the chemical mortars were brought up to the drainage ditches for further support. Meanwhile the 1st and 3rd battalions remained in reserve in the pine woods several miles to the rear. The 4th Battalion hung onto their new outpost line during the night.

After dark I filled a gap on the right between the Rangers and the paratroopers with three companies of the 1st Rangers. The left flank was receiving sniping fire from several farmhouses near Carroceto, so the next morning the men infiltrated forward to improve their positions. A group led by Sergeant Egan crawled toward one of the farmhouses carrying light machine guns and 60-mm infantry mortars. Machine pistol and gunfire caught several of his men, but the patrol—whittled down to four men—took the house. Under cover of the fire of the group's weapons, a Ranger ran forward to the shadow of the wall where he faded against the walls. Cautiously he threw grenades in the windows and door to clear the building.

Enemy shelling from self-propelled guns got heavier during the day, as did German air activity. Troops to the right and left were bombed and strafed while the Anzio beach and docks were plastered in what became a daily German standard operating procedure.

German resistance was getting stronger, and a German counterattack against the British at Carroceto spilled over into the 4th Ranger Battalion area. We held firm. Orders then came to dig in on a main line of resistance, including mines and wire, between Carroceto and Padiglione.

At dawn on 27 January the 3rd and 4th Ranger Battalions and the parachute battalion moved forward in a skirmish line to a road running from Carroceto eastward. The enemy was in foxholes and was using every house as a center of defense. The British, meanwhile, were being shelled in the factory area at Carroceto.

Our mortars plunked in shells, while enemy artillery shells landed sporadically among our soldiers. Sergeant Campbell said of the mortar support, "There was one time we saw a German come out of his foxhole for a minute, and as the mortars were zeroed in we gave him concentration No. 3. He must have had some ammo in that hole because the next thing we saw of that Jerry, he was about twenty feet in the air, turning end over end."

Enemy activity increased on the morning of 28 January with parties operating along our front. Shells were bursting over our heads, and the men were constantly making quick jumps for their foxholes to avoid the shell fragments streaking down. A heavy weapons company had come in behind the Rangers, and the situation was beginning to tighten up. The beachhead half-moon was only about ten miles deep—not extensive enough to keep the heavier enemy artillery from laying shellfire on the docks at Anzio. Shells dug into the sandy beaches, and many threw up waterspouts as they sought the pier. At this time the big Allied smoke generators that could lay a protective cloud over the beachhead had not begun to operate.

The Ranger front line now ran from Carroceto to Spaccasassi along a dirt road. Beyond that we established an outpost line of patrols to warn of enemy attack; to our rear the 1st Ranger Battalion manned the main line of resistance in the drainage ditches. In event of a strong German attack, the outpost line would be pulled in; if the 3rd and 4th battalions were driven out of their forward positions, they would retreat to the main line of resistance. Between that main line and the Anzio beach there was some seven to ten miles of flat countryside. That was to be the extent of the Anzio beachhead for the following four months.

The navy was our lifeline. Their ships sped from friendly territory at Naples past hostile coast and then back to the friendly area at Anzio—which itself wasn't any picnic. The navy ships were giving what gunfire support they could to the shallow beachhead at Anzio; but the Germans, using E-boats and midget U-boats, made the waters extremely dangerous. The Allied antiaircraft system was good, but it wasn't good enough. Nor was the fighter protection complete. The navy and the soldiers had good reason to thank the air defense, but all German sneak air raiders could not be kept from launching their damnable radio-controlled glider bombers against Allied ships. Several of these caused severe damage.

About 1600 on the afternoon of 28 January, the American 3rd Division, to which my Rangers were attached, sent orders that a British reconnaissance unit would relieve us during the night. My men were to move south and east behind the 3rd Division front. Something was cooking. The men said farewell to the parachute battalion, picked up all the equipment that could be carried by marching men, and swung into the Ranger stride down to an assembly area near Nettuno. The 3rd Division troops were plainly preparing to jump off in another attack.

As veteran soldiers we knew that the situation in the beachhead wasn't duck soup. Enemy resistance was developing according to pattern, and their artillery was sticking airbursts where they wanted them above this billard-table battle area. Enemy patrols were increasing their activity. They also were appearing in the houses near the front line and were operating a considerable number of armored vehicles on the roads northeast of Carroceto.

The Rangers didn't have too much time to consider all the pros and cons of the situation however. They knew the beachhead was shallow—that the British 1st Division and their own 3rd Division were not advancing their front lines toward the Appian Way. Fortunately the beachhead area had good flank protection in the Alban Hills to the north and the reclaimed crisscrossed Pontine Marshes to the south. Trouble lay ahead where the shadows of the mountains extended across the Appian Way.

The Rangers in Sicily and Italy

Photograph by Phil Stern

A training exercise for the Sicilian invasion; Zeralda, Algeria, June 1943. Gen. Terry Allen, commanding general, 1st Infantry Division, and an aid keep in stride with Colonel Darby and Capt. Roy Murray, commanding officer 4th Ranger Battalion.

The invasion of Sicily: Rangers of the 1st Battalion man a halftrack at intersection in the port city of Gela. July 10, 1943.

Victorious Rangers move through the streets of Gela after capturing the city's defenses. Later the Rangers helped hold off a concerted enemy tank and infantry attack that for a while threatened to throw the Americans back into the sea.

Rangers of the 4th Battalion spot enemy tanks of the Hermann Goering Division on the Gela plain the day after the Sicilian landings.

14 January 1944: Preparation for the landing at Anzio. *Top:* Men of Company "F", 1st Ranger Battalion, move through smoke screen in street of Pozzuoli, Italy, during street fighting maneuvers. *Bottom:* Rangers load into British LCAs for beach landing maneuvers near Naples.

Prior to departure for the Anzio beachhead. *Top:* Lt. James Altieri, C Company, 4th Ranger Battalion, being checked off by Capt. James Lavin, adjutant of the 4th Battalion, as the unit lines up to board LCIs. *Bottom:* Members of the 3rd Ranger Battalion loading aboard LCIs.

XI

Cisterna—
Death at Dawn

29 JANUARY 1944

PERSPECTIVE At Anzio the VI Corps had come ashore on the coastal plain between the beaches and the Alban Hills. Formerly this area had been called the Pontine Marshes, a land that had been partially reclaimed by the Italian government and made into a fertile farming region through a system of drainage canals and ditches. In the center of the plain was the largest waterway, the Mussolini Canal, which in military lingo was designated "a prime tank trap." Gen. John P. Lucas of the VI Corps used the Mussolini Canal as his right flank protection. South of the canal the ground had been flooded by the Germans as an obstacle to invasion forces.

Almost due north from Anzio, Highways 6 and 7 skirted the northern and southern edges of the Alban Hills, which had been formed by a great volcano, long since extinct. The rim of the crater, which had a diameter of eight miles, encircled two large lakes, fertile fields, and wooded hills, some of which rise hundreds of feet. Possession of this natural barrier gave the Germans perfect observation of the entire Anzio beachhead.

Had General Lucas's VI Corps taken Albano and Valmontone, they would have cut the two main highways linking the German 10th Army in southern Italy with Rome. His corps would then have been at the gates of the Eternal City. But Lucas, at the outset, was more interested in building up his beachhead than in expanding it. He devoted his primary attention to putting the Anzio Harbor into operation to handle incoming troops and supplies.

Gen. Mark Clark had visited the beachhead on the morning of D-day of the

Anzio landing and spent two hours ashore. Obviously he was well satisfied with the landing; but by the next day he was already impatient and wrote a letter to Lucas asking how far his patrols had moved forward and what his intentions were for immediate operations. In his diary, Clark said, "Lucas must be aggressive. He must take some chances. He must use the 3rd Division to push out."

General Alexander had also visited the Anzio beachhead on the first day of the landing and again on 25 January. He seemed optimistic about future prospects and complimented Lucas, who reminded Alexander that the task was hardly complete. However, Lucas felt that a beachhead nearly ten miles deep was not a bad accomplishment.

On 25 January, Clark had suggested that Lucas move at once to take Campoleone on the road to Albano and Cisterna on the road to Valmontone. He realized the value of these places for offensive action was not great, but they were important anchors for a defensive line. Intelligence indicated that the Germans had about three full divisions at Anzio and a fourth possibly en route. Clark cautioned Lucas to be alert for counterattacks and promised him more troops.

General Kesselring, the German commander, realized that if Lucas took Albano, the Allied forces would have direct access to Rome by way of Highway 7. But he believed that Lucas was too cautious to aim for that objective, and so he concentrated his troop strength in Cisterna. The 3rd Division had moved to within four miles of Cisterna, but the closer it got, the more resistance it met. In contrast, the British 1st Division had gone steadily ahead on the Albano Road and, by 25 January, had taken Aprilia. This settlement controlled a network of roads that had become vital because rain had turned the fields in the Anzio plain into a vast bog. Four miles beyond Aprilia was Campoleone, which was still only lightly defended by the Germans. But Lucas was still cautious, saying, "I must keep my feet on the ground and my forces in hand and do nothing foolish."

On 27 January Lucas met with his division commanders to discuss taking the offensive. Prospects for enlarging the beachhead appeared excellent. The 3rd Division was within three miles of Cisterna, and the 1st British Division had repulsed a German counterattack at Aprilia.

Clark urged Lucas to launch his offensive immediately since the delay would permit the enemy to build up more forces. The time seemed to him to be ripe for boldness because no definite enemy line of resistance had as yet been developed, according to intelligence estimates. (Mackensen of the German Fourteenth Army later wondered, "Every minute was precious for the Germans and Allies alike. What would have happened had the enemy [the Allies] advanced boldly immediately after landing, if he had occupied the Alban Mountains and thrust onto Valmontone, thereby cutting off the vital supplies roads of . . . the Tenth Army?")

On 29 January, the eighth day of the invasion, Lucas at last felt strong enough to launch a full-scale attack. He requested extensive naval and air support and directed heavy artillery fire. He assured General Clark that he would go all out, but added with his usual caution, "If conditions warrant."

Lucas projected a two-pronged advance with the British 1st Division making the main effort toward Albano. He wanted the 1st U.S. Armored Division, which had left Combat Command B in the Cassino area, to exploit British gains in the direction of Rome. The 3rd Division was in the right part of the corps zone and was to take Cisterna—thereby cutting Highway 7—and be ready to drive on Valmontone. The 504th Parachute Infantry and the 6615th Ranger Force (Provisional) were attached to the 3rd Division. Fifth Army's formation of the 6615th Ranger Force had finally given Darby his coveted separate headquarters, but had diluted the leadership of the battalions just before the Anzio landing, weakening their combat ability. Darby and Dammer went to Force Headquarters, which caused Lt. Col. Jack Dobson and Maj. Alva Miller to be appointed commanders of the 1st and 3rd Battalions, respectively.

The attack of the British 1st Division was successful. The troops seized the railroad embankment and continued steadily to Campoleone, which they captured by the end of 31 January. The 1st Armored Division could get nowhere. The fields were muddy and the gullies impassable. Lack of cover prevented the tanks from exploiting the British gains in any way.

On the right side of the beachhead, General Truscott called upon the Rangers to spearhead his 3rd Division attack towards Cisterna. He instructed Colonel Darby to infiltrate two of his three Ranger battalions into the town during the night of 29 January; the other battalion was to clear the road for tanks and infantrymen that would rush forward the next morning to block Highway 7 in strength. The 7th Infantry on the left and the 15th Infantry on the right were also to attack by infiltration and were to cut the highway above and below the town of Cisterna.

¶ ABOUT MIDNIGHT ON 28 JANUARY MY THREE Ranger battalions, leaving the front lines behind them to the west, marched back the ten-odd miles to the assembly area at San Antonio, arriving there before dawn of 29 January. Our assembly area was about four miles from the coast where the 3rd Division had landed. Due north some eight miles was the town of Cisterna di Littoria, its stone and cement houses spread out along the Appian Way. At that time Cisterna was about four miles outside the Allied beachhead in the country known to the troops as "Jerryland."

At daybreak of 29 January we scanned the surrounding countryside from our position near San Antonio. Close to our right, two miles away, was the Mussolini Canal running along the west side of the Pontine Marshes. Nettuno and Anzio were off to our left rear and barely visible in the distance. The entire beachhead area was as flat as a billiard table, crisscrossed by roads, streams, and canals. Due

CISTERNA—DEATH AT DAWN

north beyond Cisterna and on the far side of the Appian Way were the first ridges of the mountains. The hill mass was called Colli Laziali.

Colli Laziali is a dominating terrain feature. It is the western flank of the rugged Apennine range which held memories of the bloody mountain battles of Cassino and Venafro. Down on the plain where the Allies were trying to extend their beachhead, they were under the observation of the enemy on the heights. For that reason, as well as for flank protection, the Allies had to have the Colli, twenty-eight hundred feet high.

During the day we lay at ease in our bivouac, cleaning our bayonets and knives and inspecting our rifles and automatic weapons. A few of us were shaving off a growth of beard, and many others were lined up for a haircut.

Meanwhile the Ranger staff studied the plan of attack, Gathered around maps in the pine woods, we planned how we would infiltrate the enemy lines and get into the town of Cisterna. Our job was to occupy the town, capturing or killing any enemy, while awaiting reinforcements from the 3rd Division which were scheduled to arrive in the late afternoon of 30 January. There was no opportunity to send out reconnaissance patrols since we were to attack after dark the same day. From intelligence sources we were informed that the Germans were showing no intent of counterattacking; on the front of the 3rd Division, few signs of enemy concentrations had been reported. The front was still fluid, or appeared so, even the day before we made ready to drive toward our objective at Cisterna.

Toward evening, the Rangers who had been lolling on pine branches in the bivouac area rolled up their bedrolls and piled them on a tent canvas. They dropped their barracks bags in the same pile, leaving this gear in charge of several Ranger cooks and truck drivers who were ordered to stay behind. By this time all of us were acquainted with the maps of our march that night.

The plan itself was not an unusual one for my Rangers. In fact it was down our alley and one that would have delighted the heart of Major Rogers in pre-Revolutionary days. The 4th Battalion was to move up a secondary or one-way road bearing northeast towards Cisterna. Farther to the east was a similar road that approached Cisterna with a slight inclination to the west. We were to operate in this triangle.

Proceeding along the road, the 4th Battalion was to move through the villages of Femina Morta and Isola Bella; to their right, the 1st and 3rd Battalions were to infiltrate in the area between the roads.

Jumping off one hour before the 3rd Division, the fast-moving Rangers were expected to gain four or five hours during the night. Behind us one regiment was to be on the right, a tank battalion in the center, and another regiment on the left.

At nightfall, after a quick supper, the Rangers were ready to move out. We were accompanied by a tank-destroyer company and a cannon company as well as our friendly companions of the 83rd Chemical Mortar Battalion. The riflemen carried two bandoliers of ammunition strung over their shoulders and grenades stuffed in their pockets. The mortar crews carried three rounds for each weapon. Machine guns were left behind. Other than our rifles and automatic weapons, there was a plentiful supply of sticky grenades and many antitank rocket launchers scattered throughout the Ranger force. They would probably be needed, as the good road network leading into Cisterna and the flat terrain of the beachhead offered the Germans ideal tank country.

The men were in good spirits as they swung out for their seven-mile march from the assembly area to the line of departure. At midnight the three battalions with their accompanying troops had reached a road junction about four miles from Cisterna. I called my subordinate commanders together for a final conference on communications and ordered that radio silence not be broken until the troops had crossed the line running east through Isola Bella, less than two miles from Cisterna. My headquarters, accompanying the 4th Battalion, was hooked in by wire and radio with the 3rd Division.

The Rangers, concealed by a moonless sky, were almost completely hidden in the deep irrigation ditches leading north to Cisterna. In the advance the 1st Battalion, on the right of the line, had orders that under no circumstances were they to stay and fight. They were to keep moving toward Cisterna. The 3rd Battalion in the center had practically the same mission—though it was to fight if forced to in order to permit the 1st Battalion to continue. We continued moving forward after one o'clock in the morning. Although the night was dark, the men were at ease since night operations were second nature to us. Also we were fighting with the 3rd Division—no new experience to the Rangers.

There was no hint of disaster as we plodded ahead, passing enemy machine-gun and mortar nests, which fired occasionally off to their flanks. The Germans showed no hostile intent and gave no signs that they knew we were sifting through their defenses.

"We passed two batteries of screaming meemies," said Cpl. Ben W. Mosier. "We heard them giving orders in German and could have wiped them out. We weren't showing our hand."

"We could see their sentries," said Sgt. Thomas B. Fergen. "But they didn't see us. We had to keep quiet."

While the 1st and 3rd battalions were advancing in the drainage ditches toward Cisterna, the 4th battalion—on the left flank—began to run into difficulties along the road. There was determined resistance from houses, farm buildings, and dug-in emplacements less than a half mile north of the road junction where the Ranger conference had been held. This was the first intimation that all was not well, for information of the enemy had indicated that there were very light German forces between the beachhead and Cisterna.

Next the 4th Battalion ran into a roadblock made by two damaged jeeps and an Italian truck. They pulled these wrecks to the side of the road, and six to eight medium tanks came up behind the Rangers to support their advance. All night the 4th Battalion had a running fight, and by dawn they were still short of the town of Isola Bella, the key point for opening of radio communications.

As the triangle narrowed toward its apex at Cisterna, the 1st Ranger Battalion went into the lead with the 3rd following immediately behind. The formation was single file, Indian column. In the darkness the Rangers had difficulty keeping quiet as they occasionally stumbled or brushed their equipment against the sides of the winding drainage ditch. About two miles out from the town of Cisterna, the two battalions lost contact. About a half mile farther on, the 1st Ranger Battalion split, three companies going forward and three halting because of the lost contact to the rear. The commander of the three halted companies sent a runner to the rear to find the 3rd Battalion.

The runner returned with the information that the battalion's commanding officer, Maj. Alva Miller, had been killed by a shell from an enemy tank. Major Miller, like all Ranger officers, was in the lead in the drainage ditch when an enemy tank suddenly appeared from around a bend. Both sides had opened fire instantaneously at point-blank range. The leading Rangers were killed or wounded. The tank was knocked out by a sticky grenade, and the 3rd Battalion continued advancing to catch up with the 1st.

About 0700 the 1st Battalion, following orders, broke radio silence. The commanding officer, Jack Dobson, reported that he was located in an open field about eight hundred yards south of Cisterna where three German self-propelled guns were giving him a good deal of trouble. The 3rd Battalion was strung out just east and to the rear of him. Daylight caught them in this exposed area immediately outside the town.

Meanwhile the 4th Battalion was taking out dug-in emplacements and enemy sniper resistance slowly and surely. The junior commanders had moved ahead, with their radio operators alongside carrying walkie-talkies. My Rangers were in a hard fight at the town of Isola Bella, so half-tracks and tank destroyers were ordered to help the 4th Battalion attempt a breakthrough at the town. The vehicles moved out but were halted by a minefield south of Isola, and two of them were lost. The mortars, meanwhile, had been brought up behind the 4th Battalion and were shooting into the town.

In front of Cisterna the 1st and 3rd Battalions were facing enemy snipers and mortar troops holed up in farmhouses. As they came to a halt three hundred yards from the enemy, they spotted two enemy tanks hidden in bushes on the opposite side of the road some fifty yards away. One tank began moving, and its cannon turned ominously in the direction of the Rangers. Two soldiers armed with rocket launchers slid forward, hidden by bushes, and knocked out the tanks at practically pointblank range. By this time the 3rd Battalion and half the 1st Battalion had joined the leading group of the 1st Battalion fighting the enemy. Colonel Dobson of the 1st Rangers had sent two of his companies to face the enemy along the combat front and the other company to crawl around the left flank to get at enemy mortars and self-propelled artillery.

To the immediate front in heavy woods, one hundred yards distant, were two 20-mm machine guns and three smaller caliber machine guns. To the left front were two more machine guns plus a few

CISTERNA—DEATH AT DAWN

enemy riflemen, attempting—in turn—to infiltrate through the Rangers. They were members of a German parachute division that had much the same experience and training as the Ranger battalion. It was apparent, though, that behind them were larger numbers of troops than were available to the Allies in the Anzio beachhead.

"One tank came out of a driveway behind a house ahead of us," said Sergeant Fergen. "One of my squad climbed aboard it while it was moving and dropped an incendiary grenade into the open turret. At the same time a bazooka gunner hit it head on, and I was up beside it with a sticky grenade. The grenade exploded while I was getting away. I ducked in time to see the tank blow up and start burning. One of the crew got out and tried to get under the tank, but I shot him."

When the sun came up, the two Ranger battalions at Cisterna were surrounded. Between sunrise and 0700, when radio silence was broken, we came to the realization that the battle was lost. Sunrise doomed us and marked the beginning of the hopeless, heroic fight that continued until the last Ranger was killed or captured, until the last few members of the two battalions made their escape.

"When it got light, we saw one big building ahead with trees around it," said Corporal Mosier. "Behind us there was one tank and when we saw it, we cheered. We thought it was ours. We couldn't see very well, and then it opened up on us."

What happened next, happened fast. The Rangers attacked the tank, set it aflame with a sticky grenade and a bazooka, shot and killed the crew when they tried to climb out of the turret. At the same time other Rangers were blowing up a German ammunition dump by shooting and grenading it. But with this tank gone, ten more appeared to take its place, and those ten were followed by German infantry armed with automatic weapons.

When radio silence was broken, the first action reports were given to my headquarters. Colonel Dobson of the 1st Battalion had been wounded; the commanding officer of the 3rd Battalion had been killed. Both battalions were surrounded and fighting for their lives. They asked about the expected division support from the flanks.

All around Cisterna the Germans, who had shown no sign of strength twenty-four hours before, had moved in large numbers of soldiers. Their artillery sent its blistering fire into our attackers.

Houses, once invitingly empty, were now nests for snipers and machine guns. The Germans had reinforced their lines on the exact day the Allies had selected for attack. The German reinforcements stopped the American combat teams cold and surrounded and decimated my two Ranger battalions.

About 0800, after communications had been disrupted for an hour, I was able to talk to the 1st Battalion. I was told that the men fighting to gain a foothold in the outskirts of the town near the railroad station were receiving heavy fire from enemy artillery.

"The sun was up when they let loose with their artillery," said Corporal Mosier. "We were in the woods, not much of a woods, and they were firing into us. After the first volley, you felt naked. You knew they could see you, and you couldn't do anything about it."

"The tanks caused most of the trouble," said Sergeant Fergen. "I was in a field with the rest of my men when the tanks moved in. They came from Highway No. 7, swinging into the field, racing after us. You could run about twenty yards and then hit the ground. If you waited longer, they got you. They got three next to me with a direct hit."

The three who were hit, like the others, had tried the impossible—to tackle a tank barehanded. But for some, the impossible was done. Other men who returned told of Rangers hurling themselves on tanks, exploding the tank and themselves with sticky grenades. Gunners using their rocket launchers under direct fire crept up to tanks to blast off their treads, while riflemen following them shot the crews that emerged.

These Rangers called back for artillery concentration on the northern and western sections of the town. Their idea was one that we had used previously at Arzew with mortar fire. They would ask the artillery to register well beyond them and then by observation call for a decrease in the range until the shells were landing where they wanted them—just in front. They had no observation capability that would assure them of accuracy, however, and after a few rounds gave up this method of attack.

It was evident that the Rangers in Cisterna were not going to be relieved that day. The infantry regiments had jumped off as scheduled during the night but were stopped dead in their tracks. Later intelligence showed that the enemy had some twelve thousand men at the town of Velletri, twelve miles from Cisterna. Also, that morning's air observation showed artillery positions in some number behind Cisterna. The plan had been all right; the difficulty was that the Germans had anticipated the Allied action, countering with vastly superior numbers of troops.

The 4th Battalion and all of us at my headquarters realized how desperate the situation was. Everything possible was done to crash through Isola Bella and help our comrades. On the outskirts of Cisterna the 1st and 3rd Battalions went through at least five hours of the hardest kind of fighting, under attack by machine weapons, tanks, and artillery, and surrounded on all sides by overwhelming numbers of Germans.

The whole story of this action may never be known. When Ranger prisoners of war return, they can add their pieces of information about the Ranger stand of the next few hours. It is a grim but proud story.

At 0830 the 1st and 3rd Rangers radioed back that they were surrounded and had suffered heavy causalties. They were attempting to hold a few buildings on the outskirts of Cisterna, but the Germans were closing in. The 4th Rangers kept pushing all morning, finally getting through Isola Bella but were stopped at Femina Morta. The 1st Ranger Battalion formed a line in the fields near Cisterna with the 3rd Ranger Battalion in reserve initially. They were still attacking, and the company of the 1st Battalion that had been sent out on the enveloping movement was able to blast out the machine guns on the flank.

Walkie-talkie radios sent back increasing evidence of the crucial last-ditch stand. One company commander was killed, another seriously wounded. Casualties were becoming very heavy. The enemy had the Rangers pinned down with automatic fire in an area about three hundred yards in diameter, while snipers were zipping single shots into their midst. Patrols that had been sent out were drifting back to this perimeter defense. By this time, due to casualties among the officers, a single captain commanded both battalions. This young officer was equal to the situation, immediately closed the gap in the rear of the circle and ordered the men to dig in. The call went out for reinforcements in the hope that the 3rd Division might reach them before they ran out of ammunition.

A battalion first-aid station was set up in a building where the radio was kept—some twenty-five yards from the combined command post. Rangers were straggling in, many of them torn by shell fragments, and others hit in arms and legs by small-arms fire.

The fighting kept on, with the Rangers using every trick they knew to get a German every time they fired. The men up front who were meeting the enemy's main strength kept asking for more ammunition to the forward line.

Enemy artillery was ranged in on the defense area, and self-propelled guns were roaming outside the circle, much like the Indians around a desert caravan drawn up in bivouac. In many ways the fighting for the Rangers wasn't much different from that encountered by the plainsmen before them. The snipers were the same as in past wars. The pace, though, was swifter; machine guns and other automatic weapons spewed hot lead in streams like fire hoses. The artillery and the self-propelled guns were modern additions to the battle.

Continually the Rangers asked for help. There was no idea of giving up, although they had decided not to attempt another forward advance since it would be suicide. They had neither the ammunition nor the heavy weapons to cope with the enemy. Their plan was to hold on to what they had until help came. The calls for assistance from the 1st Battalion radio came through clearly to my headquarters, which was bogged down and sweating it out at Femina Morta. We, too, were surrounded by large numbers of Germans but had not lost the initiative completely. "SOSs" were relayed to the 3rd Division, whose regiments were battling against heavy odds in attempting to reach Cisterna on time.

The captain talking to us from the 1st Battalion was overwrought and weeping, so I called for one of their sergeants whom I knew would be nearby. This husky, top-grade fighting man from Brooklyn had been with us through every engagement. He clicked over his radio connection and in an unexcited voice stated simply: "Some of the fellows are giving up. Colonel, we are awfully sorry." Then, unhurriedly but sympathetically, "They can't help it, because we're running out of ammunition. But I ain't surrendering. They are coming into the building now." The radio went wham, wham—and was dead.

CISTERNA—DEATH AT DAWN

The Germans immediately took advantage of the situation and in overwhelming strength began to close on the 1st and 3rd battalions. Allied attacking forces were held up elsewhere. It was clear that the enemy intention was to capture or wipe out the Ranger battalions at Cisterna. Germans were in trees, houses, foxholes, and dug-in emplacements prepared beforehand, completely surrounding the two battalions. The advantage of the terrain was with the enemy, who also had superiority in artillery and heavy automatic weapons. All the while, the Germans were pressing in from both flanks and in a vise-like attack.

This went on all morning of 30 January; sometime during the afternoon the Germans attacked with considerable numbers of tanks. But the Rangers still stood their ground—practically barehanded, for they were very low on antitank rockets and sticky grenades. They took on the tanks one by one, clambering over them, dropping grenades through the hatches, and firing bazookas at pointblank range. The 1st and 3rd battalions used up a large part of their scant supply of ammunition, but they knocked out fourteen tanks.

While the tanks and Rangers were milling around, the Germans captured ten men of the 3rd Battalion. About 1330 in the afternoon the Rangers saw some of their own men as prisoners with their hands in the air at a position about two hundred yards to the rear, toward the coast. The Ranger captain in command went back to investigate and found that the men were his.

The action was so close it was like sitting in a movie house and watching a newsreel. German paratroop infantry had the prisoners surrounded, and two German personnel carriers—a type of armored vehicle for carrying combat troops up front—were also shepherding the men along. Sporadic shots rang out around the position. Two of the German guards slumped and collapsed in the dirt.

Then the story grows even more difficult to follow and more fantastic. There is one account that the Ranger prisoners were marched directly toward our own lines with the Germans calling to the Rangers nearby to surrender. Instead the company is said to have ambushed two more of the guards. The Rangers were running out of ammunition.

"I saw a man whose face was cut up," said Sergeant Fergen. "He said he didn't want to be taken prisoner and asked me to shoot him. 'Are you crazy?' I said. He answered, 'We're finished and I don't want them to get me.' 'Don't be crazy,' I told him."

"But he wasn't so crazy," Sergeant Fergen went on. "He knew what it was. Out there in the field, the tanks kept chasing us and then from the houses around the field, the snipers tried to pick us off. They were using machine guns, machine pistols, and rifles, and they were firing straight."

On the bloody field, in the irrigation ditch beside it, and in the farmhouses on the edge of town, the battle went on. In the Ranger-held farmhouses—now the targets of all German guns—the medics cared for their wounded.

The battalion surgeon was a big man with a lantern jaw and a long record of Ranger combat. Rangers recalled him offering encouragement as long as there was hope. Then his face took on the grim set look of the others. Like the rest, he carried on at his job.

At 1430 the sergeant major of the 3rd Battalion reported that he was destroying his radio. The 1st Battalion radio had been silent for an hour. The sand in the hourglass was running out. The Rangers knew it, as did the Germans.

Bitterly, the last orders were given by the battalion commander. The battalion doctor, taken prisoner while caring for his wounded, protested. The German soldier ignored him. The doctor seized the German's pistol and shot him. As he tried to return to his wounded, he was killed.

Corporal Mosier remembered his company commander, a tall, bespectacled, thin-faced West Pointer, telling his men to go. "I hate to do this," the captain said, "But it's too late now. That direction is south. Take out and God bless you."

The platoon leader, the only lieutenant left in this company hollered, "Good Luck," as the handful of men started out.

"There were eight of us together," said Mosier. "The lieutenant told me that he wouldn't be captured and showed me his two bandoliers of ammunition. He was loaded up and firing to cover us with his carbine when we set off.

"We headed for the ditch. All this time the tracers were flying close enough to stop them with your hand. Along the ditch there were snipers all the way."

When Sergeant Fergen's company officers and first sergeant became casualties, he took command, leading the way to the ditch while shells and snipers' bullets followed him. When the group had passed through the German lines, only two men were left: Fergen and Technician 5th Class Joseph Yytarchik, a machine gunner in his section.

All the rest of 30 January the 4th Battalion fought on bitterly, knowing in their hearts that the 1st and 3rd Battalions were surrounded and taking terrific punishment. Nevertheless they clung to a hope born of their training and experience that they would be able to get through and relieve the other two battalions.

That afternoon I brought up the Cannon Company in an attempt to swing around Femina Morta and reach the beleaguered battalions. The young captain in charge was aquiver with excitement about his task. Four times he took his half-tracks in towards Cisterna; each time one or more of them were knocked out. Three times he came back, loaded up with ammunition, and went in again. After the fourth attempt the captain came out weeping, saying that he couldn't do any more for the surrounded Rangers. He went into the Ranger force command post to report his story; as he walked out the door, in the depths of despair, he was hit through the head by an enemy sniper.

The 4th Battalion was still surrounded the next morning. The night had been difficult. The command post was set up in a captured house, and all night long enemy snipers fired at it. One of the officers told of looking cautiously out the window in the middle of the night to see a German soldier walk past, a few feet away. But strangely the Germans didn't try to get in, probably because they knew that most of them would pay with their lives. They couldn't use artillery or mortars against the Rangers because their own troops were mixed up among the Americans.

On 31 January a regimental combat team fought its way up to the 4th Battalion, and together they cleaned out Femina Morta, taking two hundred and fifty prisoners—one hundred and fifty Germans of the 1st Parachute Division and one hundred of the Hermann Goering Panzer Division.

Of the 1st and 3rd Ranger Battalions only six escaped. Of the group who returned one said, "We're Rangers. You can never wipe out all the Rangers, we've been through too much for that. They paid for the ones they got and they'll keep on paying. And we'll be around to see that they do."

XII

The Rangers
Live On

PERSPECTIVE   The situation in which Darby's Rangers found themselves was a result of poor intelligence by the Allies and careful planning by the Germans. The Germans had concentrated considerable strength in Cisterna in preparation for a counterattack scheduled for 2 February. This was overlooked by American intelligence, which interpreted the German intentions in the area to be defensive in character. Kesselring was astute enough to see the possibility of an American attack on Cisterna and moved forces in to counteract it. A captured German officer later stated that Cisterna had been reinforced on the night of 29 January.

An attempt was made to warn the Americans of the ambush. There were a number of Polish troops with the German army, and one young man deserted to the Rangers and tried to explain about the German preparations. No one could understand him, and they evacuated him to the rear. His full story was developed later when he was finally interrogated at Fifth Army's headquarters.

Also unknown to Darby was that the Germans had seen the 1st and 3rd Ranger Battalions moving northward about a mile south of the triangular field. The appearance of three German tanks on the Rangers' rear, while Dobson was briefing Shunstrom, indicated that the 1st and 3rd Ranger Battalions were being surrounded.

Darby blamed himself for the disaster at Cisterna, believing that the outcome of the operation would have been different had he been with the forward battalions. He had pleaded with his men not to give up and exhorted them to infiltrate back. But he was told that they couldn't return because they were surrounded. At that, Darby "put his head down on his arm and cried . . . he broke down," said Sgt. Carlo Contrera, Darby's jeep driver who had been with him since the Rangers were in Africa. "Darby had always put the safety of his men first, and he couldn't stand the thought of what was happening to them."

In the final analysis, only six of the seven hundred and sixty men who infiltrated to Cisterna made their way back from the battle. The rest were killed or captured.

The VI Corps attack was ended on 1 February. The next day Alexander and Clark informed Lucas that he was to prepare for the German counterattack believed to be imminent. None of the Allied commanders knew at the time that the attack had caused fifty-five hundred German casualties and had forced the Germans to commit all their reserves. In fact, the Allied attack came very close to success for it had upset the German plans to counterattack, delaying them two days.

¶ MEMBERS OF THE 4TH BATTALION RETURNED TO the coastal area in the Anzio beachhead and joined the remnants of the 1st and 3rd who had slipped away from Cisterna. These men were shell shocked. At first they would tell their story only to their own cooks and truck drivers who had remained behind. We all had lost too many comrades and friends in the ill-fated assault to want to discuss the experiences with outsiders.

The Rangers blamed no one for their losses. The infantry troops had run into the same reinforced enemy defenses, had jumped off, hit something solid, and recoiled. Slipping through enemy lines, my raiders had met the same strengthened enemy and were surrounded.

In the shell-torn Anzio beachhead and at Naples, time and the necessities of war brought those of us remaining back to the realities of life. We began to talk more freely about our experiences at Cisterna, once the horror of it was far enough in the past.

There was something to be proud of in the grim story—something that welled up in the heart of every soldier who heard the Rangers' story: They had done their duty, had fought to the limit of human endurance, and almost inevitably—as with other groups of soldiers in history who had taken the long chance by raiding into enemy-held territory—they had met their fate. The British Commandos who raided St. Nazaire had had a similar experience.

There was a pioneer American savor to the story. How often in our early days had other groups of fighting men—selected, hard fighting, experienced men—found themselves in the Rangers' position on that fateful 29 January at Cisterna. In this fight were elements of Custer's last stand, of the Alamo, even of Major Roger's Rangers in the French and Indian War. The gallant Rogers band had fought and died in raids into enemy country. They had made raid after raid, but the sands of time ran against them. They were too few, too courageous, too well versed in the art of warfare—not to have realized that time and fate were holding the high cards.

Eventually the remaining Rangers of the 1st, 3rd and 4th battalions were brought home. There was no band to salute us on our departure—no one at home in the United States who paid special heed to our return. Yet deep in our hearts we knew we had always led the assault against the enemy.

The Rangers had gone overseas in the spring of 1942, opened the North African campaign, fought against overwhelming odds in Tunisia. We had landed against concentrated hell at Gela and been in on the final kill at Messina. At Sorrento we had played the gambler's odds on the far left flank, standing off forces superior by at least eight to one and, more than that, an enemy equipped with heavy supporting artillery and air power. The Rangers had known, too, the bitter static fighting in the cold, dreary Italian mountains in the winter of 1943. Finally at Anzio and Cisterna, we had found we could fight a hard defensive fight while still believing—in the American spirit—that we would take the offensive and carry the fight to the enemy.

In this war the Rangers had asked only for the opportunity to fight. An average group of Americans, my men had prepared themselves physically and mentally for combat. If there is no other lesson in their combat it is that American youths, so much maligned during the prewar years, could condition their bodies physically to meet the rigors of blitzkrieg and could condition their minds to the individual responsibilities of modern warfare. Weapons they knew intimately. Battle preparedness was their continuing study and practice. They learned the tricks of modern war: improvising ruses, how to stalk a sentry, how to blow up a pillbox. When tanks and heavier weapons were brought against them, they fought them with their infantry weapons—with rocket launchers and sticky grenades thrown from up close.

The name Rangers was aptly chosen—my men lived up to it with the full measure of their willingness and spirit. They were proud soldiers, confident warriors, and evidence that the spirit of battling against any odds still lives strong among the American nation.

Though the Ranger force had asked for no special recognition, two of the battalions received the Presidential Citation for gallantry, the 1st Battalion meriting that great honor twice. On the record they are credited with four engagements: the landing in North Africa; the Tunisian combat; the Sicilian operation, including landing and cleanup; and the landing in Italy at Sorrento. Though the Anzio beachhead battle and the fighting on the Italian Peninsula were not designated as separate campaigns, the Rangers knew intimately the strength required for those combats.

No Ranger received the Medal of Honor—in fact, many of our deeds are unknown, unheralded. Twenty-seven Rangers were commissioned from the ranks on the battlefield, however; we provided our own rewards for our finest soldiers.

Nineteen officers and one hundred and thirty-seven enlisted Rangers returned to the United States. Not all of these men had been through all the engagements in which we had fought. There had been replacements. The 1st Ranger Battalion had been expanded to three. At my last count there were eighty-seven Rangers remaining of the original five hundred who successfully completed the training at Achnacarry. That number may be somewhat increased since some of the original Rangers were taken prisoner at Dieppe, in Tunisia, in Sicily, and in Italy.

The Rangers still live, and as one sergeant said: "We'll go back, and we'll take more of the enemy than we lose."

EPILOGUE

Darby's Later Assignments

AFTER THE DEFEAT AT CISTERNA, THE RANGER FORCE consisted of only the 4th Battalion plus a few cooks and drivers who had been ordered to remain behind when the three battalions moved toward Cisterna. The 4th Battalion was placed in 3rd Division reserve and then was attached to the 504th Parachute Regiment and placed on the line.

Darby, who had been slightly wounded by a bomb fragment on the night of 15 February, was relieved as commanding officer of the Ranger force and assigned to the 3rd Infantry Division. On the following day he was sent to the 45th Infantry Division and given command of the battered 179th Infantry Regiment. On 17 February, the 179th was forced back to the Anzio beachhead line. At that time the hard-pressed Allies had 160,000 men in the Anzio beachhead confronting some 125,000 of the German Fourteenth Army.

When Darby looked over his regiment, he found one battalion seriously understrength, a second at less than half strength, and a third practically without men. Although he seemed to have rebounded from the disaster at Cisterna and his confidence and enthusiasm quickly invigorated the new headquarters, he was not able to do anything to alter the condition of the regiment, which almost disintegrated later in the day when the Germans stepped up their counterattack. Darby called the 45th Division Headquarters that evening to describe the situation and to declare his intent to withdraw. Maj. Gen. William W. Eagles, commanding general of the 45th Infantry Division, wouldn't permit Darby to pull the regiment back, insisting he stand fast on the final beachhead line. The Germans fortunately didn't continue their pressure on the 179th Infantry; otherwise that unit might have been destroyed, too. The Nazis directed their attack against a neighboring regiment, and on 20 February the five-day counterattack ended.

Darby's service as commanding officer of the 179th Infantry Regiment at Anzio lasted for approximately two months. He was a good leader during that period and exhibited an appreciation of firepower that had been one of his characteristics in past battles. He made lavish use of artillery support all during the German counterattack. Always careful about men's lives, he was willing to experiment with anything that would help save them. Roy Murray, the commanding officer of the 4th Ranger Battalion, visited Darby one day and found him testing a grenade-throwing slingshot made from inner tubes.

Gen. Mark Clark, who had personally decorated some twenty men with the Medal of Honor, believed that they and other soldiers with formidable combat records were probably used often in a reckless way because of their reputations. Fearing for their lives, he wrote a letter to General Marshall asking that certain of these exemplary combat soldiers be returned to the United States and sent on tour for inspirational purposes. Darby was among those recommended; and in early April he was assigned to the Operations Division of the War Department General Staff in Washington.

Darby took home with him memories of his two-month service with the 45th Division, his bitter memories of Cisterna, and recollections of gallant days and landings at Arzew, Gela, Sorrento Peninsula, and Anzio—plus tough fighting in the mountains at Kasserine Pass, Djebel Ank, and Venafro.

General Clark sent Darby home thinking that he deserved a rest. Darby joined the Operations Division, War Department General Staff in Washington, D.C. This was General Marshall's command post for the army and the agency through which orders relating to strategy and operations were issued. Operations Division was divided into Strategy and Policy, Theater, Executive, and Logistics.

The Theater Group was the staff agency that exercised the chief of staff's command function in each operational theater and was organized into sections corresponding to the theaters around the world. Because of his experience, Darby was initially assigned to the North African and Mediterranean section. Part of Operations Division function was to check out the quality of the troops being trained in the United States for duty overseas, so he went on training inspections to Fort Meade, Maryland, in late April; and in late May to Camp Butner, North Carolina; Camp Croft, South Carolina; Fort McClellan, Alabama; and Fort Benning and Camp Wheeler in Georgia.

On his return to Washington, he prepared a report of the inspection and his evaluation of the training. When he viewed the patrolling and camouflage techniques at Fort Benning's Infantry Replacement Center, he was pleased with that emphasis, but he remarked that a training exercise that involved an attack on a town was not realistic because the town was in a thick forest rather than in a clearing. This gave the attacking forces more concealment than they would find in actual combat. At Fort McClellan for example, Darby thought that the training was excellent, but he felt that the quality of instruction was poor because the officers were inexperienced. He recommended that German mines and also German uniforms and weapons be brought from Italy so that the training would be more realistic.

In June 1944 Darby was off for visits to Camp Robinson, Arkansas, and Camps Fannin, Wolters, and Hood, in Texas. In one report he expressed approval of the realism of the training, saying that the training in American camps was now far more developed than it had been at the British Commando Depot that the Rangers had known at Achnacarry. The army had come a long way in two years.

While Darby was at Camp Butner on 19 June, he visited with those Rangers who had returned after Cisterna and was with them to celebrate the second anniversary of their activation. Later he had leave with his family in Fort Smith, and in mid-December he visited Camp Ritchie, Maryland.

Darby's forceful and agreeable personality very quickly got the attention of his chiefs and he became executive of the entire Theater Group. That same fall of 1944, Darby received orders awarding him decorations including the Legion of Merit, the French Croix de Guerre, Soviet Order of Kutuzov 3rd Class, and Oak Leaf Cluster to the Purple Heart.

Darby didn't like staff work, and he wrote to General Clark, still Fifth Army commander, asking if he could arrange to have him assigned back to Italy. But Clark was unable to help, or perhaps unwilling to bring back a man who had done as much soldiering and combat as Darby had.

Officers from Operations Division were continually being sent overseas to take part in operations and also to report on the situation around the world. On 29 March 1945 Darby finally got his overseas assignment. He was sent on a ninety-day tour of the European theater with the main purpose of evaluating aerial support of ground combat. The orders were ammended to allow him to visit other theaters if he felt that was necessary.

Before his departure for Europe, he intimated to his sidekick, Dammer, that he was going to Italy to join the 10th Mountain Division, which had been organized and trained especially for mountain warfare and was therefore appealing to him. Darby, who had great faith in Dammer, explained that once he was established in Italy, he would use his influence in an attempt to have Dammer transferred there too.

Darby left Washington for Europe on 31 March 1945 and, after other visits, made his way to Italy where he visited the 10th Mountain Division. There he found that the commanding officer was Maj. Gen. George P. Hayes, Darby's commander of the 99th Field Artillery Battalion (Pack) as a lieutenant colonel in 1940 and 1941, when Darby had commanded that battalion's Battery A. Hayes's good impression of Darby and his knowledge of what Darby had accomplished with the Rangers in the Mediterranean made him a key prospect, and Hayes said he would be happy to have Darby under his command again. Coincidentally, a vacancy was created a day or two after Darby's arrival when the assistant division commander, Brig. Gen. Robinson E. Duff, was wounded and evacuated. Hayes asked General Clark whether Darby might be assigned as assistant division commander. Clark, knowing that the war was drawing to a close and that the assignment might mean a brigadier generalcy for Darby, consented and obtained orders from Washington authorizing the transfer.

This was one of General Clark's last official acts as Fifth Army Commander. On 14 April the army command was taken over by Maj. Gen. Lucian K. Truscott, Jr., formerly division commander of the 3rd Infantry Division—a unit to which the Rangers had at various times been attached. At the time that Darby took over the new command, the Allies had encircled the Ruhr in Germany and were advancing to the Elbe; the Russians in the east had taken Vienna. In Italy, the Germans were being pursued northwest of the Senio River by McCreery's army and north of the Via Emilia by the Fifth Army in the latter part of an Anglo-American offensive that had begun on 9 April. The 10th Mountain Division had advanced to the Po River by 24 April and there established a bridgehead.

Darby was assigned officially as assistant division commander and given a task force with the objective of taking Verona. Task Force Darby, as the provisional force was named, included the 13th Tank Battalion, some engineers with bridging equipment, the 86th Mountain Infantry Regiment, Company B of the 701st Tank Destroyer Battalion, and Company B of the 751st Tank Battalion. Also included was a field artillery battalion and a medical battalion.

All three regiments of the 10th Mountain Division were north of the Po River by nightfall of 24 April. They patrolled in every direction but noted little enemy activity.

The next morning the 85th Mountain Infantry advanced forty miles to the Villafranca Airfield without meeting any enemy resistance until they reached the airfield itself. There they had to overcome the enemy troops protecting it. Due to a delay in setting up the bridging equipment needed for the tanks, Task Force Darby was late crossing the Po and was unable to advance until noon. The task force reached the Villafranca Airfield at night and arrived at Verona at 0745 hours the following morning but found the city already in the hands of anti-Fascist partisans. No serious resistance had been encountered by the task force, and once Verona was in their hands, the group was dissolved. It was now apparent that the Germans were withdrawing to the Adige River.

Further advances beyond the Villafranca Airfield were to be on both sides of the Adige and on the west side of Lake Garda. The German army was withdrawing along these same routes from Trento and the Brenner Pass, so General Hayes directed the 10th Mountain Division to attempt to outrun and head off the retreating Germans by pushing up the east side of Lake Garda and taking Trento, where all three routes of the German withdrawal converged. He ordered that each of the division's three mountain infantry regiments would lead the advance for eight hours and then rest for sixteen hours, while the other regiments took their turns leading the force. He hoped by this method that he would have fresh troops in the vanguard to keep up pressure on the retreating Germans.

As had been true throughout Italy, the Germans had the terrain in their favor. The road running up the east side of Lake Garda was restricted by the lake on one side and high ground on the other; towards the northern end of the lake it passed through seven tunnels. Hayes planned to overcome enemy obstruction by using DUKWs to bypass and encircle any enemy units.

The 10th Mountain Division began its attack up the east side of Lake Garda at 0700 on 28 April. By noon of the twenty-ninth the town of Torbole at the northeasternmost point of the lake was entered by units of the 3rd Battalion, 86th Mountain Infantry. There was heavy resistance from German tanks, artillery, and machine guns that kept the entire battalion from entering Torbole until late that night. The town was finally taken in close combat after a heavy artillery bombardment.

A simultaneous attack upon the neighboring town of Nago by the 1st Battalion, 86th Mountain Infantry, had been less successful; the unit was unable to advance beyond the outskirts of town.

At 0100 hours on 30 April the Germans launched a counterattack against both Torbole and Nago with armor and infantry. After a time the American position became so difficult that Hayes authorized the 86th Infantry's commander, Col. R. L. Cook, to withdraw if necessary. Although the troops at Nago pulled back about fifteen hundred yards, those defending Torbole held their ground. By 0230 hours the German counterattack was broken.

When the Germans withdrew, Cook's command post moved into Torbole and occupied a hotel toward the north end of town. Darby, as the assistant division commander, visited the command post to assess the local situation for Hayes. Cook briefed Darby, who was ready to leave by 1745 hours. Before returning to division headquarters, Darby and the division artillery commander, Brig. Gen. David Ruffner, planned a visit to one of the tunnels along the east side of the lake where a battle had been fought. M. Sgt. John T. Evans, regimental sergeant major, volunteered to take them in Cook's jeep. The vehicle was brought to the command post by Lt. James H. McLellan of the regimental staff. McLellan parked directly in front of the hotel where Darby, Cook, Evans, and a few other men were standing. There had been no enemy shelling of the command post since the regiment's arrival, and no one seemed to think they were taking an unnecessary risk by standing in the open.

Then without warning, one round from a German 88-mm antiaircraft gun struck about thirty feet from the group at the side of the hotel. The gun was depressed to fire like a rifle. Evans, almost decapitated by a large shell fragment, died instantly. Cook was hit in the left hip by a small fragment, and McLellan fell with severe thigh and ankle wounds. Darby received a shell fragment in his heart and was carried back into the command post by Cook, who was so dazed by the blast concussion that he had not yet become aware of his own wounds. Darby was laid on a cot, under the care of two medics. Two minutes later, without having spoken or having regained consciousness, he died. The shell fragment was about half the size of a dime.

When Darby died on 30 April 1945, he was just thirty-four years old. The terrible irony was that his death came just a few days before VE Day, the end of World War II in Europe. Two days before, Mussolini had been slain by Italian partisans in Milan; and Vietinghoff, the German commander, agreed to the unconditional surrender of all German forces in Italy effective at noon, 2 May.

Lt. Gen. Lucian K. Truscott, commanding general of the Fifth Army, notified the War Department of Darby's death with this note, "Never in this war have I known a more gallant, heroic officer." On the same day Darby was killed, his name appeared on a list of nominees for promotion being submitted by the secretary of war to the president. On 2 May, Secretary of War Stimson recommended to the president that, in view of Darby's outstanding record, his name remain on the list and that he be promoted posthumously. President Truman agreed, so on 15 May 1945, Darby was promoted to the rank of brigadier general.

Darby's West Point obituary read in part as follows:

> Most importantly, Bill Darby remained to the end a modest individual with an enthusiasm which communicated itself to his Rangers as well as to generals like Patton, Truscott, Mark Clark, and Terry Allen. Whether enlisted men or generals, they applauded Darby's leadership, his insight into men's hearts, his desire to have his men trained to the highest pitch. He lived his teaching that no officer would ever ask a soldier to do in combat what he himself would not be willing to do.
>
> The rise of Bill Darby from a field artillery battery commander to assistant division commander in the space of four years was phenomenal . . .
>
> Wherever classmates gather in years to come the legend of Bill Darby will ever be fresh. He lived up to every tradition at West Point and became, through his qualities, one of the finest soldiers.

The Ranger chief, Colonel Darby, was probably more decorated than any of his men. He was in every engagement, fought in the front lines in every battle, landed in the first wave in every assault. One officer who went to Sorrento to see Darby tells this story: After going ashore he went looking for Darby, asking each man wearing the Ranger insignia. Approaching one member in Ranger uniform he asked his usual question, "Do you know where I can find Colonel Darby?" A slow grin crossed the face of the husky soldier as he answered, "You'll never find him this far back."

General Darby's Message
to the Officers and Men
Who Served with the 1st, 3rd
and 4th Ranger Battalions

THE GLORIOUS HISTORY OF THE 1ST, 3RD, AND 4TH Ranger Battalions came to an end with the official inactivation of those units at Camp Butner, N.C., 26 October 1944; disbanded, after a long period of constant and agressive action against the best military forces the enemy could offer. A period during which, time and again in the face of tremendous odds, the superior courage and ability of the Ranger paved the way to decisively crush enemy resistance in the Mediterranean theater.

Whether it was in training or in battle, your unwavering, indomitable spirit forged by painstaking and diligent zeal has always persevered. Your resourcefulness and initiative have earned for you the respect and esteem of all true fighting men the world over. You have done much to aid the Allied cause in this war.

As your commanding officer, I am justly proud to have led such an outstanding group of American fighting men. Never was I more sad than on our day of parting. Never was I more content than being with you on our many exciting operations. You trained hard, you fought hard, and always you gave your best regardless of discomfort or danger. From the great Allied raid at Dieppe through the exacting, bitter campaigns culminating with the Anzio beachhead battles, the 1st, 3rd, and 4th Ranger Battalions have performed in a capacity unsurpassed by the highest traditions of the American Army. Your record speaks for itself.

We—the living Rangers—will never forget our fallen comrades. They and the ideals for which they fought will remain ever present among us. For we fully understand the extent of their heroic sacrifices. We will carry their spirit with us into all walks of life, into all corners of America. Our hearts join together in sorrow for their loss; but also our hearts swell with pride to have fought alongside such valiant men. They will never be considered dead, for they live with us in spirit.

When this war comes to an end, most of you will return to the way of life which you fought so hard to return to—to pick up the threads of your civilian pursuits. You will bring back with you many nostalgic memories of your fighting days—both bitter and pleasant. But above all, you will bring back with you many personal characteristics enriched by your experiences with the Rangers. In whatever field or profession you follow, I know that you will continue as civilians with the same spirit and qualities you demonstrated as a Ranger. Your aggressiveness and initiative will be tempered to adjust to civilian life with little difficulty. In your hearts as in mine, you will always have that feeling—of being a Ranger always.

No better way can I sum up my feelings of pride for your splendid achievements than to state this:

Commanding the Rangers was like driving a team of very high-spirited horses. No effort was needed to get them to go forward. The problem was to hold them in check.

Good luck, Rangers, and may your futures be crowned with deserving success.

William O. Darby
Colonel, U.S. Army
April 1945

The Other Ranger
Battalions

WHILE THE 1ST, 3RD, AND 4TH RANGER BATTALIONS made history in the Mediterranean, there were three other Ranger battalions who lived up to the Ranger tradition in other World War II combat.

The 2nd and 5th Ranger battalions, organized in the United States at Camp Forrest, Tennessee, on 1 April and 1 September 1943 respectively, fought in the landings at Normandy and in northern France and central Europe. The 6th Ranger Battalion, activated on 13 January 1941 at Fort Lewis, Washington, was assigned to the Pacific theatre and participated in battles in New Guinea, Leyte, and Luzon.

In the cross-Channel invasion of Normandy on 6 June 1944, the Allies had fairly easy going at Utah Beach, but at Omaha Beach there was grave doubt whether the assault had been stopped at the water's edge. Both the German defenders and the American Seventh Army believed through most of D-day that the Omaha assault had not been successful. It was many days before the Allied command could feel secure about the V Corps beachhead.

Leading the attack of General Gerow's V Corps was the 1st Infantry Division under Maj. Gen. Clarence R. Huebner. The "Big Red One" was to assault with two regiments abreast along with the 116th Infantry Regiment of the 29th Division. The beachhead maintenance line roughly followed the ridge of high ground parallel to the main coastal road and was in most places from two to three miles inland. It was planned that from this line the assault regiments would punch out to the D-day phase line. This would mean the occupation of a coastal strip five or six miles deep astride the Bayeux Highway.

The 116th Infantry was given responsibility for capturing the Pointe du Hoe coastal battery in the center of Omaha Beach. The assumption was that there were six partially fortified 155-mm guns emplaced there, which probably would not have been destroyed in the pre-D-day bombing and in the heavy naval fire directed at them just before H-hour. The 2nd and 5th Ranger Battalions, attached to the 116th Infantry, had the special H-hour mission of taking out these guns.

Three companies of Rangers from the 2nd Battalion were to land at the foot of the cliff, below the fortified battery, scale it with rope ladders, and attack the German position. Another Ranger company would land on the 116th Infantry's main beaches to the east and attack the fortifications at Pointe Raz de la Percée and then continue westward to cover the flank of the Rangers at Pointe du Hoe. The rest of the Rangers were to land at Pointe du Hoe, if they were notified that the initial landings were successful.

Lt. Col. James E. Rudder commanded the 2nd Ranger Battalion, whose companies D, E and F were to conduct the initial assault. The 5th Rangers were commanded by Lt. Col. Max F. Schneider who had been an original member of Darby's 1st Battalion when he formed the Rangers in North Ireland in 1942.

For the attack on Pointe du Hoe the Rangers had received intensive training and developed special equipment. During April and May 1944, on the Isle of Wight at Swanage, they were given hard practice in rope and ladder rope on cliffs like those of the French coast, combined with amphibious landing exercises in difficult waters. The three Ranger companies of the 2nd Battalion were to be loaded in ten LCAs. Each LCA was fitted with three pairs of rocket mounts wired so that they could be fired in pairs from one control point on the stern. Three-quarter-inch ropes were carried by one pair of rockets, which were affixed to the rocket's base by a connecting wire. The second pair was rigged for rope, also the three-quarter-inch size was fitted with toggles (small wooden crossbars two inches long and inserted at about one foot intervals). The third pair of rockets was attached to light rope ladders with rungs every two feet. The rockets were headed by grapnels.

The extension ladders were of two types. One consisted of 112 feet of tubular steel in four-foot sections weighing four pounds each. These ladders were partially assembled in advance in sixteen-foot lengths. For mounting the ladder on the Normandy cliff, a man was to climb to the top of each length and haul up and attach the next sixteen-foot section and repeat this process until the necessary height was reached. As a final auxiliary for climbing, four DUKWs were to carry one-hundred-foot extension ladders of the London Fire Department type. Two machine guns were mounted at the top of each of these ladders.

Speed and quickness were essential for the operation so the men were dressed in simple fatigue uniforms. Each carried two grenades and his rifle. A few who were first on the ropes carried pistols or carbines. The only heavier weapons were four BARs and two light mortars per company as well as ten thermite grenades for demolition work. Two supply boats would come in a few minutes after the assault wave with packs, rations, and ammunition, two 81-mm mortars, demolitions, and equipment for hauling supplies up the cliffs.

D-day weather was unfavorable for amphibious landings, since the seas were very rough. Shortly after leaving their transports, the *Ben Machree* and *Amsterdam,* the LCAs began to suffer from the heavy going. Eight miles from shore, LCA 860—carrying twenty men of Company D—was swamped in the four-foot choppy waves. The personnel were picked up by rescue craft and returned to England, rejoining their unit some nineteen days later. A few minutes later one of the supply craft sank with only one survivor. The other supply craft was soon in trouble and had to jettison all the packs of Companies D and E in order to stay afloat. The other craft, carrying the Rangers, survived with varying degrees of trouble. All the Rangers were soaked with spray and were wet, cold, and cramped during their three-hour trip. But the most serious effect of the soaking was to wet the climbing ropes and rope ladders, making them heavier.

The leading group of nine surviving LCAs were in good formation in a double column, ready to fan out as they got to shore. Unfortunately, the guide craft lost its bearings and headed straight for Pointe de la Percee, three miles east of their target. When Colonel Rudder, in the lead LCA, realized the error, he intervened and turned the column westward. The mistake cost more than thirty minutes in reaching Pointe du Hoe, so that instead of landing at H-hour, the first Ranger craft touched down about H-plus-thirty-eight, a delay that affected the whole course of action for the next two days. The 5th Battalion and two companies of the 2nd Battalion under Colonel Schneider were awaiting information about what was happening at Pointe du Hoe. When there were no signals of success by 0700, they adopted their alternate plan and landed at Vierville Beach to assist the 116th Infantry. This meant that Rudder's three companies were to fight alone for the next two days.

The error in direction had further dire consequences. The column of LCAs had to move westward roughly paralleling the cliffs and only a few hundred yards offshore, so it ran the gauntlet of fire from German strong points along three miles of coast. Even worse, the naval fire on the shore installation had been halted just before H-hour on the supposition that troops would be going ashore. When the troops were almost forty minutes late, this gave the defending Germans a chance to recover from the effects of the bombardment. As the LCAs neared Pointe du Hoe, they received scattered small-arms and automatic fire and saw enemy troops moving near the edge of the cliff. Fortunately there was no indication of enemy artillery in action.

The assault force was under the protecting guns of the British destroyer *Talybont*, which had been bombarding Pointe du Hoe at a range of 2.7 miles. When they saw the Rangers taking a wrong course and then correcting it, coming under fire from the cliff positions, the *Talybont* closed range and for fifteen minutes raked enemy firing positions with four-inch and two-pound shells. Meanwhile the U.S. destroyer *Satterlee*, twenty-five hundred yards from Pointe du Hoe, could see enemy troops assembling on the cliff and opened with her main battery and machine-gun fire.

As the nine LCAs touched down on a front of about five hundred yards, the Rangers found a heavily pitted and bomb-cratered beach about thirty yards in depth. These craters handicapped the unloading of men and supplies and put the DUKWs out of use because these craft couldn't cross the sand to get close enough to the cliff to reach it with their extension ladders. The cliff face, eighty to one hundred feet high, showed extensive marks of naval and air bombardment and huge chunks had been torn off the top. As the Rangers were forming on the beach, a few grenades were thrown down or rolled over the edge, and enemy small-arms fire came from scattered points along the cliff edge. The assault went forward with Ranger casualties on the beach totaling about fifteen, most due to fire from their left. In less than ten minutes, however, the first Ranger parties were getting over the cratered edges at the cliff top.

At the instant of their landing, the men in LCA 860 fired their rockets with the ropes and grapnels. All the ropes fell short of the cliff because they were thoroughly soaked. The men therefore carried some hand rockets ashore. The first went over the top of the cliff and caught. Pfc. Harry W. Roberts started up the hand line bracing his feet as he went. He made about twenty-five feet when the rope slipped, or was cut, and he slithered down. A second rocket was fired and the grapnel caught. Again he went up and this time made the top, estimating his climbing time at forty seconds.

He pulled into a small cratered ditch just under the edge. In a couple of minutes, five men including Lieutenant Lapres joined him. Without waiting for further arrivals, the six Rangers started for their objective—the heavily constructed observation post at the north tip of the fortified area.

The next group up the cliff ran into heavy explosions, but fortunately they had no effect on the climb. Very quickly four more Rangers came up, found Roberts's party already gone, and followed inland.

LCA 862 had better luck with its rocket-firing ropes, actually getting a couple operative on the top. Five men got ashore quickly and up the ropes. Following standard Ranger tactics, these five moved off without waiting for the rest of the team who came up a few minutes later.

The Rangers at Pointe du Hoe were astonished at the wasteland on top of the cliff. The ground was literally torn to pieces by bombs and navy shells. Landmarks were gone, with craters and mounds of wreckage everywhere, obscuring what had been paths and trenches. They had been studying these few acres for months, using excellent photographs and large-scale maps, but now they found themselves in danger of losing their way as soon as they made a few steps inland from the ragged cliff edge.

The attack followed a well-defined plan and order with each platoon having definite objectives. Each man knew what his mission was and where he was to go. The first objectives were the gun emplacements and the observation post near the end of the point, and these were taken quickly. One party after another reached its allotted emplacement to make the same discovery: the open gun positions were pulverized, and the casemates were heavily damaged; there was no sign of the guns. Evidently they had been removed before the period of major bombardment. The only fighting took place at the tip of the point at the observation post which the Rangers eventually captured. Actually, two small groups of Rangers had been attacking the observation post from opposite sides, but neither was aware of the other's presence.

The D-day fighting at Pointe du Hoe developed into two main groups: the Ranger force that reached the paved highway and took positions there and other Rangers who remained on the cliff at Pointe du Hoe. Some were diverted from going inland by circumstances and others by the revival of German resistance near or in the fortified area. Many of the men from Company F stayed in or near the fortified area.

Colonel Rudder had gone on top at 0745 and established his command post in a crater between the cliff and the destroyed antiaircraft gun emplacements. Most of the assault parties had left the fortified areas on their different missions, so Colonel Rudder could only wait for reports. Eight or nine Rangers had been captured in a German ambush. Enemy snipers were active, many of them operating inside the fortified area, and efforts made to eradicate them were only partly successful. Rudder sustained a thigh wound from sniper fire during the morning.

For the next two days it was small-unit action, many times with Ranger patrols not knowing if other Ranger patrols were nearby. The revival of German resistance at the point was unknown to the first Rangers to cross it, since they had drawn only scattered fire from the western flank. As they passed beyond the fortified area, some artillery and mortar shells began to drop near them, and they were aware of light small-arms fire from just ahead to the south. This slowed the leaders down, and the original parties of two and three men began to merge into larger groups until eventually about thirty men from Companies E and D had gathered together. Without waiting for the others to arrive, they started down an exit road taking as much cover as possible in a communications trench along its edge, keeping in single file. The German artillery were searching the area with time fire, and from the assembly area onward the Rangers began receiving enemy machine-gun fire from the right flank and small-arms fire to their left. They suffered serious casualties in the next few hundred yards, with seven killed and eight wounded. Despite these losses, the total size of the force was increasing as it caught up with small advance parties who had moved inland earlier.

By 0815, barely an hour after the landing, the Rangers had reached their objective, the paved highway a half mile inland and paralleling the beach. They had made good time, even though enemy opposition had clearly suffered from disorganization.

Eventually the Rangers at the paved highway numbered about fifty men, with all three Companies, D, E, and F, being represented. Their mission was to block movement along the coastal highway, so they expected to see the 116th Infantry and the 5th Rangers arrive at any moment on the Vierville Road. But their main concern was the highway west toward Grandcamp. Enemy resistance seemed to be coming from the west and south, so they made their dispositions accordingly.

They began active patrolling, setting up combat outposts with BARs and grenade launchers. At about 0900 a two-man patrol, Sergeants Lomell and Kuhn from D Company, walked into a camouflaged gun position where they found five of the enemy's 155-mm guns that were missing from Pointe du Hoe. These guns were in position to fire toward Utah Beach but could easily have been switched to fire on Omaha Beach. Piles of ammunition were at hand, but there was no indication of recent firing. Not a German was in sight, and occasional sniper fire from a distance could hardly be intended as a defense of the battery.

With Kuhn covering him against possible defenders, Lomell went into the battery and set off thermite grenades in the recoil mechanism of two guns, effectively disabling them. After bashing in the sights of a third gun, he went back for more grenades. Before he could return, another patrol from Company E finished the job. A runner was sent off at once to the point to give word that the missing guns, the primary objectives at Pointe du Hoe, had been found and neutralized.

The enemy had gathered more strength around the antiaircraft position, and the Rangers moved against it. A white flag suddenly appeared over the German emplacement, and two Rangers on the right of the skirmish line stood up in the open. The warning yell from the other men was too late to save them from a burst of machine-gun fire, and the fight was resumed.

German artillery also came into action from somewhere inland. Later this attack resulted in four men being killed, and as the Rangers withdrew, two more were killed by snipers. So that was the last effort of the day to assault the antiaircraft emplacement.

The Rangers had no success in communicating with friendly ground forces. Consequently, Rudder was in complete ignorance of the progress of the great assault at Omaha Beach. Between noon and 1300, he sent a message saying, "Located Pointe du Hoe, mission accomplished—need ammunition and reinforcements—many casualties."

Two hours later the 116th Infantry replied saying it was unable to decipher the message. About that time a destroyer at sea relayed in reply a brief message from the 1st Division commander, General Huebner, saying that there were no reinforcements available.

The Germans made two attacks against the point during the afternoon of D-day, both of them hitting the small Ranger force on the south and west. The first attack came over the fields, and the Rangers spotted riflemen coming through the craters with at least one machine-gun section. When the enemy reached the hedgerow one field south of the Rangers' position, they set up the machine gun and started a fire fight that went on for an hour. There was some artillery and mortar fire supporting the effort, but most of the enemy shells were "overs." The German attack was met and stopped by concentrated rifle fire.

A still more dangerous attack occurred about 1600 at a time when the small Ranger force had insufficient ammunition and weapons to fend it off. The Rangers' mortar opened at sixty-yard range, and the first shells burst right on the advance group of the enemy, driving them into a hasty withdrawal. Shifting its fire, the Ranger mortar flushed out another German party who suffered casualties as they ran for cover.

Meanwhile the Ranger group at the paved highway was being joined by small parties, so that by noon there were over sixty men to hold the forward positions a half mile inland from the point. Among the arrivals were three paratroopers from the 101st Airborne Division. They had been scheduled to drop early that morning fifteen miles away at Carentan, but had landed instead at Pointe du Hoe.

The action during the rest of the day near the highway consisted of combat patrols of six or seven men going out on the flanks of the highway position. The Rangers found no organized enemy positions and encountered no strong forces. They did run into a number of Germans who evidently had been bypassed near the point and were trying to work south. They straggled into the Rangers' position from the seaward side and were killed or captured. All day the Rangers kept running into small groups of Germans, and altogether about forty prisoners were taken in and grouped under guard in the field near the command post.

During the late part of D-day, Ranger patrols found evidence that Germans were present in some strength south and southwest of their highway positions, but there was no sign of preparation for a counterattack. Rangers who attempted to go back to Colonel Rudder's command post were usually engaged by snipers. Sometimes they had to fight their way on both trips as German resistance revived near the point. Lieutenant Lapres went back to Colonel Rudder's command post twice, once getting ammunition and another time for a radio that failed to work. On the morning trip, Lapres drew heavy fire from the west of the exit road, but his attempts in the afternoon were entirely blocked by Germans who had infiltrated between the two Ranger groups.

The 5th Ranger Battalion, led by Col. Schneider, and two companies of the 2nd Rangers, had made their alternate landing on the beaches above Point du Hoe. Companies of the 5th Battalion met intense mortar, artillery, and machine-gun fire, and several assault boats were hit before reaching the beach. Despite bitter opposition,

Fifth Battalion Rangers secured positions to the left of Vierville. To the right, the 116th Regiment of the 29th Infantry Division was pinned down against the sea wall. So serious was their predicament that Gen. Omar Bradley was seriously considering abandoning Omaha Beach and sending all supporting forces to Utah Beach, approximately eight miles away on the Cherbourg Peninsula.

It was then that Gen. Norman Cota, commander of the 29th Division, summoned Schneider and gave the historic order to break out of the slender beachhead: "Lead the way, Rangers." Across the barbed-wire obstacles, up the pillbox-rimmed bluffs, through minefields, the 5th Rangers advanced, knocking out machine guns, light-artillery positions and several trenches lined with bitterly defending Germans. The Ranger breakthrough penetrated four miles of stiffly defended enemy lines and opened the breach through which the supporting infantry forces poured.

About 2100, still two hours before dark, a party of twenty-three men from Company A, 5th Ranger Battalion, came into the 2nd Ranger Battalion lines from the east. This platoon's fight from Omaha Beach to Pointe du Hoe is one of the sagas of D-day.

The platoon became separated from the 5th Ranger Battalion near the first penetration of the German beach defenses between Vierville and St. Laurent about 0815 hours. Unaware that its battalion had become involved in a fire fight just inland from the beach, the platoon made its way south of Vierville to the battalion assembly area. Finding no friendly troops there, Lieutenant Parker concluded they must have preceded him and set out west. After fighting in two hot actions, one of which netted a score of prisoners, while the other nearly trapped his platoon, Parker moved all the way to St. Pierre-du-Mont and walked into the 2nd Ranger position at the highway. He was surprised to learn that the 5th Rangers had not arrived, but he was sure they must be close behind him on another route. A patrol was sent in at once to Colonel Rudder with this encouraging news, and Parker's men stayed with the group at the highway as they prepared their night defenses.

As night approached with still no word from Omaha Beach, Rudder faced a difficult command decision as to the disposition of his meager forces. Of his original two hundred men, more than one-third were casualties. Ammunition was low, especially grenades and mortar shells. The Germans were still holding the antiaircraft position close to the point on the cliffs and had shown themselves in some force on the eastern flank as well. Communications between the point and the highway group had been precarious. That force numbered more than half of the Rangers—men from Companies D, E, and F and the platoon from the 5th Rangers—and was particularly exposed to counterattack that might cut it off from the shore. In that case, both Ranger positions would be in danger.

Rudder decided to shorten up the position so that it formed a right angle facing southwest with equal sides about three hundred yards long on two fields running back to the highway. Thirty or forty German prisoners were put in foxholes in these fields not far from the command post, with two Rangers considered a sufficient guard. As they settled in for defense that night, the main worry was that their ammunition supply was running short, especially for the Browning automatic rifles. There were only a few grenades left, although the Rangers were picking up a plentiful supply of German potato-masher grenades. A few of the Rangers had lost their rifles but were using German weapons for which ammunition was in good supply. Company E had captured three German machine guns as well. The Rangers had had little to eat since leaving ship, but because of the excitement of the day, few seemed to feel the need for food.

At about 2330 the Rangers along the highway were startled by a general outburst of whistles and shouts close by on a slope of the orchard. Enemy fire opened up immediately and in considerable volume. The men saw tracer fire from a machine gun to their right and only twenty-five yards from Company D's side of the angle. South of the corner, the Rangers spotted another machine gun about fifty yards from Company E's defensive line. Neither outpost had seen or heard the enemy approach through the orchard. Only a few minutes after the firing began, an immense sheet of flame shot up over the west near the position of the abandoned German guns. They guessed that somehow more powder charges had been set off in the ammunition dump. The orchard slopes were fully lit up, and many Germans could be seen outlined against the glare. The flare died almost at once, and so did the firing from the enemy.

About 0100 on 7 June the Germans came in with a stronger effort, hitting again from the south and southwest against the right of Company E's line. The Germans got through the same orchard to within fifty yards of the Ranger position without being spotted. The attack opened with heavy firing, including machine guns, near the angle of the Rangers' lines.

The third German attack came at some time near 0300 with heavy and inaccurate fire involving machine guns that sprayed the hedgerow and the field beyond. Mortar fire increased somewhat in volume but was falling in the area where the prisoners were grouped.

The enemy pressure extended farther eastward this time, reaching into the wheatfields south of the command post. Enemy machine guns were spotted in the orchard below the second platoon of E Company and also directly south of the command post. There was a great deal of fire, much of it indirect, which confused the defense. One group of Germans worked through the orchard close to the Rangers, and their automatic fire ripped through the hedgerows keeping the defenders down. The fighting seemed to go for about an hour, and eventually the enemy broke into the field, capturing about twenty Rangers of E Company, most of them wounded.

All was confusion among the remaining Rangers, and some went ahead with a plan to withdraw. Word kept coming in that the Germans had broken the positions, and the report was confirmed by enemy fire that seemed to come from the field inside the Rangers' angle.

As the volume of enemy fire built up again from the south crest, indicating a new attack was at hand, the word was passed for a withdrawal back to the highway and to Pointe du Hoe. Some Rangers failed to get the information and were temporarily left behind.

As the men arrived at the blacktop highway there was no sign of any pursuit, and an effort was made to reorganize the Rangers at hand. All told, about fifty men got back to the point shortly after 0400 and were put at once on an improvised defense line. Very little could be done to organize the positions before daylight.

Colonel Rudder was told that the remainder of the Ranger force had been destroyed. Strangely though, some of the Rangers were still back along the highway, including men from Company D scattered along 250 yards of hedgerow. They had had no notice of a withdrawal. When they realized it was under way, they had no chance to

APPENDIX B

move because of Germans in the field to their rear and flanks. Daylight was near, and twelve men stayed in a deep drainage ditch, overhung with the heavy vegetation of the hedgerow. They had delivered no fire during the attack and could only hope that the Germans had not spotted their position.

The Company D men lay hidden in the hedgerow near the highway all the next day, D + 1. No enemy search of the area was made, and they saw only a few Germans during the period. Their main cause of worry was fire from naval guns supporting the beleaguered point. From time to time friendly shells came close enough to bounce the men around in their holes, but there were no losses. The next morning they were relieved by the 116th Infantry Division, which had been fighting for over a day to reach Pointe du Hoe from a distance of only one thousand yards.

On D + 1, Colonel Rudder's force at Pointe du Hoe consisted of about ninety men able to bear arms. Restricted to a few acres, including only a part of the fortified area, they expected to be the target for heavy concentrations of artillery and for assault by enemy ground forces. With the support of strong naval fire, the Rangers held out during the day. Later that afternoon their situation was improved by the landing of craft with food, ammunition, and a platoon of reinforcements. By night they were in touch with patrols of a relief force that had reached St. Pierre-du-Mont, only one thousand yards away. The relief on the point came the next morning on D + 2.

The 2nd and 5th Ranger Battalions that participated in the D-day landings on 6 June 1944 on Omaha Beach in Normandy accomplished their mission of capturing Pointe du Hoe and German coastal batteries. The two battalions later assisted in the capture of Grand camp and the mop up of scattered enemy opposition between Grandcamp and Isigny.

The 5th Ranger Battalion also participated in operations on the Bay of Brest area. Operating on the left flank, they captured three of the numerous defenses which extended seven miles to the town of Recouvrance.

Later, in September 1944, the 2nd Battalion, attached to the 29th Infantry Division, drove through numerous strong points to reach the German main line of resistance. The Le Conquet Peninsula was the 29th Division's next objective. The Rangers participated in this by breaking into a German 280-mm gun position, forcing the surrender of the garrison of 814 men.

During the Rhineland Campaign, from 6 to 8 December 1944, the 2nd Ranger Battalion operating in the Heurtgen Forest captured critical heights near Bergenstein and created a salient in the German lines. Although counterattacked five times and subjected to continuous artillery fire, the unit held the ground that offered observation of the key town of Schmidt as well as of the Roer River dams. This salient created by the attack reached the most easterly point to which the Allies had driven by that time.

In February and March 1945 the 5th Ranger Battalion, while attached to the 94th Infantry Division, accomplished a mission of great consequence to the success of Allied operations in the Saar River basin. Under cover of darkness, the battalion infiltrated the enemy front-line positions and seized the high ground commanding the main German military supply route west of Zerf. Two counterattacks were repulsed, and after five days of fighting the 5th Ranger Battalion had killed some 380 men, wounded about 550, captured 562 more, and destroyed two armored vehicles. Seizure of their assigned objective aided the armored breakthrough which overran Trier and brought elements of the XX Corps to the banks of the Rhine River.

The 6th Ranger Battalion operated in the Pacific rather than European theaters of war. It was the only Ranger unit fortunate enough to have been assigned to just those missions most applicable for Rangers. All its missions, usually task force, company, or platoon size, were behind enemy lines and involved long-range reconnaissance and hard hitting, long-range combat patrols. The three most noteworthy were during campaigns in the Philippines.

This battalion was the first American contingent to return to the Philippines with the mission of knocking out coastal defense guns, radio stations, radar stations, and other defense installations in Leyte Harbor. On A-day minus three days, the Rangers were landed from fast attack-type converted destroyers in the midst of a storm on islands in Leyte Bay. Their mission was successfully accomplished with hours to spare.

A reinforced company from the 6th Ranger Battalion formed the entire rescue force that liberated American and Allied prisoners of war from the Japanese prison camp at Cabanatuan in January 1945. They made a twenty-nine-mile forced march into enemy territory, obtained the support of local civilians and guerrillas, and determined the enemy's dispositions. They crawled nearly a mile through flat open terrain to assault positions, destroyed a Japanese garrison nearly double the size of the attacking force, and in the dark assembled over five hundred American prisoners of war. They were evacuated from the stockade area within twenty minutes after the assault began.

The last mission for the 6th Ranger Battalion was a 250-mile march behind enemy lines by B Company to the city of Aparri on the northern tip of Luzon. It was the last seaport and major city held by Japanese forces. For twenty-eight days behind the lines, the Rangers successfully infiltrated and reconnoitered the Japanese defenses. They prepared the landing facilities at the nearby airfield for the 11th Airborne to make one of the major airdrops of the Pacific campaign. Following this successful drop, the Rangers initially supplied the point and later the flank security for the 11th Airborne Task Force driving southward along the Cagayan River to link up with the 32nd Infantry Division, and thus end the Philippine Campaign.

The three battalions—the 2nd, 5th, and 6th—lived up to traditions developed by Darby's own Ranger Battalions in the Mediterranean fighting. In every mission they performed successfully. Darby would have been proud had he been leading them.

LIST OF ABBREVIATIONS

BAR	Browning automatic rifle
CP	Command post
DUKW	Self-propelled, boat-like amphibious truck
HE	High explosive
LCA	Landing craft, assault
LCI	Landing craft, infantry
LCS	Landing craft, support
LCT	Landing craft, tank
LSI	Landing ship, infantry
LST	Landing ship, tank
MG	Machine gun
OP	Observation post
OPD	Operations Division (War Dept. General Staff)
RAF	Royal Air Force
RCT	Regimental combat team
SOP	Standard operating procedure
WP	White phosphorus shell
WTF	Western Task Force